AMERICAN CAESAR

ALSO BY BRADLEY B. ONISHI

Preparing for War

The Sacrality of the Secular

AMERICAN CAESAR

HOW THEOCRATS AND TECH LORDS ARE TURNING AMERICA INTO A MONARCHY

BRADLEY B. ONISHI, PhD

ST. MARTIN'S ESSENTIALS
NEW YORK

First published in the United States by St. Martin's Essentials,
an imprint of St. Martin's Publishing Group

EU Representative: Macmillan Publishers Ireland Ltd, 1st Floor, The Liffey Trust Centre, 117–126 Sheriff Street Upper, Dublin 1, D01 YC43

www.stmartins.com

Designed by Omar Chapa

The Library of Congress Cataloging-in-Publication Data
is available upon request.

ISBN 978-1-250-42792-2 (hardcover)
ISBN 978-1-250-42791-5 (ebook)

First Edition: 2026

10 9 8 7 6 5 4 3 2 1

To Kasia
stubborn, defiant, divine

CONTENTS

PROLOGUE

JESUS IS KING!

The gymnasium smelled of teenage body odor and sweat. Earnest adults were busy shushing chatter and shepherding everyone inside. We sat on the wood floor, facing a makeshift stage under one of the basketball hoops. It was a Sunday night, sometime in the late summer of 1996. After a dinner of pizza and soda and a game of dodgeball, it was time for the devotional part of our youth group's gathering.

"Now, I'm going to bring up Brad Onishi to share what's in his heart for the new school year," Rick said. As I made my way to the stage, I could feel the surprise in the room. Rick, our youth pastor at Rose Drive Friends Church—an evangelical megachurch of two thousand people in North Orange County, California—hadn't told anyone that I would be speaking. I hadn't either.

This was my first sermon, given a week or so into my sophomore year of high school and about eighteen months after my conversion to evangelical Christianity. Standing in front of the eighty teenagers in our youth group, I wasn't nervous. God had given me a message—it was time to deliver it.

"One of the things I learned recently," I began, one hand on the cordless mic, another in the pocket of my corduroy surfer shorts, "was that salmon swim upstream in order to spawn. Many of them die in the process, losing their lives to reproduce themselves. For them, it's worth the sacrifice to ensure life for future generations."

Though caught off guard by the metaphor, my audience quickly understood the point. As we swung into the new school year, it was our duty to make more Christians, to evangelize to the increasingly godless world around us, to sacrifice our vanity and insecurity to ensure future generations had eternal life.

Without me knowing it, my sermon fit into an emerging movement in evangelical circles—a missional understanding of the church in the world. Spreading the Gospel wasn't new. American born-again Christians have been doing that for centuries. What was new was the understanding that we Christians were doing so in a culture no longer accurately described as Christian. If America was no longer a godly nation, then we were missionaries to a secular culture, not the proponents of our society's dominant ethos. And two years later, in 1998, the movement found its central text in *Missional Church: A Vision for the Sending of the Church in North America,* a series of essays that called on Christians to see Western culture—the world that many of them still assumed to be predominantly Christian—as a post-Christian society in which they were not the majority cultural group but a holy remnant sent to evangelize in the same way as those in India, China, or Kenya might do. The missional paradigm spread to Southern Baptist congregations, Reformed circles, and nondenominational churches across the country. In this framework, Christians would have to embrace their roles as countercultural disciples of Jesus swimming upstream in a current no longer moving toward or with Christianity.

The missional church model fit within larger trends in religion and politics from that era. Throughout the late 1990s, evangelical men attended Promise Keepers rallies in stadiums across the nation, where speakers emphasized racial reconciliation and the responsibilities facing Christian fathers. Promise Keepers wasn't as much about converting souls as transforming how evangelical dads viewed their place in society. Speakers asked attendees to take stock of gender roles in the home and in the country. The movement remained patriarchal—and in my view deeply problematic—but nonetheless it was based on multiculturalism (at least in name) and vulnerability (men were often seen weeping at these rallies). By the early 2000s, George W. Bush was arguing for a compassionate conservatism that would enlarge the GOP base by recognizing the need to make room for Americans of different ethnic and racial backgrounds.

To be clear, I have no interest in paying homage to these religious or political trends. My goal is neither to reminisce upon nor restore the legacies of the missional church movement, Promise Keepers, or George W. Bush's presidency. Rather, these touchstones from my evangelical youth serve to draw a sharp distinction between where we were a quarter century ago and where many in evangelical and other conservative Christian spaces have arrived today. Currently, there is little room in the evangelical world for seeing the church as swimming upstream in an increasingly secular society. There is even less appetite for compassion and reconciliation—whether in racial, gender, or any other terms. Instead of a call for a missional church made up of countercultural, self-sacrificial disciples, now the crusade is to restore Christendom through the eradication of diversity, the cultivation of ethnonationalism, and the use of brute force. This call is coming not only from evangelical leaders but from Catholic intellectuals, Silicon Valley technocrats, and Reconstructionist theologians who support Trump as an instrument for moving the country toward the pure nation they envision. But what many of them really want is an autocratic leader—a CEO or Christian prince—who will go even further than Trump ever imagined.

* * *

Jake Lang, a portly White man in his thirties, is wearing a tactical military vest over his blue-and-white flannel. It's November 2025. Lang is marching down Michigan Avenue in Dearborn, Michigan, protesting what he calls the "Islamification" of the United States. Lang holds a JESUS CHRIST IS KING OF DEARBORN banner as he strides through the city with a small entourage. "Today we mark America a Christian country. Today we mark America a European Western civilization that the Muslims have no part in. . . . This is our country."[1]

Dearborn is a suburb of Detroit. About 55 percent of Dearborn residents are Muslim. In 2023 it became the first majority Muslim city in the US. The city's profile makes it a symbol of what civilizational chauvinists like Lang think is wrong with the United States. He arrived in Dearborn to provoke its citizens and gain media attention for his Senate campaign in Florida.

Later Lang spoke at a Dearborn city council meeting where

he unloaded a vile xenophobic rant against Muslims: "We have been taken over without a single shot fired. You guys are insidious parasites on the American way of life," he screamed into the microphone. Standing in front of seated city council members, Lang berated them. "You will never look like us. You'll never eat like us. You won't build buildings like us. You are nothing. You can build nothing. Just like President Trump's great American friends have said, you guys are not us, and get the fuck out! America First, America only! God bless America! Jesus is king!"[2]

Lang is a J6er, one of the fifteen hundred people pardoned by President Trump for their crimes and alleged crimes at the January 6, 2021, insurrection. He is by most accounts not a serious person. His rhetoric consists largely of cruel slurs and racist talking points. His tactics seem designed for shock, not change. His most apparent interest is in public conflict. It is difficult to see that Lang has any investment in the flourishing of anything but his social media and bank accounts. But what caught my attention was the way he mixed civilizational rhetoric with the phrase "Jesus is king." He shouted this repeatedly as law enforcement escorted him out of the city council meeting. "Jesus is king. Jesus is king. King. King. King. King. King. Jesus is king. Jesus is king."

Lang didn't lead a team into town in order to proselytize to its Muslim citizens. There was no sense that bond building, persuasion, and clear evidence from the Christian scriptures would be the best way to lead Dearborn's residents to Christ. Lang was not a Christian missionary. He was a Christian colonizer, an emissary of King Jesus sent to root out a people he considers unassimilable invaders. He framed the situation as a war between the King of the US and Muslim interlopers, invoking the authority of Christ as the monarch of the United States who will not abide by "infidels" in his kingdom.

It would be easy to write off Jake Lang as a J6 extremist—a Christian shock trooper of little consequence to the national profile of the United States. But Lang is a representative of a broad movement among a strange coalition of religious and quasi-religious Western supremacists whose power and influence go all the way to the White House. Rather than a radical outlier, he is downstream from an influential set of Catholic, Protestant, and technocratic luminaries who want to seat a king in the United States. Some of them, like Lang, see Jesus as the American monarch and themselves as his authoritarian representatives on earth. Others want a human to take the American throne, whether as an extension of Christ's monarchical rule or as a CEO who owns the people and land over which he reigns. Either way, democracy and pluralism are things of the past. Autocracy is the future.

* * *

Between the time I gave my first sermon in 1996 and the moment when Jake Lang began his "protest" march in Dearborn, the trendy image of Christ among evangelicals and their allies transformed from a "missional" Jesus to King Christ. There are a number of causes for the shift. One clear one came in the 2010s, when White Christians officially became less than half of the American population.[3] For the first time in the nation's history, they were the minority. This coincided with the second term of the first Black president, building momentum for legalizing same-sex marriage, and a continuing decline in religiosity across the United States. It might have been one thing to view the church as a countercultural force in American society back before White Christians lost their demographic majority and executive exclusivity. Since then, Protestant, Catholic, and technocratic figures have emerged to give voice to a Western Christian supremacy bent on regaining power through non-democratic means, fortifying White identity by denying the political equality of those not like them, and calling for the political denigration—and in some cases, excision—of non-Christian people.

It seems that they were never going to settle for the title of "missionary" in their own country, never going to let what is Caesar's be his, never going to accept the reality of American multiculturalism. Instead, they declared themselves settlers and demonized immigrants, started calling for a monarch to replace the Constitution, and proclaimed other cultures a dangerous hodgepodge and a blight on the United States.

This book is the story of how these movements went from the ignored outskirts of our society to the halls of power in Washington, DC—and are shaping the future of the planet.

INTRODUCTION

THE END OF "WE THE PEOPLE"

I no longer believe that freedom and democracy are compatible.

—Peter Thiel

They make an odd pair. The conversation feels like two friends of the bride—the BFF from childhood and the college roommate—awkwardly trying to connect and bond in order to plan the bachelorette party, a connection that should work in theory but turns out to be an unsteady fit in real life. White and in his early fifties, Kevin Roberts is bald, stout, and forceful. Dressed in cowboy boots and a matching stylish blazer, he looks more like a Texas high school football coach than the leader of the Heritage Foundation. Dwarkesh Patel—a Gen Z podcaster in his early twenties who has managed to enmesh himself with the biggest names in tech—is of South Asian descent. Dressed in a navy suit and white dress shirt, no tie, he is the emblem of the young Silicon Valley nerd, exuberant over Big Tech and AI. His enthusiastic naivete is evident in his goofy smile and bold proclamations about how they will make the future of humanity idyllic. At one point Roberts asks him why he's excited about superintelligence. "Like twenty percent economic growth a year, expanding through space," Patel responds. "And then on Tuesday we'll look at some more stuff," he finishes, letting out a dorky belly laugh.

It's September 2024, less than two months before the presidential election that will put Donald Trump back in power. Roberts and Patel are on stage at "Reboot 2024," that year's iteration of an annual tech conference held in San Francisco. Reboot hosts big names from academia, politics, and Silicon Valley. The sponsors of this year's gathering are the Heritage Foundation—the powerful right-wing think tank Roberts leads, and the infamous publisher of Project 2025—the tech monarchist Curtis Yarvin's Sovereign House, the Manhattan Institute, and a bevy of like-minded others. There are the panels on pronatalism and population anxiety with professors from Catholic universities, issues not normally featured at tech conferences with audiences steeped in venture capitalism and AI innovation. Finally, there is Roberts himself. He had been billed as the special surprise guest—the big reveal that was supposed to excite attendees. Instead, his fireside chat with Dwarkesh Patel falls flat—as if everyone was expecting Taylor Swift and got Bob Dylan.

In the first three minutes Roberts compares Senator Mike Lee of Utah to Thomas Jefferson, making it clear that this is going to be an absurd discussion. Roberts is prone to saying ridiculous things, but this might be his worst. Eight minutes into the interview things get tense when Patel asks Roberts, "Why aren't you more positive on Big Tech? They're like the greatest institutions in the country; they produce all this innovation, all this surplus; a lot of small businesses like mine would not be possible without Big Tech. Shouldn't we celebrate them more?"

Roberts doesn't miss a beat. "They're not the greatest institutions in this country. The greatest institution in this country is the nuclear family." Patel's face sours as Roberts says this. "I believe as a conservative that too many people in Big Tech have their priorities misordered," Roberts continues. "And the success of a lot of the innovations in Big Tech comes at the expense of Americans."

In order to find common ground, Patel turns to AI, a subject where they find a loose agreement. "Rather than be the kind of dinosaurs that the left characterizes us to be . . . we really ought to think about how, for the sake of the common good . . . conservatives and those of you in tech . . . are kindred spirits," Roberts explains. "I'm really excited about artificial intelligence if it is virtuously developed and virtuously implemented."[1]

This moment isn't enough to turn the interview around entirely. Though it is clear there are ideological overlaps between Big Tech and Christian nationalists, it's an awkward pairing in practice.

This should have been expected. Roberts is a firebrand conservative Catholic who oversaw the publication of Project 2025 and has ties to Opus Dei. He had showed up as the featured speaker at a tech conference funded by Silicon Valley luminaries like Peter Thiel, an openly gay man. The Heritage Foundation is a Capitol Hill think tank with a half-century record of advising presidents on policy, lobbying congresspeople to vote for "family values," and doing everything possible to reduce taxes of all kinds. Roberts views the nuclear family as the foundation of American society. He doesn't believe gay marriage should be legal. His previous role was as president of a liberal arts college. Silicon Valley is not his natural habitat. This raises the question: What is behind this awkward blind date between Big Tech and Christian nationalism?

* * *

A king is the antihero of the Declaration of Independence and the Constitution—the thing that we exist against and in spite of. Until now. At this moment, theocratic religious radicals and Silicon Valley technocrats are leading movements calling for something like an American Caesar. We are by any measure a young country. Yet the United States is among the world's oldest continuous democracies. The rule by the many, rather than the few—or the One—is fragile and rare enough that our system is often referred to as an experiment, one that began 250 years ago with a famous Declaration:

> We hold these truths to be self-evident, that all men are created equal, that they are endowed by their Creator with certain unalienable Rights, that among these are Life, Liberty and the pursuit of Happiness.

This is perhaps the most famous sentence in American history. As the heart of the Declaration of Independence, it is the basis of the document that declared freedom from the British monarchy and the intention to form a new government rooted in We the People. It was the beginning of the power-sharing agreement that we call American democracy—one based on the "unalienable rights" of all human beings, including the pursuit of life, liberty, and happiness. We can argue about cuisine and whether or not baseball is still America's pastime and if the Dallas Cowboys are really America's team (they are not). There is no argument, however, that democracy, or at least the idea of it, is the most American thing imaginable. We the People is the core of our national identity; it defines who we are and who we were meant to be this whole time.

By contrast, there is nothing less American—nothing more diametrically opposed to this imperfect, unachieved, audacious experiment we've been conducting for two and a half centuries—than a monarch. A king and his religious myopia were what the Puritans supposedly escaped. Tyrannical monarchy is what the colonies refused. "I was much an enemy to monarchy before I came to Europe. I am ten thousand times more so since I have seen what they are," Thomas Jefferson wrote to George Washington in 1788. "There is scarcely an evil known in these countries which may not be traced to their king as its source, nor a good which is not derived from the small fibres of republicanism existing among them."[2]

* * *

"Christian nationalism" has become a buzzword since Trump's first election victory. Rep. Marjorie Taylor Greene said in a 2022 interview that "we need to be the party of nationalism and I'm a Christian, and I say it proudly, we should be Christian nationalists." Books by ultraconservative theologians like Andrew Torba and Stephen Wolfe make the case for Christian nationalism as the way to save America. Christian nationalism is a cultural identity that seeks to privilege Christians in the United States over all others by way of historical narrative and ideology. In short, Christian nationalists propose that if one were to sit at a round table where all types of Americans, in terms of racial, ethnic, sexual, gender, and other forms of identity, were represented, a Christian nationalist would claim authority in some way over everyone else by dint of their Christian faith. For the Christian nationalist, since the country was formed as a "Christian" nation, it is the Christian (and only the right kind of Christian) who should have the most say in how the country's present and future should look. Thus, Christian nationalists evoke the long-held call for America to "return" to its foundation as a Christian nation. Make America Great Again is often code for Make America White and Christian Again.[3]

Along with other academics, journalists, and ex-practitioners, I have tried to warn audiences about the threats that Christian nationalism poses to American democracy and American Christianity. In my 2023 book, *Preparing for War: The Extremist History of White Christian Nationalism—And What Comes Next,* I told the story of my conversion to evangelicalism, my becoming a White Christian nationalist, and my exit from both those movements. In *Preparing for War* my story is a prism through which to see a larger one—the modern history of Christian nationalism in the United States from the Christian nationalist backlash to the progress of the 1960s and how it led all the way to January 6.

For most of us, the sixties were a time of progress, albeit unfinished, when the Civil Rights Act, the Voting Rights Act, immigration reform, the Stonewall uprising, *The Feminine Mystique,* and so many other touchpoints made the American public square more inclusive and equal. For the White Christian nationalist the 1960s were the tipping point when those who didn't deserve to inherit or represent the country "stole" it from the real Americans. Since then, Christian nationalists have protested, fought, and rioted in order to take "their" country back. In their minds, if this country was founded as a Christian nation, then it should return to its original state, and for many of them, if that requires brutality or violence, then so be it.

There has been plenty of extremism among Christian nationalists for decades. However, what we are witnessing now is a frightening escalation to something more radical. In order to understand Trump's potential coalition—and the reasons for picking JD Vance as his vice president—in the months before the 2024 election I surveyed corners and niches in various Christian supremacist, authoritarian, and antidemocratic movements: Calvinist Protestants, reactionary Catholics, tech monarchists, and others in the MAGA orbit. Everywhere I looked, it felt like something different was emerging—something unhinged from the dominant modern lineage of Christian identity politics. Eventually, I began to see a pattern in the noise: the desire to replace We the People with a Red Caesar, a Protestant Franco, or an Enlightened Tech Founder. In other words, a second American revolution, but this time to seat someone like a king, rather than to break away from one.

This, in many respects, is no longer a Christian nationalist movement, at least not in the way we often think of it. Whether it was Jerry Falwell Sr. in the 1980s clamoring for a return to traditional values, or Fox News hosts in the Obama era griping that "we can't say Merry Christmas anymore," or MAGA pastors during Trump's first term proclaiming the return of American greatness, the call for Christian nationhood has been a call to a return—a going back to our supposed origins as a New Israel chosen by God to play an exceptional role in human history. A 2016 study from the Public Religion Research Institute found that seven out of ten Trump voters believed that the country had changed for the worse since the 1950s; 74 percent of White evangelicals agreed with this statement.[4] One of the ways to read Trump's first election was as a mission to restore the country to its pre-1960s contours—a country where Jim Crow still flourished, voting taxes and tests were in place for Black citizens, immigration was reserved mainly for Europeans, women couldn't divorce their husbands without court approval, and there were no anti-discrimination protections for LGBT citizens. This is a xenophobic, racist, and retrograde vision for the country. *But, now the mission has changed. And not for the better.* The dream is no longer to return to a time when White Christianity went hand in hand with America; a restoration of the supposed Pax Americana of the 1950s. The outlook now is more grim and more extreme.

In the face of demographic change, cultural progress, and global crises, Christian Reconstructionists, reactionary Catholics, and Silicon Valley magnates long to replace American democracy with a postconstitutional Caesar who will rule without the burden of checks and balances or the sharing of power in any meaningful way. They retain the racism, xenophobia, and misogyny of the old Religious Right, but are explicit about their desire to achieve their ideal social order through an authoritarian dictator.

This brings us back to the question of why Kevin Roberts was in Silicon Valley months before the 2024 election.

◆ ◆ ◆

The purveyors of the autocratic mission to refound America go well beyond the category of White evangelicalism. Since 2016, many have associated Christian nationalism with White evangelicals, envisioning the latter as the religious kernel of

MAGAism with little understanding of the other religious and quasi-religious groups who have supported Trump for the last decade. But there are nuances to MAGA religious populism.[5] To understand the rise and ambitions of the postliberal American Right, we must first grasp the complex forces that have brought it into being.

* * *

Kevin Roberts is a busy man. Just weeks before he appeared at Reboot 2024, he was a guest on Steve Bannon's *War Room* podcast. "We are in the process of the second American revolution," Roberts proclaimed, "which will remain bloodless if the left allows it to be." The statement came a few days after the Supreme Court ruled that presidents acting in their formal capacity as head of the executive branch are immune from prosecution. Roberts praised the ruling, saying the immunity provision would mean the president would not have to "second guess, triple guess every decision they're making in their official capacity."

Roberts's choice of words is important. He doesn't say that we are in the midst of a restoration. He doesn't believe that changes to the executive branch will reset the country to its original greatness. Instead, it's a second revolution based on seemingly unlimited trust in an unbound president. Roberts is a postliberal Catholic. Heritage was founded by another Catholic, Paul Weyrich, in 1973. He believed that Vatican II dismantled the Church's political power and signaled submission to pluralism and liberalism. "We are revolutionaries," Weyrich once said, "here to overturn the present order."[6]

Roberts and Weyrich represent a reactionary strain in American Catholicism focused on ordering society around

God's natural law and the Church's authority. "Anything that violates nature, if conservatives are going to be intellectually honest are going to stand against that," Roberts says in his fireside chat at Reboot 2024. "It is also most importantly about the common good and about human flourishing." Throughout the conversation with Patel, Roberts repeatedly describes himself as a conservative, rather than as a libertarian. He is not a laissez-faire capitalist. Instead, he admits, "I'm a little more willing to use the federal government's power on a limited basis for the common good."[7] In other words, he is a leader in a new generation of conservatives who think *government is the solution, not the problem,* to humanity's woes—as long as the right Father figure is the president sitting at the head of the table.

In other words, Roberts is part of a lineage of postliberal Catholics who believe that the government should be designed not to foster the freedom of the market or the freedom of individual choice, but as a tool—or a weapon—to instill God's law in American society. Writing in the wake of the 1960s, the antidemocratic Catholic intellectual L. Brent Bozell Jr.—whom we will meet in the next chapter—explained in the right-wing Catholic magazine *Triumph* that if America were to be a true Christian society, it would need to undergo a governmental revolution.

> The first citizen of the city would of course be the Church. She would not govern directly the way a President or Congress does, but she would be the anchor for the whole public thing. Her articulation of divine and natural laws would be the constitution of the city with which any human legislation would be expected

> to comport. Her ceremonies and feasts, her penances, would set the rhythm of the public life.[8]

For Bozell, as we shall see, the models for this type of government were medieval papal states, led by kings, and Franco's Spain.

Influential contemporary Catholic figures maintain this vision. As Fr. Edmund Waldstein, a leading Catholic postliberal figure, articulates it, the goal is "to work towards something like High Medieval Christendom. . . . It makes no sense to distinguish Church and state as separate spheres at all; rather there was one single kingdom in which spiritual and temporal authorities cooperated."[9] Establishing something akin to a papal state is different from returning America to its Christian roots. This is not a desire for the good old days of Christian America. It's a vision for refounding the American government as a subservient vassal within Christendom 2.0.

Postliberalism isn't limited to Catholic circles. Since the 1960s, Protestants, many of whom look and sound like evangelicals but who often despise this label, desire a similar refounding of the nation. Instead of calling for a papal state like their Catholic counterparts, they envision something more like a Christian commonwealth led by a magistrate or prince who oversees a hierarchy designed to enforce the public Christian ethos, laws, and policies of the government. This group of Protestants is often labeled "Reconstructionists," because they believe that American society must be reconstructed from the ground up in order to base it in biblical law. They believe that God has absolute dominion over all of creation. Reconstructionist leaders see themselves as extensions of God's total authority over earthly life, including the political, economic, and cultural domains. Their role is to colonize Earth for the Creator. The strategy is not persuasion, but domination.

Joel Webbon, currently a pastor in Austin, Texas, is part of an influential cadre of Reconstructionist Christian leaders who would like to return to a state governed by "biblical law" through the power of a strongman leader. "We're degenerates. The constitution, it's not suited for governing degenerates," Webbon said on his podcast in May 2024. "But I think for our population that is degraded morally and culturally, religiously, as far as we have, you need power. Men must be governed. You need a Caesar type. . . . I don't think constitutioning even harder is going to get us out of our current mess."[10] For Webbon, there can be no restoring American greatness through democratic means. Instead, we need a Caesar who will rescue our fallen citizenry from themselves by taking over the shambles of our society as a benevolent Christian autocrat.

Webbon often appears on panels and podcasts with Doug Wilson, an elder statesman in the Reconstructionist movement. Pete Hegseth, the Fox News host turned Secretary of Defense, attends a church in a denomination founded by Wilson, who believes that women should not have the right to vote. In other words, the head of the Department of Defense is a theological acolyte of a strain of Reformed Protestantism in which leading lights regularly call for a Red Caesar, a strongman figure who will reconstruct the nation after the dissolution of the current constitutional order. When Hegseth led a prayer at the Pentagon in May of 2025, he addressed it to "King Jesus."

Reconstructionists like Hegseth are hardly alone in their adoration of "King Jesus." Their project is increasingly shared—and amplified—by powerful figures in the tech world, whose wealth and influence give this theology real political force. In September 2025, the Commonwealth Club—the historic San Francisco venue that for decades has hosted lectures and fireside chats with entrepreneurs, tech moguls, and intellectuals—held a series of talks by Peter Thiel. "You are warmly invited to a series of four lectures by Peter Thiel addressing the topic of the biblical Antichrist," the event description promised eerily. An honest version would have read: "Come hear one of the richest men in the world talk about the Antichrist in deeply unsettling ways. Get a cookie and a glass of wine. It will be a nice way to spend a Monday evening if you like obscure readings of Revelation by a man who is the cofounder and board chair of an apocalyptic AI surveillance company in bed with the federal government." Instead, the official invitation explained that "his remarks will be anchored on science and technology, and will comment on the theology, history, literature, and politics of the Antichrist."

The lectures were off the record. Recording the event was not allowed. However, leaked notes and audio revealed that Thiel drew on a motley crew of intellectual influences, including the Nazi Carl Schmitt, the philosopher René Girard, and the prophet Daniel, to warn the audience that those worried about the existential threats we face as humans—an activist like Greta Thunberg or Pope Leo XIV—are possible Antichrist figures. When Thiel's lectures were announced, their subject shocked many in the public who were baffled at Thiel's fascination with Armageddon and the Antichrist. But Thiel has not only been talking publicly about these issues for years, he has been developing an idiosyncratic techno-theology since the turn of the millennium. Thiel may be the figurehead of the

PayPal mafia, but he is also a monarchist theologian. "I no longer believe that freedom and democracy are compatible," Thiel proclaimed in 2009.[11]

Thiel is one of Silicon Valley's most influential figures, even if Elon Musk, Mark Zuckerberg, and others are more often in the spotlight. As we shall see, Thiel is somehow more religious than spiritual. He draws on Christian scriptures and symbols to develop a heterodox theology more focused on the Antichrist than Christ himself. His monarchist cohorts are less theological than him, but many share the belief that in order to save the United States and the West, democracy must be sent to pasture in favor of a new model of governance led by a tech autocrat.

◆ ◆ ◆

And this explains why Kevin Roberts was the featured guest at Reboot 2024 in San Francisco. Roberts's appearance at the conference represented the public alliance of Big Tech and the most prominent Christian nationalist think tank on Capitol Hill. However unlikely their coalition may appear, Christian Reconstructionists, reactionary Catholics, and Silicon Valley technocrats are increasingly united by a shared worldview that frames pluralism and democratic governance as problems to be overcome rather than values to be defended. Their diagnoses of what ails the United States—and Western society more broadly—are rooted in grievance, hierarchy, and fear of social change. Their proposed "solutions" center on consolidating power rather than expanding rights. Across these movements, five common ideological commitments repeatedly surface: hostility to liberalism, a turn to postlibertarian politics that abandons individual freedom in favor of hierarchical control, contempt for democratic institutions, a desire for autocratic rule, and Western supremacy.

* * *

At the heart of the contemporary convergence among Protestant Reconstructionists, reactionary Catholics, and certain technocratic elites lies a shared conviction: Liberalism is the fundamental cause of civilizational decline. For these groups, liberalism is not simply a flawed political philosophy or an incomplete governing framework—it is the primary antagonist undermining the foundations of Western society. They argue that liberalism's emphasis on individual rights erodes the common good, weakens social bonds, and creates societal disorder. Liberalism's embrace of multiculturalism and immigration is seen as a direct threat to cultural cohesion, opening the door to "foreign" influences that are supposedly destroying "our way of life." They also rage against the limitation of executive power by the courts and Constitution. In sum, liberalism is the unifying villain across three movements that otherwise disagree on theology, history, and governance.

I use the term "postliberal" throughout this book to describe figures in all three of these movements. While the category "postliberal" emerged from a specific group of Catholic intellectuals, it is helpful for conceptualizing how leaders and thinkers across these movements have mainstreamed the turn away from liberalism and embraced an openly illiberal political worldview.[12] Historically speaking, there are different theoretical lineages that have merged to create the current postliberal coalition. For simplicity's sake, however, we can say that today postliberals share the belief that the government should curtail personal liberty in order to cultivate collective virtues, impose social order, and protect the "American way of life" through economic and cultural isolationism. While there are wrinkles of difference, the three movements' shared resentment of liberalism is the foundation for everything else.

As these groups articulate their response to what they view as liberalism's failures, they increasingly reject the libertarian ethos that once dominated right-wing politics. The shift away from libertarianism to strains of autocracy represents one of the most striking ideological realignments of the past decade. When I was growing up in 1980s Southern California, the public religion was Reaganite conservatism. The doctrines were small government and low taxes. The mission? Spreading democracy and capitalism across the globe.

Reagan's orthodoxy has been replaced. While the figures analyzed in the following chapters are all considered "conservative" in the American context, they are not advocates of a small government or for the wisdom of laissez-faire economics. As former libertarians, they now argue that minimal government and market freedom are insufficient to sustain a moral or Western Christian social order. Key figures in these movements have come to see libertarianism as an impotent ideology, incapable of cultivating virtue, protecting the nation from demographic change, or guarding society from moral collapse. In place of the invisible hand of the market, they want the ruthless fist of the strongman. Individual liberty is no longer a political priority; instead, the state is reimagined as an instrument for enforcing religious and/or civilizational norms and safeguarding White heritage. This means a turn away from libertarian ideals and toward advocacy for government restrictions on commerce, speech, and personal conduct. They subjugate economic freedom, once sacrosanct, to the demands of cultural and religious control.

Underlying these shifts is an even more radical conclusion: For postliberals, democracy is the problem, not the solution to saving the United States and Western civilization. Across these movements, democracy is increasingly portrayed as a system that enables moral degradation, cultural dilution, and political instability. The claim is that ordinary people—especially those newly included in the political process since the 1960s—lack the capacity to govern themselves wisely and thus don't deserve rights conferred by citizenship. Some argue explicitly that political participation by women, non-Whites, immigrants, or secular citizens erodes social order and national cohesion. Many are openly calling for the repeal of the Nineteenth Amendment and the negation of birthright citizenship. In terms of replacing democracy, their proposed alternatives range from Protestant theocracy to an American government subservient to the Catholic Church to various forms of technocratic dictatorship. What unites their visions is the belief that Americans require external authority and coercive power to maintain a well-ordered society—that We the People should give way to the One True Leader. In their view, the children are out of line and the women have run amok. A free market and the ballot box won't fix that. They'd rather have order than liberty.

If your national family is out of whack, you need Daddy to take over. So, the men in these movements pine for the figure of the strongman—an autocrat who can circumvent democratic restraints and impose the necessary cultural, religious, or civilizational order. Because they view liberalism and democracy as inadequate, they cast a strong executive as the only viable way to secure borders, suppress ideological enemies, and reverse moral decline. For postliberal Protestants, Catholics, and technocrats, the strongman becomes both a political and symbolic solution: a protector of the nation against internal and external threats, empowered to wield the state aggressively on behalf of "the people." This is the kind of leader who authorizes his personal military to enter your home without permission to look for migrants or other "traitors," regulates what you do in the bedroom for the "common good," and controls your body in the name of natural law.

The drive to save America is not grounded in the sacrality of We the People, but in a different ideological foundation: the belief that Western civilization, as embodied in the United States, is superior to all other forms of human society. This ideology does more than defend Christian nationalism; it frames political struggle as an existential battle over the survival of Western Christian civilization itself.

Some scholars use the term "civilizational populism" to describe a worldview that elevates Western (and especially European Christian) civilization as inherently superior to all others, and that sees non-European, non-Christian, or non-White populations as fundamentally incompatible with the West's cultural foundation. In this narrative, "the people" are defined not simply as citizens but as the rightful heirs of a European Western Christian heritage. Their opponents are cast as corrupt elites or culturally "foreign" groups who threaten the integrity of the national body. The emphasis on Western civilization, rather than on a Christian nation, makes room in the coalition for nonreligious technocrats and White nationalists who align themselves with a mythicized Western past. This worldview imagines the United States as the end of a genealogical tree that started in ancient Greece, flowered in the Roman Empire, actualized in medieval Christendom, and then became global through the colonial efforts of early modern Europeans. It is Western supremacy: the belief that those who are part of Western civilization are naturally superior to every other human society on the planet.

The theology matters less than the mythology. You don't have to go to church to be a Western supremacist. You just need to believe that Western civilization—White, Christian-rooted, European-derived—is morally superior, yet somehow under existential threat. Elon Musk is not a Christian in any meaningful sense. White House adviser and shadow president Stephen Miller invokes "civilization," not Christ. Yet both fit comfortably in the center of this ideology. This is the key difference from more recent iterations of Christian nationalism. In recent decades, Christian nationalism ran on the notion that the United States is "a Christian nation" built by and for Christians. This is an exclusionary vision. It demands that non-Christians—Muslims, Hindus, Buddhists, Jews, pagans, atheists—take a subordinate position in public life and assimilate into an implicitly White, Protestant cultural order. If Christian nationalists say everyone can sit at the American table but Christians must always sit at an elevated position at the head of it, Western supremacy says many people can't sit at the table at all. Christian nationalism was already an antidemocratic threat to a pluralist, multiracial, multiethnic United States.

The rhetoric now shaping the postliberal American Right is no longer satisfied with demanding privilege for White Christians. It demands supremacy for an entire "civilization"—a supposedly homogenous Western, European, Christian-rooted people who are imagined as superior to the rest of the world. This is more expansive and more volatile. It turns whole populations into existential enemies. It transforms immigration into invasion. It marks millions—sometimes on sight, often based solely on ancestry—as incapable of loving or contributing to the nation. While it may be tempting to write this off as distilled White nationalism, the story is wider in scope—at least to those who adhere to it. The "Christian" dimensions of Western superiority are key. Christianity is the nucleus of the West, the transcendent story that anchors it. In order to be part of that story you do not need to read the Bible daily or attend mass regularly. You must simply find a role to play in the battle against the seditious elites and incompatible outsiders destroying the West's noble culture.

In sum, the ties across postliberal Protestant, Catholic, and technocratic movements are held together by a coherent ideological structure. Liberalism is condemned as the source of cultural decay; libertarianism is dismissed as too weak to uphold moral order; democracy is rejected because the masses cannot be trusted; authoritarian leadership is embraced as a necessary corrective; and civilizational populism provides the theoretical and moral justification for remaking America as a hierarchical, exclusionary, Western-Christian polity. These movements do not merely critique the American founding—they envision a new American order grounded in hierarchy and civilizational purity. They aren't new. But they are now mainstream. The fringe has become the fabric.

Thus, as much as I would like to, we don't have the luxury of writing off the American postliberal right as a set of crackpots. Not only do figures like Thiel, Hegseth, and Roberts hold tremendous influence over our public square, but they also have an ally in the White House. Donald Trump is sympathetic to their ideologies as long as it keeps him in power—and puts billions in his pockets. But the true believer in the postliberal cause is JD Vance, who was mentored by Thiel, is a close friend of Roberts, and is adored by Christian Reconstructionists like those in Hegseth's denomination. As the political scientist Julian Waller says, Vance "has referred to himself as a postliberal and is very well read on the entire diverse ecosystem of postliberal thought, from its Catholic postliberal end to Silicon Valley's burgeoning tech-right."[13] Vance is the "poster child" of the postliberal cause—a devout Catholic, former Silicon Valley investor, and rabid Western supremacist. He is the figure who stands at the center of the Venn diagram composed of the three movements I trace in the following chapters.

* * *

To comprehend how we arrived at a moment when the heir to the presidency is an open postliberal, it's necessary to tell the story of how tech monarchism, Catholic integralism, and Protestant Reconstructionism became mainstream movements in American political discourse. What emerges from this story is not a culture war but a multipronged counterrevolution.

The roots of this movement lie in a strand of American Catholicism that never accepted liberal democracy in the first place. For decades, integralist thinkers built an intellectual and institutional case against liberal rights, insisting that the state must ultimately answer to divine authority rather than popular consent. What began as a marginal rejection of the Enlightenment made its way into elite legal theory, policy networks, and conservative organizing. That vision now shapes real policy agendas, staffing pipelines, and the machinery of power surrounding the White House.

Alongside this Catholic project runs a parallel Protestant one, even more explicit in its ambitions. The language of "King Jesus" is a declaration of intent: Christ as sovereign, biblical law as civil code, and democracy as heresy. A theology once considered too extreme even for evangelicals has been rehabilitated, translated into activist strategy, and carried into military, media, and political institutions. Its architects do not seek reform. They seek replacement. Their goal is a society governed by divine command.

If this were only a religious movement, it would be dangerous enough. But it is reinforced by something colder and somehow even more bizarre: Silicon Valley techno-theology. Influential tech elites have fused apocalyptic Christianity, civilizational panic, and startup logic into a vision of governance by the One, with the few, *against* the many. In this world, monarchy rebrands as innovation, founders elevate to sovereigns, and citizens become property.

These religious and technological projects may someday compete for the crown, but for now they are converging. Catholic postliberalism reemerges in elite law schools, think tanks, and policy shops, openly arguing that liberal rights must give way to a single, enforced moral vision—whether the public agrees or not. Protestant Reconstruction mutates into ethnonationalism, with preachers and theologians calling for a "Christian prince" or Protestant Caesar to save the nation from women's suffrage, multiculturalism, religious pluralism, and migrants of any kind. In their imagined past and desired future, only White Anglo-Saxon Protestants truly belong;

everyone else exists as second-class subjects or removable threats. Meanwhile, for tech monarchists surveillance becomes a tool for civilizational dominance. The strategy? Construct a state strong enough to enforce order, then hollow out democracy from within. The goal is rule without accountability. The characters involved may seem ridiculous, even cartoonish. But their ideas are already shaping how our leaders understand power and justify violence, and who is considered "one of us." The frightening part is not that these movements exist. It is how close they are to winning.

1

VIVA CRISTO REY

> **If you polarize, people either agree with you or they don't. Polarization is an essential political tool.**
>
> **—CONNIE MARSHNER**

They share a worldview, but Connie and Bill Marshner seem to come from different worlds. It's September 2023, and they're seated on stage for a fireside chat at the Catholic University of America in Washington, DC.

Wearing a simple blue and white dress that matches her matter-of-fact demeanor, Connaught "Connie" Marshner is energetic and pragmatic. She reads like someone who spits fire with a smile on her face; one whose wrath you'd never want to witness in a board meeting or on the other side of an angry phone call. Everything I've read about her makes me think that she's never one to lose herself in daydreams or wasted afternoons; Connie is a task-oriented planner who leaves no detail unchecked, whether it be the family day trip to the beach or a conservative takeover of the Republican Party.

By contrast, William "Bill" Marshner looks the stereotype of a nutty professor—what an American would dress up as if he were playing the role of a nineteenth-century Cambridge don. His cream seersucker jacket is mismatched with dark pinstriped pants and a gray tie. He carries a cane and wears a beard that would make Dumbledore jealous. Bill speaks in a languid tone, seeming to pluck each word from the heavens, mashing it into an imperfect earthly manifestation. His natural habitat appears to be an archive containing obscure works by Thomistic theologians or an office overflowing with the books, papers, and other paraphernalia of an analog scholarly life. You would not be surprised to find out that he still uses a landline.

But as different as they may appear, Connie and Bill Marshner have been married for fifty years. However, the story is not about how they have made their domestic life function, but how they represent two wings of an illiberal Catholic movement that has served as the central nervous system of Christian nationalist policy, principles, and mobilization since the late 1960s—one that culminated in the Heritage Foundation's Project 2025, the policy engine of Trump's second term. The casual observer would never guess it looking at this elderly couple on stage reflecting on their lives and careers. But there would be no Trump presidency without the Marshners and the institutions they've spent their lives serving.

From the early 1970s, Connie was the confidant and professional partner of Paul Weyrich—the founder of the Heritage Foundation, the Council for National Policy, and the Free Congress Foundation, not to mention the engineer of Jerry Falwell's Moral Majority. Weyrich's legacy cannot be overstated: He masterminded the modern Religious Right. At the same time, Bill became one of the youngest contributors to *Triumph*, a traditionalist Catholic magazine started by L. Brent Bozell Jr.—Barry Goldwater's ghostwriter, Joseph McCarthy's dedicated apologist, and the best friend of William F. Buckley. The Marshners are a bridge between a once-in-a-generation political organizing movement spearheaded by Paul Weyrich that took over the GOP and an obscure Catholic intellectual project led by Brent Bozell that is now the inspiration for influential postliberals like JD Vance. They are two different antidemocratic vectors designed to come from opposite directions, converging in order to destroy liberalism, the separation of church and state, and democracy as we know it. Viewing them together, it's possible to understand how postliberal Catholic extremism eventually made its way all the way to the White House in 2024.

Brent Bozell was born in 1926; Paul Weyrich in 1942. They each viewed the defeat of conservatism from FDR to Eisenhower as ruinous for America, and the modernization of the Catholic Church by way of Vatican II as disastrous for the Kingdom of God. They both believed the order of society was crumbling because of the triumph of liberalism and the weakness of the Catholic Church. Their goals were to reinstitute proper social order in American political and cultural life, respectively. Weyrich and Bozell were traditionalists in the sense that they recalled former times when this order was supposedly present. As the scholar Chelsea Ebin argues, they were revolutionary in that such order—maintained through the weaponization of the government by religious actors and the imposition of Christianity on all people—had never been present in the extreme form they imagined. It was not a historical reality to revive. It was a fantasy conjured by insurgent Christian supremacists. They wanted an America more akin to Christendom, not Christian America as it had ever been manifest.

* * *

In the 1950s, the story goes, William F. Buckley birthed the modern conservative movement. Buckley, a cradle Catholic and the founder of the *National Review*, became the figurehead of a new American right that fused libertarian economics with Christian patriotic spirit. Smaller government at home, a mighty military abroad, and Christian identity throughout: These were the ingredients to the takeover of the GOP that created Barry Goldwater's presidential nomination in 1964, birthed Reagan's political career, and inspired the likes of Marco Rubio, Mike Pence, and countless others to run for office. But alongside Buckley's fusionism another reactionary political movement took root, led by his brother-in-law. Many Americans are still quite familiar with Buckley. Yet almost no one knows about L. Brent Bozell Jr. Bozell helped Buckley found the *National Review* in 1955. However, while Buckley grew into the role of a clearinghouse of conservative orthodoxy, Bozell became a Catholic extremist who wanted to model the United States after Franco's fascist—and exclusively Catholic—Spain.

* * *

L. Brent Bozell Jr. was born into an affluent family in Omaha. After winning a nationwide competition for best high school orator and completing a short stint in the Navy, he enrolled at Yale in 1948. His rhetorical skills translated to the Yale debate club, where he partnered with William F. Buckley to become one of the most fearsome debaters in the university's history. Bozell and Buckley became best friends—and more. When Bozell decided to convert from the Episcopalianism of his childhood to Roman Catholicism, Buckley was his sponsor. After graduating from Yale, Bozell married Patricia Buckley, William F. Buckley's sister; they welcomed their first child, Christopher, in 1950. Soon thereafter Buckley and his wife, also named Patricia, welcomed a child. The couples served as godparents for each other's children.[1]

During his time at Yale, Bozell developed the foundations of his political worldview. He despised the New Deal as government overreach and considered communism a threat to American life—and to human civilization as a whole. One of Bozell's abiding concerns, even more so than Buckley, was the formation of a sense of "we" based on transcendence and virtue in the face of the communist collective formed around immanence and devotion to the party. For Bozell, it was not a matter of the individual against the group, but a question of which group had the correct values and worldview—and thus the right to rule.

Buckley and Bozell were entranced by the infamous Wisconsin Senator Joseph McCarthy, who was also Catholic. In 1950, McCarthy claimed that the United States government was infested with communist traitors. Soon, he would claim he possessed a list of those "Reds" and begin a nationwide crusade to root out Marxists in government, Hollywood, and beyond. Working with his aide, Roy Cohn—who would later become Donald Trump's mentor in business and politics—McCarthy spearheaded the period of anticommunist witch-hunting now known as McCarthyism. From 1950 to 1954 he leveled unfounded attacks on government officials and cultural icons, creating a "Red Scare" that pervaded American society as well as a purge of queer individuals from the US federal government known as the "Lavender Scare." "As McCarthy's activities stoked fears of anticommunist subversion, thousands of additional Americans, by some estimates, lost their jobs, their freedom to speak or travel freely, and even their lives for being suspected of left-wing beliefs or associations," writes the historian A. Brad Schwartz.[2]

* * *

Even in 1954, after his censure by the Senate and fall from grace, McCarthy was revered by Bozell and Buckley. With the help of their Yale professor Willmoore Kendall, the pair wrote a defense of McCarthy's record in the Senate and of his anticommunist crusade, published as *McCarthy and His Enemies: The Record and Its Meaning*. They acknowledged the Senator's mistakes and overreach, but concluded that "men of good will and stern morality" could properly "close ranks" around a leader such as him. For Bozell and Buckley, the ruining of reputations and destruction of careers at the hands of McCarthy's quixotic quest were worth it if it meant rallying the American "We" against the threat of godless communism. Taking the job once held by Roy Cohn, Bozell went on to become one of McCarthy's top aides and served as his final speechwriter, even living with the senator at his home before his death in 1957.

Buckley and Bozell identified McCarthy as the kind of conservative needed to break the liberal establishment and the centrist hold on American conservatism. Instead of bridge-building and middle-of-the-road politics, they wanted guerilla warfare from the right. McCarthy's resentment against those he deemed to be un-American had a lasting effect on both men.

"Trolling the libs, denouncing political correctness, and overthrowing the deep state," writes the historian Jacob Heilbrunn, were the lessons of political insurgency Buckley and Bozell took from McCarthy's political career.[3]

◆ ◆ ◆

Buckley became a national figure after the overwhelming success of his book *God and Man at Yale,* which argued that conservatives were marginalized on the Ivy League campus, reflecting the national trend of leaving God-fearing Americans behind. Firmly in Buckley's shadow, Bozell nonetheless became part of the inaugural team for the *National Review* in 1955. Bozell and Buckley saw themselves as conservative beacons in a time when the Republican Party was hopelessly centrist—a muddled mass without principles or a spine. They were staunch anticommunists, foreign policy hawks, and advocates of traditionalist religious values. More than anything, they despised the liberalism behind the New Deal and the creation of the American social safety net and expansion of the federal government. Thus, it was necessary to stake out a coherent intellectual conservatism to counter the country's ballooning federal government and the erosion of traditional religious and family values. One way to think of Buckley in this era is as a kind of antecedent to Charlie Kirk: a fearless debater who became a prominent right-wing figure in his twenties and started an organization that became a cornerstone of conservative political thought and action. Like Kirk, he was young and precocious, but so influential that aspiring candidates and those up for re-election needed his support.

Unlike Buckley, who benefited from family money and the success of his bestselling book, Bozell needed an inexpensive place to live while he finished a manuscript on the Supreme Court. He woke up one day in 1960 and told his wife Patricia that they should move to Spain so that he could finish his book without distraction (and in a place with a much lower cost of living). Though taken aback, Patricia agreed; soon the Bozells decamped to a home near El Escorial, outside of Madrid.

Spain was not a random choice by the Catholic convert. It held a special place in the American Catholic imaginary during this period. Many of Bozell's colleagues, friends, and mentors had either visited there with great enthusiasm or spent time living in the country. Spain represented that which America had never had: an officially Catholic society with deep ties to medieval Christendom and a social order based on family and faith, rather than individual choice or diversity. The time in Spain proved a decisive chapter in Bozell's journey. It was a "magic kingdom," as Bozell's biographer puts it. "The half-historical, half-mythical Spain of conquistadors and mystics, crusaders and missionaries."[4] There the couple found Catholicism integrated into public policy and public life. Later Patricia would observe that in Spain Bozell became "swept away . . . by the concept of Christendom."[5] Francisco Franco, Spain's authoritarian dictator, became a model of sorts for the type of leader Bozell imagined the United States needed. Jacob Heilbrunn summarizes his enchantment with Franco's Catholic regime:

> He was smitten by Franco's readiness to crush dissent. . . . Living in Spain instilled in him the conviction that the Christian West wasn't simply at odds with liberalism, but in a fight with it to the death. The authoritarian Spanish model was worthy of emulation.

> The Spanish regime had promoted the power of the Catholic Church and banned other religions. Abortion, contraceptives, and divorce were prohibited by the church. The throne-and-altar conservatism that he witnessed, coupled with a wider medieval piety (and poverty), left him agog.[6]

Unlike the United States, Franco's Spain wasn't founded on the idea of individual liberty. Instead, it was directly tied to Christendom—the Christian civilization that emerged from the work of the Church to build a society imbued with monuments, rituals, and saints based on patterns of divine order. It was not a pluralist state wherein religious minorities called for equal representation or in which congress forbade prayer in schools. Franco was an unabashed authoritarian, but for Bozell the illiberal state was justified in order to form the "We" he had searched for in McCarthyism and ultimately Catholicism. Spain enchanted him because it was a unified society formed on the foundations of family, security, and devotion to Christendom.

It's hard to avoid characterizing Bozell as the apotheosis of two infernally grating characters—the zealous convert and the American study-abroad student. Bozell converted to Catholicism at Yale, and then carried his faith to extremist ends in a manner condemned by the cradle Catholics around him. It was as if Catholicism was a magic circle that offered an escape to a different world that could be real if the Church and the American people had the fortitude to create it. Spain became his possibility model—the historical blueprint of that world filled with real-life memorials, monuments, and cathedrals to the Christendom he wanted to resurrect. But Bozell was far more than a naive college sophomore trying to make America into the Europe he saw during a semester overseas. He was a determined intellectual with the clout to make a lasting imprint on American politics.

During his time abroad, Bozell had a grand Spanish realization: The way to save society is not through laissez-faire capitalism, but through a government formed in subservience to the Church—two hierarchies integrated into a functioning whole, one designed for earthly life, the other for eternal ends. In this sense, Bozell became what is known as a Catholic integralist. Catholic integralism operates on the notion that the Church's authority should be integrated into the government, thereby giving priority and privilege to Catholic religious values in policy and public life. Integralists are generally opposed to pluralism and liberal democracy. For them, government is less about individual freedoms than collective virtue formed through public religion and policies in line with the Church's teachings. Integralism is not theocracy, in the sense that integralists do not propose that the Pope lead the government. Rather, integralists desire a government directed by the Church, with the former working as a subsidiary temporary power subservient to the Church's eternal authority.

* * *

You can observe the integralist leap Bozell made in Spain in his famous 1962 response to *National Review* contributor Frank Meyer. Meyer was a proponent of conservative fusionism, the coupling of free market libertarianism with traditionalist views on social issues. For the libertarian, the markets should decide everything and the government should do little more than protect the nation from foreign threats at home and abroad. For the traditionalist, the government should be in the business of imposing traditional values through policy—ensuring that their views of family, sex, gender, and religion are protected and even enforced by governmental channels. Bozell put it this way: "The fused position . . . maintains that the duty of men is to seek virtue; but it insists that men cannot in actuality do so unless they are free from the constraints of the physical coercion of an unlimited state."[7] At some point, the capitalist and the Christian have to fuse their respective conceptions of the state's role in forming—or not forming—the public square.

But there is an inherent contradiction in this coupling. "If freedom is the 'first principle' in politics, virtue is, at best, the second one," writes Bozell. What is virtue? "God desires—for its own sake—a human order that conforms to the transcendent order," he maintains.[8] If individual freedom supplants virtue, then society is based on the primacy of human choice, rather than on the purpose of carrying out God's will. In other words, the marriage of the free market and traditionalist Christian values was always destined for divorce. You cannot merge Christian virtue with unfettered capitalism, because the latter gives people choices that might lead them away from the traditional values Bozell believes must be the foundation of society.

Bozell uses the example of Spain as a country that prioritizes human order in the image of God's will over individual liberty. In the Spain of 1962, divorce was illegal. As Bozell points out, a Spaniard who wanted to get a divorce would have to travel abroad, which would be costly. He would then be a social pariah and have few opportunities for remarriage. As a result of the government's guardrails against divorce, the man remains married. The libertarian would argue for divorce to be legal, since the government shouldn't regulate personal choice. But, Bozell argues, isn't it better for the state to limit freedom in order to instill virtue? After all, "When a commonwealth builds according to the divine patterns of order, then it is in a position to help man conform to his nature, which is the meaning of virtue."[9]

There is a direct line from Bozell's admiration of Franco and Spain's state-sponsored Catholicism to his break with the foundations of American conservatism as expressed by Meyer, Buckley, and the other voices at the *National Review*. In his post-Spain years, Bozell argued that if the purpose of government is to cultivate virtuous citizens, then individual freedoms should be curtailed in favor of public religious imposition. The government cannot be a hands-off guarantor of limitless individual freedoms and the backbone of Christian civilization. It must choose one or the other.

* * *

As time went on, Bozell's ideas only became more extreme. In 1966, he ventured out of the shadow of Buckley and the *National Review* in order to start *Triumph*. As historian Patrick Allitt puts it, Bozell and his team, which was made up almost entirely of Catholic converts, were monarchists who wanted to refound the United States. "What they could not find in the United States they searched for in Spain instead," Allitt writes. "*Triumph* became a bulwark of Hispanophile Catholics in the nine years of its regular publication (1966–1975)."[10]

For Bozell, the problem with American conservatism was that it was a branch on the same tree as liberalism. Like contemporary Catholic radicals such as Patrick Deneen,

Adrian Vermeule, and Kevin Roberts, Bozell believed both conservatives and liberals mistakenly founded their politics on the notion of individual human freedom. But, as we have seen, in Bozell's view guaranteeing freedom is not the point of government. It is an illusion, as he says in "Letter to Yourselves," a 1969 essay aimed at the American Right, that the "ordering of public life—can proceed without references to God."[11] Conservatives may fight to preserve religious liberty, but in Bozell's eyes all that it preserved was religion as an individual matter, degrading the spiritual dimension of public life, creating elites who could pursue the lofty goal of self-fulfillment, but leaving behind the common man. Religion is restricted to "a compartment," rather than being a shared public good.

In an essay titled "Politics of the Poor," Brent Bozell defines the poor not as those without economic means, but as those poor in spirit who do not have the strength to live the Christian life in the face of persecution or pluralism. In other words, those without the spiritual fortitude to be baptized when the faith is not reflected in the culture around them—the cultural Christians who follow the masses to mass. It is the Church's duty, then, to create a civilization wherein the divine patterns of order are publicly embodied so that even the spiritually poor are brought into the Church's arms. For Bozell, following the Christian nationalist French priest Jean Daniélou, "The world must speak of God; otherwise, man can normally have no access to him."[12] The point of government is neither individual liberty, nor the protection of religious liberty for all citizens regardless of their creed or confession. Rather, it is to be a "training ground for sanctity."

This conclusion led Bozell to question the very founding

of the United States. By the early 1970s, he not only observed "that America today is not a Christian country" but questioned whether it ever had been, since its public square never "had a distinctively Christian character."[13] The answer to America's woes, in other words, was not to go back to her Christian roots, since from the beginning "God was made the patron of America in much the same sense that Catholic countries adopted this or that saint as their patron." Instead of reform, the country needed to be refounded on a model wherein the "The first citizen of the city would of course be the Church."[14] This wouldn't mean direct rule by the Vatican, but instead that the Church "would be the anchor for the whole public thing. Her articulation of divine and natural laws would be the constitution of the city with which any human legislation would be expected to comport. Her ceremonies and feasts, her penances, would set the rhythm of the public life."[15] For Bozell, Christ is king of every commonwealth, and thus religious pluralism and diversity is a war on the rightful monarch of the nation. His vision is in essence not returning to the America that was once a city on a hill, but to a country that has yet to exist, but could.

Bozell was not alone in this assessment. William Marshner, like Bozell, converted to Catholicism while at Yale. Eighteen years younger than Bozell, Marshner was no less zealous for the integration of the state into the Church. Following his theological hero Thomas Aquinas, Marshner argues in "Liberty and Social Order," a 1973 essay in *Triumph,* that the social order is part of the natural order, and thus Christian order must triumph as it did in Christendom. This is the only way to true freedom. The problem with America is not too much liberty, "but that it has almost no liberty" because its social order is diseased.[16] The only way to liberate the United States, according to Marshner, is to place religion above the state as the transcendent anchor of the public square. America has never been either a Christian country or a free nation because it has never allowed the Church its proper role in public life. The Church, not the individual, Marshner maintains, "is the very fountainhead of human freedom."[17]

* * *

By the early 1970s Bozell was a marginal figure on the American Right, a zealous convert who had allowed his enchantment with Spain and newfound faith to lead him into extremism. Even Buckley, his brother-in-law and confidant, castigated him publicly for views that appeared to many as theocratic. Bozell didn't want rule by We the People, but by King Jesus.

In its heyday, *Triumph* made the *National Review* look like *The New Republic*. Bozell and his colleagues argued consistently that the Founders had laid a false foundation full of idols by leaving God out of the Constitution and treating him like a patron saint of America, rather than its transcendent authority. They called for a new American founding in which the state and the divine will would be integrated, raging against the separation of powers and democracy itself—something like Franco's Spain, rather than Reagan's America. Fittingly, Bozell summed up his political theology with the slogan "Christ is King." However, by 1976 *Triumph* was forced to close its doors. As Bozell and his team became more radical, readership dwindled and financial backers slipped away. Unlike today, it was not politically prudent in the 1970s to call for the end of separation of church and state and the takeover of our government by the church.

✦ ✦ ✦

Historically in the United States, Protestants have persecuted Catholics. As the majority, the former have characterized the latter as both un-American and heretical. When Irish, Italian, Polish, and other Catholic Europeans arrived here in the twentieth century, they were seen as neither White nor Christian. The KKK, an overtly Protestant and vehemently anti-Catholic organization, enrolled millions of members in the 1920s. When John F. Kennedy was elected the first Catholic president, Protestants wondered aloud if he would have allegiance to the flag or to the Vatican. While there is now a politically fruitful alliance between American Protestants and Catholics, when Paul Weyrich set out to revolutionize American society in the name of God's truth in the early 1970s, Catholics were not only a minority in the Christian American cosmos, but also considered by fundamentalists and evangelicals to be an untrustworthy denomination. How would it be possible to create a political bond between the two groups that would use Catholic natural law and conservative family politics as the backbone of a political machine built on the component parts of celebrity evangelical preachers, mass media, and denominational networks? It was one thing for Bozell to create a Catholic magazine dedicated to radical Catholic politics. But it would be another to forge a coalition that united Catholics and evangelicals into a voting bloc that could take over the Republican Party.

With the help of Connie Marshner, Paul Weyrich took

inspiration from the Catholic anti-abortion movement to create a "pro-family" platform based on a simple but powerful idea: *The nuclear family is the bedrock of American civilization—and the basis of any flourishing society in human history.* Thus, it's the government's role to safeguard the nuclear family as the basic unit of society. This may seem like common knowledge or historical inevitability; something that is true and has always been true: conservative Christians claiming that their version of the family—a heterosexual reproductive couple with one or more kids—is the only God-approved model, and claiming victimization at the suggestion of any alternative. But before the mid-1970s, there was no conservative political coalition founded on the idea that American freedom is based not on individual liberty, but on protection of the nuclear family.

As the historian Seth Dowland observes:

> The triumvirate of political positions that came to constitute the core of "family values" opposition to abortion, feminism, and gay rights did not command much attention from evangelicals before 1975. In fact, most evangelicals who spoke publicly about these issues in the early 1970s supported the Equal Rights Amendment and equivocated on abortion. Gay rights, to be sure, never found favor among conservative Christians, yet it seemed a marginal issue until the end of the decade. In short, on these three issues, evangelicals in the early 1970s seemed ambivalent.[18]

There were evangelicals who were deeply concerned about abortion and the rising numbers of women entering the workforce, as well as increasing divorce rates, but the evangelical world was neither united to stop them, nor unanimous in their positions toward them.

For example, in the 1960s and 1970s Southern Baptists and other historically conservative Protestant denominations held that abortion was not only permissible, but also should be left to individual choice. In 1968, a group of evangelical leaders from a variety of denominations wrote in a document titled "A Protestant Affirmation on the Control of Human Reproduction" that they could not agree whether or not abortion is sinful outright, but they could agree "about the necessity of it and permissibility for it under certain circumstances." They even argued that "the preservation of fetal life . . . may have to be abandoned to maintain full and secure family life."[19] A few years later, in 1971, the Southern Baptist Convention issued a joint resolution calling for Southern Baptists "to work for legislation that will allow the possibility of abortion under such conditions as rape, incest, clear evidence of severe fetal deformity, and carefully ascertained evidence of the likelihood of damage to the emotional, mental, and physical health of the mother."[20] This resolution was in accord with Baptist views on abortion at the time. As the Baptist Press, a news service affiliated with the Southern Baptist Convention, wrote in 2015:

> In 1970, a poll conducted by the Baptist Sunday School Board found that 70 percent of Southern Baptist pastors supported abortion to protect the mental or physical health of the mother, 64 percent supported abortion in cases of fetal deformity and 71 percent in cases of rape. Three years later, a poll conducted by the Baptist Standard news journal found that 90 percent

of Texas Baptists believed their state's abortion laws were too restrictive.[21]

This all changed by the end of the 1970s, when evangelical ministers such as Jerry Falwell, Tim LaHaye, Ralph Reed, and others forged the Moral Majority with Paul Weyrich and other Catholic organizers. "Over the course of the 1970s, however, a small cadre of evangelical ministers developed a political philosophy that connected defense of the 'traditional family' with opposition to abortion, feminism, and gay rights," Dowland writes. Christian right leaders defined traditional families as those with two heterosexual parents, with the husband as the head and, preferably, the primary breadwinner.[22]

The source of the pro-family worldview came from the Catholic universe. It was a political tool wielded by Paul Weyrich and Connie Marshner to unite conservative Catholics with their evangelical and fundamentalist siblings. As Ebin explains, they "utilized the politically charged signifier of the family to generate new coalitions and produce a vehicle for the NCR (New Catholic Right) to ride into the mainstream of American politics via Republican Party incorporation."[23] This meant mobilizing Catholics and evangelicals against civil rights for nonstraight people, rallying to defeat the ratification of the Equal Rights Amendment, and vowing to do everything possible to ensure *Roe v. Wade* would be overturned. It also meant arguing that men were the natural authorities in the home, church, and world. As anthropologist Sophie Bjork-James observes in *The Divine Institution*, when one considers the heterosexual, patriarchal, reproductive nuclear family to be an unquestionable theological-political component of God's plan for creation, issues of sexuality, marriage, reproduction, and gender rise to the level of doctrine.[24] Where one stands on abortion, gay marriage, and women's rights become litmus tests for both political and theological orthodoxy. In place of Protestant and Catholic dividing lines, the nuclear family became the boundary that separated "real Americans" and "real Christians" from everyone else.

The nuclear family as a "divine institution" is the core idea that built the unprecedented alliance among conservative and traditional Catholics and Protestant fundamentalists and evangelicals in the 1970s (one that eventually included many Latter-day Saints and some Jews and even Muslims). While they disagreed on church structure, biblical hermeneutics, and theological doctrines, they could all agree that the nuclear family was the basis of human society and American greatness. If one displaced or disordered the nuclear family, Connie Marshner and Weyrich argued, our society would crumble, our children would be overrun by predators and perverts, women would be attacked, and God would be forgotten. Thus, "family" became a code word for a religious conception of society that "good" religious Americans could agree on.

* * *

This is exemplified most powerfully in the case of the White House Conference on Families proposed by Jimmy Carter when he ran for president in 1976. Carter was a born-again Southern Baptist who proudly identified as an evangelical Christian. However, when he entered office, he quickly fell out of favor with Weyrich, Falwell, and their Catholic-evangelical coalition. Carter was not an abortion hardliner, he was sympathetic to the fate of single mothers, he promoted more women and people of color to the judiciary than any president before him, and he would not use the government as a weapon against queer Americans. He was a dyed-in-the-wool evangelical who taught Sunday school and quoted the Bible, but his stance on the nuclear family crossed the red line Weyrich had drawn in the religious-political sand.

As I wrote in my 2023 book *Preparing for War,* "Carter's goal" at the White House Conference on Families "was to examine 'the strengths of American families, the difficulties they face, and the ways in which family life is affected by public policies.' The organizers who led the conference took this as a mandate to explore how 'nontraditional' families, including single-parent and LGBTQ households, were navigating the social and professional landscapes."

As a result, when Carter kicked off the Conference in the summer of 1980, Connie Marshner built a campaign to discredit it as anti-American and anti-Christian. She spearheaded a protest at the conference. Marshner wrote to participants to encourage them to endure "some of the most unpleasant [days] of your life" in the name of "our agenda for the American family."[25] She also coordinated a walkout from the conference and organized a "pro-family" gathering in response. As the political scientist Chelsea Ebin observes, "promotional materials for America's Pro-Family Conference suggested the (Protestant) Christian Right had taken the lead on 'pro-family' issues." A Moral Majority report claimed that Carter's conference "heaped scorn on the traditional family." Alabama governor Fob James said it opposed "Judeo-Christian values."[26] While the Catholics organized behind the scenes, the Protestants headlined the events. "It is here," Ebin continues, "that we see the 'pro-family' agenda and ideology developed by the Catholic New Right become the 'pro-family' platform of the New Christian Right."[27]

The controversy Weyrich, Marshner, Falwell, and others manufactured around the White House Conference on Families exemplified the wider revolt against Carter. While Carter was undoubtedly a Bible-believing and church-attending Christian, his social values didn't match the "pro-family" agenda at the heart of the Catholic-evangelical political alliance. Thus, as has been well chronicled, in the 1980 election Weyrich and Falwell mobilized the Moral Majority in favor of a divorced Hollywood actor from California, Ronald Reagan, against the Southern Baptist military veteran from rural Georgia, Jimmy Carter. When Reagan won the presidency, the Moral Majority claimed victory.

◆ ◆ ◆

Weyrich's hopes for social change were soon dashed by Reagan's prioritizing of economic issues over "Judeo-Christian" values. As Bozell had feared two decades earlier, it seemed that in conservative politics the libertarian wing of the party—led by big business interests—would always trump the religious traditionalists when it came to policy and budgetary priorities.

"The Religious New Right had an enormous opportunity to change the situation in America, politically if not culturally, but it utterly failed to do so," Weyrich wrote in a 1990 conference paper. "The Religious New Right failed, first of all, because it had a ghetto mentality about what it was. Immediately after Ronald Reagan was elected . . . the administration announced that its social agenda would have to be postponed for several years. In response to that blow, evangelical and fundamentalist leaders refused to say anything."[28] In the wake of Reagan's victory, Weyrich was not satisfied with having access to the White House. He wanted to see real social change in the name of God.

> The leaders told me that I was much too harsh and that they rather agreed with the notion that economic issues were important. They thought Reagan had a good point, that he had to deal with the economy first. I'm not a theologian; I'm a politician. But I'm talking to people who are supposed to be politicians and telling them, "No, you settle matters that pertain to God first—that's the proper order." I was told, "No, absolutely not, we have to have credibility first," and so on.[29]

Weyrich's retrospective on the Reagan presidency corresponds to the historical record.

In 1987, the Free Congress Foundation, under Weyrich's leadership, published a manifesto by William Lind and none other than William Marshner outlining a clear vision for the United States based on the "pro-family" agenda Weyrich and Connie Marshner had established a decade earlier. Lind and Bill Marshner maintained that the "politics that carry us into the twenty-first century [would] be based not on economics, but on culture."[30] That culture, they argued, was based on the nuclear family, which was, "put simply, the basis of a civilized society" and the "bedrock of civilization."[31] After calling for the overturning of *Roe v. Wade*, an end to no-fault divorce, and the prohibition of sex education, they demanded "a new national agenda" as the way to "nothing less than the restoration of our national greatness."[32]

Despite efforts to find a suitable traditionalist candidate to take the reins from Reagan, by the late 1990s Paul Weyrich was disillusioned. After the lackluster presidency of George H. W. Bush and the election of Bill Clinton, Weyrich saw the conservative movement as in shambles. Clinton's affair with Monica Lewinsky proved a tipping point. "I no longer believe that there is a moral majority. I do not believe that a majority of Americans actually shares our values," Weyrich wrote in a 1999 letter to religious leaders. "I believe that we probably have lost the culture war. . . . This is why, even when we win in politics, our victories fail to translate into the kind of policies we believe are important."[33]

In response to the failure of politics, Weyrich advocated for creating separate institutions that would function beyond the "collapse of culture" he was witnessing in mainstream America. After decades of organizing, mobilizing, and coalition-building on Capitol Hill and in statehouses across the nation, Weyrich was advocating for a retreat in order to regroup and attack from a different angle. He had arrived at the same conclusion as Brent Bozell had two decades earlier: "The Constitution has not only failed; it was bound to fail. The architects of our constitutional order built a house in which secular liberalism could live, and given the dominant urges of the age, would live. The time has come to leave that house and head for home."[34] This wasn't a call for renewal. It was a rally to a refounding.

Two years later, Weyrich's new strategy appeared in a manifesto by Eric Heubeck commissioned by Weyrich at the

Free Congress Foundation. When Weyrich began in politics, he had wanted to create institutions that would provide the channels for organizing conservative Americans into an unstoppable voting bloc. He had partnered with name-brand evangelical ministers like Jerry Falwell to build an unbeatable grassroots religious movement that would become the engine of the Republican Party. Yet, by 2001 Weyrich was disenchanted. Heubeck's manifesto calls for destroying existing institutions. Instead of building a majority that will defeat the left electorally, the plan is to "attack the very legitimacy of the Left" in order to be "intimidating," "feared," and to impose a "cost" on those who oppose them publicly.[35] The methods would be "guerrilla tactics" used "to undermine the legitimacy of the dominant regime."[36] He argues that an "us-versus-them, insider-versus-outsider mentality is a very strong motivation in human life" and thus must be employed. This follows on a remark Connie Marshner made ahead of the White House Conference on Families: "If you polarize, people either agree with you or they don't. Polarization is an essential political tool."[37]

Instead of working to convince the masses, the document calls for recruiting elites who will feel as if they are part of an exclusive club with a secret body of knowledge—an American gnosticism formed around wealthy donors and those with political and public influence. In a striking paragraph, Heubeck outlines how the elites are more important than the masses because "the ideas of the masses never come from the masses."[38] In *Shadow Network: Media, Money, and the Secret Hub of the Radical Right,* the journalist and scholar Anne Nelson calls the document "a virtual declaration of war on American culture and governance—shocking in its ruthlessness and antidemocratic spirit."[39]

By the new millennium, Weyrich was convinced that there was no moral majority of Americans who would buy into his radical vision for American society. The majority was not on their side—and given demographic change, trends in American church attendance, and the rising favorability of gay rights, it seemed it never would be. It's no coincidence that during the late 1990s, after the fall of the Soviet Union, Weyrich began taking regular trips to Russia in order to build relationships with elites. Officially, the goal was to create goodwill between the nations and encourage President Putin to continue his efforts to westernize Russia. However, the ventures proved enlightening. "For Weyrich, remaking the United States as the city on a hill would require foreign help from Russia," I wrote in *Preparing for War*. "Authoritarians like Putin have become the model leader for a segment of the American population who have lost their majority but want to maintain the purity of the American body. For them, democracy is not the ideal form of governance if it doesn't yield the political and cultural hierarchies they desire." As the journalist Sarah Posner explained in a 2020 interview: "In the early days of Putin, Weyrich kind of admired him and thought it was okay for a strong leader to dispense with some of the procedures and protocols of democracy in the service of advancing that kind of ideal of a Christian nation. This was not something that was really on the radar of many rank-and-file Christian right activists until the Trump era."[40] By the 2000s, Weyrich's hatred of liberalism seems to have made him illiberal. Like Bozell, he now considered democracy as an obstacle, rather than the pathway, to saving America.

◆ ◆ ◆

Most analyses of Weyrich portray him as a shrewd politico who used evangelicals and fundamentalists in order to win elections and pass legislation. But, like Bozell, Weyrich was not a libertarian but a religious traditionalist who sought to create a government that would use its coercive power to order society according to God's ordained hierarchies. Like Bozell, he didn't want to return America to a golden age, but to create a country that had never before existed—one shaped by the contours of conservative Catholic theologies of the family, gender, sexuality, and religion.

Whereas Bozell and his fellows at *Triumph* articulated a throne-and-altar vision for transforming the United States into Franco's Spain, Weyrich and his partners used a kitchen table model to re-Christianize society. However, the differences between them were ultimately a matter of scale. By the time Weyrich reached the last decade of his life, he expounded an antidemocratic and ruthless vision for burning down the institutions that govern America and recreating them in the image of a ferociously conservative Catholic civilization. Both men believed that human society should be structured according to God-ordained hierarchies. Bozell worked on the macro level, fighting the battle on the most grandiose front through a vision for a second American revolution that would transform the country into a Christian nation for the first time. Weyrich worked from the ground up, focusing on the divine institution of the nuclear family as a basis of human society as a whole. For him, the family was a microcosm of the government and the Church.

Similarities aside, it would be easy to conclude that Weyrich's legacy overshadows Bozell's. After all, Weyrich and Connie Marshner accomplished through organizing, alliance building, and ingenious political maneuvering what Bozell could not do through intellectual guerilla warfare: They transformed the Republican Party and the American Right into a religious-traditionalist vehicle infused with Catholic theologies of family, sex, gender, and reproduction. However, their visions for the American government and society were never disparate from Bozell's. They wanted the same things—a state shaped by—and willing to enforce—God's fundamental social and familial hierarchies.

* * *

On the surface, they advanced a muscular public Christianity. In reality, their visions for the Church and the United States represented desperate flailings of patriarchal men and women anxious in the face of social change. Nobody turns to anger like an authoritarian dad who has lost control of his children in public. Weyrich's and Bozell's anxieties about the changing contours of the American public square led them respectively to the idea that forced faith and government imposition were the answers to moral uncertainty and demographic change. In taking this position, they forgot key lessons from the history of the Catholic Church—ones that informed the American founding. When belief becomes required, the Church becomes a hollow institution, full of people and void of real community. The separation of church and state not only protects the nonreligious from government imposition, it protects religious institutions from the corrupting influence of state power.

They also ignored the reality that no matter how far the government goes to enforce family structures, divorce laws, and gender conformity, it cannot reach the soul. Coercion is not conversion. Baptism by law is not a baptism of the spirit.

Families forced together by fear of punishment are not strong; they are as fragile as the authoritarians too frightened to allow the stunning diversity of human love, care, and devotion to emerge into public view. You can't make people love God or each other. When you try, the result is resentment and rebellion, not submission.

Not only does this vision denigrate the power and beauty of the human spirit, it puts the Church in a precarious position in relation to the state. Bozell and other integralists offer a model wherein the government is a subsidiary of the Church. Yet, the annals of history reveal that autocrats rarely, if ever, bow to the authority of the Church. Instead, the Church becomes reliant on the power and goodwill of the strongman, forcing it into a subservient role. When Franco died, the Church was no stronger for his help. Many Spaniards abandoned the institution altogether, because Catholicism and authoritarian rule had become synonymous during his reign.

Overall, Weyrich and Bozell (as well as Connie and Bill Marshner) forecasted a return to "family values" and public religion through a pyrrhic religious victory based on manipulated morals and dependent on political favor from secular strongmen. Unfortunately, these lessons have been unheeded by the contemporary postliberal Right. Weyrich, Connie Marshner, and those who helped them build the apparatus of right-wing institutions laid the populist groundwork for Bozell's intellectual vision to take root in the American public. Bozell's ideas were not lost to history—they've been inherited by a new generation of postliberal conservatives who want the government to be a weapon in the fight against liberalism, fusionism, and what they see as the secular degradation of the United States. One of those postliberals is the vice president, JD Vance.

The work done by Weyrich, Connie Marshner, and their cohorts steered history to a point at which the radical ideas outlined in *Triumph* could be received into the political mainstream. Their work primed both the masses and elites for the eventual reception of Bozell's grandiose integralist vision. As we see in chapter 4, it also set the stage for contemporary Catholic radicals to call for a return to Christendom and a second American revolution.

2

KING JESUS

> **All transgression faces ultimate judgment; capital offenses require the death penalty here and now, by civil authorities.**
>
> —R. J. RUSHDOONY

> **Women are the kinds of people that people come out of.**
>
> —DOUG WILSON

"King Jesus, we come humbly before you, seeking your face, seeking your grace, in humble obedience to your law and your word."

These are the opening lines of the prayer Secretary of Defense Pete Hegseth offered at a Pentagon worship service in May 2025. After being introduced by a uniformed colonel, the leader of the American armed services took the podium wearing a simple dark suit. The slickness of his signature coif belied his tone and body language. Hegseth looked and sounded like the guy who had taken a job for which he was not qualified, but which he was trying to convince the world—and himself—he could do. Gone was the smooth cadence and macho charm of the former Fox News host. This was the Hegseth who speaks rapidly, flails his hands constantly, and yells to make sure you know he is the right guy to be talking to. He touted the event as the first monthly voluntary service for members of the Department of Defense. "This is exactly where I need to be," the former Fox News host said, "and exactly where I think we need to be as a nation in this moment—on bended knee in prayer recognizing the providence of our lord and savior Jesus Christ."

The service was held on the grounds of the Pentagon, the headquarters of the United States' military forces. It took place at twelve noon, the heart of the workday. Hegseth encouraged those in attendance to tell their friends and invite others. This was no doubt an overstep in terms of the commingling of church and state. Hegseth imposed a certain strand of Christianity on a military and government that is meant to serve all Americans, and which employs one of the most diverse bodies of personnel on Earth.

In order to understand how we arrived at a place where the leader of our military is asking American soldiers to worship God with him, we have to look closer at how he prayed.

"King Jesus," he began. "We come humbly before you, seeking your face, seeking your grace, in humble obedience to your law and your word." To the casual observer, this may seem like a standard way to open a Christian prayer. But as a former insider in the evangelical world and someone who has been studying American Christianity for two decades, it immediately caught my ear. "King Jesus" is how a particular brand of American Protestants often address God in their prayers. Whereas others might begin with "Heavenly Father," or "Dear Lord," those from Reconstructionist-influenced backgrounds almost always begin with "King Jesus." They also never forget to include a mention of God's law. Reconstructionism is a Christian paradigm that broadly pushes for a complete reconstruction of American society according to the ancient biblical law given to Moses in the Hebrew Bible (Old Testament). Reconstructionists are sometimes called theonomists, since "theos" in Greek means God, and "nomos" means law. While many might call this model "theocracy," that label isn't accurate. Reconstructionists don't want the church to be in charge of the government (theocracy). But they do want the government to be modeled after biblical law and for it to be led exclusively by Christian men (theonomy).

In 2023, Pete Hegseth, who has been married three times and began his relationship with his current wife while he was married to his second wife, moved his family from New Jersey to Tennessee in order to attend Pilgrim Hill Reformed Fellowship, which is part of the Communion of Reformed Evangelical Churches (CREC). Hegseth enrolled his children at Jonathan Edwards Classical Academy, a member of the American Association of Classical Christian Schools (ACCS). Both the CREC and the ACCS have direct ties to Christian Reconstruction by way of a pastor named Doug Wilson, who helped to found both the denomination and the association of schools.

In the late 1970s, Wilson took over a church founded by his father in Moscow, Idaho. After reading Reconstructionist theologians in the 1980s, he began to contour the church according to their theologies. Wilson eventually built a multifaceted empire designed to advance his militant theology, including the CREC, a private school network, his publishing house Canon Press, and a university—New Saint Andrews College.[1]

Hegseth said in an interview that when the time comes, he would prefer to send his kids to New Saint Andrews College rather than to Princeton, his alma mater, or another Ivy League school. He is not alone in his enthusiasm for Wilson's work. Wilson has been a controversial figure for decades, yet he has seen a mainstream resurgence over the last few years. He did interviews with Tucker Carlson and Charlie Kirk in 2024, then appeared that same year on stage at NatCon, a right-wing conference that features White nationalists, conspiracy theorists, theocrats, and Republican US senators and other elected GOP officials (some of whom are also White nationalists, conspiracy theorists, and theocrats).

It wasn't always like this for either Wilson or Christian Reconstructionism. Until recently, Reconstructionists have been largely reviled by both secular and Christian critics alike, condemned as extremists who want to apply ancient laws in order to commit unspeakable acts of violence in God's name. The Christians to the right of the Religious Right, Reconstructionists see mainstream American Christianity as more interested in popularity and maintaining relationships with the powerful than obeying God's word. In other words, they view someone like Paul Weyrich, who spent much of his career building coalitions with elected officials, as a political sellout whose theology and politics were bent to the mainstream will, rather than faithful to the Gospel. Evangelical luminaries in Weyrich's circles warned their followers to avoid Christian Reconstructionists lest they become politically toxic. Now Wilson is not only Hegseth's spiritual holy father, but has been called "the New Right's favorite pastor."[2]

How did a radical brand of American Protestantism—one too extreme even for the Moral Majority—ascend to the place where the leader of the American armed forces openly and enthusiastically embraces it? How did Reconstructionism go from the American spiritual desert to the DC Promised Land?

The answers lie beyond Doug Wilson. We have to go past him to R. J. Rushdoony, the man the religion scholar Julie Ingersoll calls the "crazy uncle" of American evangelicalism.[3] Rousas John Rushdoony spent the prime of his life on a remote piece of land a world away from the Pentagon. He didn't lead a megachurch. Wasn't a daily regular on television. Couldn't be heard every day nationwide on the radio. Never appeared in a packed stadium to convert the masses, much less in DC to counsel presidents or senators. For most of his career, Rushdoony was essentially banished not only from polite society, but also from the table of the evangelical elite.

There's a reason for that.

"For a brief moment in the late twentieth century, Rushdoony challenged anyone who would call himself or herself a conservative Christian to take the whole Bible seriously—including inconvenient verses in the Old Testament that most Christians, even biblical literalists, politely ignore," says Molly Worthen, a scholar of Reconstructionism and American religion. "He pushed a mutant strain of Calvinist theology to its logical conclusions."[4]

For Rushdoony, democracy is an "anti-faith" that denies God's absolute authority over all creation and fails to envision human beings as they are—subservient sinners in the hands of a dominant deity. In place of the "equalitarianism" imposed by liberal democracy, Rushdoony called for a complete reconstruction of American society into a theonomy based on God's laws—a restoration of a feudal Christian society "to bring every area of life and thought under Christ's Kingship." This would mean the eradication of the public school system, government support programs, and taxation. Christian magistrates would administer biblical law, requiring the death penalty for "sins" like homosexuality. In other words: *The Handmaid's Tale* meets Soviet Russia.

Unexpectedly, R. J. Rushdoony is now the decoder ring for understanding much of the evangelical religiosity of the twenty-first century—and the spiritual worldview of the man who leads the most lethal military in human history. There can be no clear conception of what someone like Pete Hegseth—and millions of other Americans like him—wants without an understanding of the Christian Reconstructionism at the heart of his faith.

* * *

Rousas John Rushdoony was born in New York in 1916 to Armenian parents. His family fled Armenia to escape political violence the year prior to his birth. Soon after their arrival, the family moved to California, where his father pastored an Orthodox Presbyterian Church (PCA). The Orthodox PCA was founded in 1936 as an offshoot of the larger Presbyterian Church of the United States. Those who founded the Orthodox PCA, led by John Gresham Machen, stood against what they took to be the modernist forces infiltrating their faith. The PCA is a small, reactionary denomination marked by theological militancy.

Though he was raised in a fundamentalist household, Rushdoony attended college at UC Berkeley, which even in the first half of the twentieth century was considered a center of liberal thought and politics. After graduation he moved on to the Pacific School of Religion, one of the most progressive divinity schools in the country, in order to attend seminary and prepare for ministry. Always the contrarian, Rushdoony envisioned himself in these institutions as a covert actor learning the tactics and strategies of his foes—theological and political liberals who in his mind were the enemies of God. In the 1940s Rushdoony answered a call to do ministry on the Duck Valley Indian Reservation on the Nevada-Idaho border. It was there, far removed from any American center of power, that Rushdoony began to construct his radical theology of law and order. Over the next five decades he would write daily, producing a prodigious output of books, pamphlets, and newsletters. At times he flirted with mainstream evangelical publications, like Billy Graham's *Christianity Today*, but he always found himself on the outs with those in charge. For a short period, he was connected to Robert Welch and the John Birch Society; he worked for some years at the right-wing Volker Foundation, a libertarian think tank. Rushdoony was even invited to the first meeting of the Council for National Policy and other gatherings of religious and corporate elites. The question was never if but when Rushdoony would find a reason to sever ties with those institutions and figures due to their compromises on key theological issues. Unlike Weyrich, who was their organizer and connector, Rushdoony was a perpetual outsider—on the margin, even when invited to the center.

✦ ✦ ✦

Though his voluminous writings cover an unfathomable range of topics, Rushdoony's worldview comes down to the simple idea that men—not humankind, but men—are called by God to hold dominion over every aspect of human society. "Every sphere of life is an area of priesthood and a place of nearness to God," Rushdoony writes in his 1964 book *This Independent Republic*. "Similarly, man under God is king or vice-regent of creation, called to exercise dominion over creation by Godly exploitation, exploration, knowledge, and activity."[5] By contrast, a woman is a "helpmeet," whose role is to submit to man as his closest aide. Since God created Adam first, and since Adam enjoyed dominion over creation apart from Eve, Rushdoony concludes that it is men alone who are called to dominion. If women had never gotten involved, Adam could have stayed in his man cave, aka Earth, forever.

The building blocks of Rushdoony's understanding of human life can be summarized as follows. God created man—not human beings, but man—in order to "subdue the earth and to exercise dominion over the earth (Gen. 1:28)." Rushdoony returns time and time again to this basic starting point in his voluminous oeuvre: Man is God's deputized king on Earth. The ultimate goal of the Christian man is to conquer society in God's name. Man sinned when he attempted to "establish separate dominion and autonomous jurisdiction over the earth" and fell into sin and death.[6] In order to redeem man, God called Abraham, Moses, and the nation of Israel to "re-establish the Kingdom of God" through obedience to the "law."

◆ ◆ ◆

The law is the means by which God will be crowned king once again—and the men who follow him are the ones who will make it happen. Thus, the 613 commandments that God gave Moses are, according to Rushdoony, the unchanging and forever binding "laws of godly society."[7] They were valid in ancient Israel, just as they are valid for contemporary human society. Christ's death on the cross did not nullify the law, but made it possible for it to be reinstituted on Earth. "The creation mandate was precisely the requirement that man subdue the earth and exercise dominion over it," Rushdoony writes. "There is not one word of Scripture to indicate or imply that this mandate was ever revoked. There is every word of Scripture to declare that this mandate must and shall be fulfilled, and 'scripture cannot be broken,'" according to Jesus (John 10:35).[8] Every iota of the law still applies to God's vision for society—including the death penalty for those who disobey their parents.

Rushdoony concludes that seventeen crimes demand punishment by death. "Life is created by God, governed by His law, and to be lived only in terms of His law-word," Rushdoony writes in the first volume of *The Institutes of Biblical Law*. "All transgression faces ultimate judgment; capital offenses require the death penalty here and now, by civil authorities."[9] Rushdoony's biographer Michael McVicar notes that most of the crimes deserving of death are related to the family. "Murder, cursing a parent, kidnapping, adultery, incest, bestiality, homosexuality, rape, and habitual delinquency all struck out against the propagative, future-oriented nature of the family," McVicar observes. "Death was necessary in these cases because each crime asserted the sovereignty of humanity over God's law."[10] In Rushdoony's America, if you were routinely late to class or mouthed off to your dad, the only fitting punishment would be the guillotine.

It's hard to imagine how the stories of the Prodigal Son and the Good Samaritan, much less the phrase "God is love" from I John 4:8, fit in here at all. I spent more than a decade in the evangelical movement. The parenting advice in that culture often endorses corporal punishment. But Rushdoony's prescriptions for putting wayward children to death are far beyond the pale of anything I learned as a young convert. Now, as a father of two young children, they disgust me to my core.

* * *

For Rushdoony, family was a matter of life and death. Like Paul Weyrich and Brent Bozell, he viewed the nuclear family as the bedrock of society. He agreed with his Catholic counterparts that it was the basis for social order. But he differed from Weyrich and Bozell in his understanding of how the family operates as the basis for national greatness. Instead of emphasizing how the family is an icon of the Church, Rushdoony centered his family values around law and order. The well-ordered family, led by a viciously authoritarian patriarch, is a microcosm of a properly constructed human culture.

Rushdoony envisions the mandate for dominion extending to every facet of human society. That means places you'd expect, like the church and government, but it also means business, the arts, and agriculture, since "every realm under God's law is an area of Kingdom activity."[11] Rushdoony's dominion theology is about dominance, submission, authority. He has no appetite for a church whose approach to culture and politics is persuasion, pluralism, or the recognition of wisdom in other faith traditions and worldviews. "Rushdoony reasoned that this knowledge had political implications: thinking is a matter of kingship, power, rebellion, and, in the final analysis, warfare," writes McVicar. "Either human thought recognizes God's sovereignty, or it does not."[12] There is no middle ground, no compromise. Any sense of vulnerability, any call for reconciliation, any need for a mutual respect across theological and political lines is abolished in the name of the absolute authority of God's law and the mandate to subdue the world in his name. Every sphere must be conquered by men who are God's representative kings on Earth.

This vision differs from the Catholic one articulated by Bozell and Weyrich. In their Catholic theology, the Church would be the final authority over a government integrated into its sovereignty, as it was in certain contexts in medieval Europe. By contrast, Rushdoony openly advocates for theonomy—the rule by God's law. This requires "godly" magistrates ready to implement justice and order. But they are not to be agents of the church. Rushdoony sees each sphere as equal in terms of the mandate to dominate, but separate in their function, authority, and structure—except for one, the family: "The family is God's basic governmental institution."[13]

The special function of the family for Rushdoony is that it

is a self-contained sphere of dominion, authority, and submission. It is the model for how each sphere should work—a prism for God's desired human order. "Because the family is the womb of life, it is also the locale of basic government," Rushdoony says. "It is man's first church and state, his first school and vocation, the first economic realm, and more."[14] Within the family, the man is the head to whom the woman and the children submit. This is the entire meaning of the family—it is the first point of contact with the hierarchical structure that governs all human relationships. "The meaning of the family is thus not to be sought in procreation," Rushdoony writes, perhaps with an eye toward his Roman Catholic counterparts, "but in a God-centered authority and responsibility in terms of man's calling to subdue the earth and to exercise dominion over it."[15] A man's authority in the household is the first defense against "social chaos."[16] The family's special status means that "in a godly society" crimes against the family are "treason." The death penalty applies to adultery and homosexuality and disobeying one's elders. In essence, if you betray the order of the family, you betray the natural order of the universe, and God himself. This is deserving of death. In sum, Rushdoony constructed a theology in which the earthly father is so like the heavenly one that disobeying him is as grave a sin as anything one could do to God himself.

* * *

Rushdoony's cutthroat approach to biblical interpretation and the family provide the theological foundation for how he understands the history of the United States. His desire to return to a barbaric state that stones people to death for not obeying their parents may only be outdone by his bonkers rendering of

American history. For most American evangelicals, and many other conservative American Christians, the Pax Americana was sometime between the 1920s and the 1950s, before the sexual revolution, the civil rights movement, immigration reform, and *Roe v. Wade*. Make America Great Again means going back a few decades to a time when racial minorities, women, and immigrants were less represented and less free. This is bad enough. But Rushdoony goes way further:

> The roots of American history go deep. Not only is it the oldest of Western countries in consecutive and unbroken inheritance in civil government, having been free of revolutions and internal chaos, but its origins are Christian and Augustinian, deeply rooted in Reformation, medieval, and patristic history. It is held, moreover, that the United States, from its origins in the Colonial period on through the era of the Constitution, represented a Protestant feudal restoration.[17]

Rushdoony's era of American greatness is more the 1650s than the 1950s. In his mind, it was the Puritans of the Massachusetts Bay Colony who embodied the godly state outlined in the Bible. He believes that the God-ordained form of civil society is a network of independent counties or territories that are run according to local laws and customs. In order to return to a "Christian America," Rushdoony maintains that authority must be restored not only away from the federal government to the states, but further to the counties. This will ensure that no incursion is made on the family. After all, "The family is to all practical intent abolished whenever the state determines the education, vocation, religion, and the discipline of the child."[18]

In a Christian state, the civil government has no role in the cultivation of morality, the education of children, or the welfare of individuals. That is left to the authoritarian men sitting at the head of the dinner table.

Civil government is nothing more than an administration of God's law. Rushdoony says, "It is not sovereign over law but is under law."[19] Magistrates of the civil government are representatives of God whose role is to administer King Jesus's law without bias or empathy. According to Rushdoony, once the United States created a centralized government, it was no longer a Christian federation. As the country developed from the Constitutional Convention into the postcolonial period, the creation of public schools, federal laws, and federal taxes represented a humanistic attempt to replace God and his law with the idolatrous authority of the state.

For Rushdoony, the Puritan colonies reflected the "biblical" model of government not only because of their feudal structure, but due to their strict laws as well: "Religious tests for citizenship, blasphemy laws, singular or plural establishments, and other religious settlements were the rule," Rushdoony observes, "jealously guarded and prized, first against British interference, then against Federal usurpation."[20] In other words, it was the ideal civil society precisely because it was not a democracy: "The holy commonwealth was a theocracy in that it rested on the sovereignty of God and His kingship."[21] Historian Molly Worthen calls the Puritan colonies the "most successful experiment in theocracy that the modern West has ever seen" in the sense that "New England Puritans built societies that functioned as totalitarian city-states ruled by God's law."[22] When Rushdoony envisioned renewing America, this is what he imagined.

What's clear when reading Rushdoony's rendering of American history is that he both interprets America as a city on a hill in the sense that it was a unique iteration of God's ideal state and also believes that every time the United States inched toward something resembling a democracy, in which the will of the people is abided and all citizens are represented, it became less reflective of God's model. All governments should be an administration of the King's law and will without regard for pluralism, diversity, or the freedom of or from religion.[23]

Although Rushdoony criticizes monarchies in which a royal sits on an earthly throne, he is a monarchist in the sense that he believes civil society should answer to King Jesus—and to him alone. This rendering of American history and the Constitution leads Rushdoony to disgusting claims about the enslavement of Black people: "Thus, in a century's time, the Negro exchanged slavery to an individual for slavery to the State. In both conditions, there are advantages, but both constitute slavery."[24]

* * *

Though he was born a decade before Bozell, Rushdoony's heyday as a writer, theologian, and pastor corresponds largely with the years that Brent Bozell was a sought-after speaker and the editor of *Triumph*. Whereas Bozell was ushered out of the spotlight by a combination of alcoholism, mental illness, and his Catholic monarchism, Rushdoony's downfall was largely the result of a coordinated campaign by his fellow evangelicals.

As Michael McVicar chronicles in *Christian Reconstruction*, by the late 1980s Rushdoony and other Reconstructionist theologians—including his son-in-law Gary North and his onetime student Greg Bahnsen—had gained traction in evangelical circles, despite Rushdoony's criticisms of mainstream figures like Billy Graham and his adversarial relationship with *Christianity Today*, the flagship evangelical publication of the era. Rushdoony appeared on television programs hosted by evangelical stalwarts and had his books endorsed by Jerry Falwell. Rushdoony was evangelicalism's most infamous frenemy, an ally and an irritant.

However, the more he became known, the more evangelical leaders feared that his stringent dominion theology would spell disaster for the budding mainstream popularity of the evangelical movement. Some, like the theologian Hal Lindsey—author of *The Late Great Planet Earth*—argued that dominion theology would lead to another holocaust.[25] In a more measured tone, Rodney Clapp made the case in an infamous 1987 *Christianity Today* article that a return to biblical law wouldn't solve complex questions of Christian ethics, but instead introduced a moral maze requiring a whole class of scribes and scholars able to parse all its details.[26] Should illegitimate children be shunned from society? Should the dowry be reintroduced? Homosexuals murdered? For Clapp it was clear that the open call for theonomy was the wrong path for the Religious Right. After all, men like Paul Weyrich had worked tirelessly to make important strides in electoral politics and to fight the culture wars. If evangelicals followed Rushdoony and his heirs into the Reconstructionist vortex, they would soon find themselves once again on the margins of society, labeled backward extremists with no business participating in the modern political arena.

It wasn't just Rushdoony's evangelical siblings who sounded the alarm. "Secular journalists are calling Rushdoony's movement 'the spark plug behind much of the battle over religion in politics today,'" wrote Molly Worthen. "If his followers have their way, these writers warn, America will become a patriarchal society with zero religious tolerance for any faith other than fundamentalist Christianity, where church and state are effectively one and Mosaic code is the law of the land, where homosexuals, adulterers, and disrespectful teenagers are executed by public stoning."[27]

While key ideas from Reconstructionism infiltrated nearly every corner of the evangelical universe, the movement—and the man behind its rise—were publicly ushered out of polite society by the new millennium.

* * *

Despite their different personas, there's a strange overlap to the lives of Paul Weyrich and R. J. Rushdoony. Rushdoony spent most of his career criticizing the Religious Right as an idolatrous form of Christianity more interested in political gains than serving King Jesus. The Religious Right is of course the political alliance Weyrich masterminded in the 1970s in order to take back American culture in the name of God.

The two did cross paths. Rushdoony reportedly attended the first meeting of the Council for National Policy. He also had various run-ins with Richard Viguerie, one of Weyrich's close colleagues in the 1970s. Yet, for the most part while Rushdoony was firing off missives from his remote compound in a far corner of California in the seventies and eighties, Weyrich was likely somewhere on Capitol Hill hosting a lunch with

GOP members of Congress, lobbying a senator, or building support among Catholics and evangelicals to champion "family values" at their state houses.

However, by 1999 Weyrich was disillusioned with electoral politics. He concluded that there was no moral majority and that a new strategy of separation, guerilla warfare, and antidemocratic strategizing was needed in order to re-Christianize society. All the optimism of a once-in-a-generation politico had vanished. It wasn't just the movement that had failed him. He now saw the Constitution itself as destined to fail from the start. This is the sentiment one would expect from Rushdoony or other Reconstructionists, not the man who led the traditionalist takeover of the GOP. While Weyrich's theology and tactics never synchronized fully with Rushdoony's, there is a stray remark in a 1999 letter by the former that highlights how Reconstructionism hovered in Weyrich's consciousness. "We don't have to become Amish or move to Idaho," Weyrich says.

By the end of the millennium, Reconstructionism had been all but banished from mainstream evangelical discourse. Popular news outlets had warned the general public about the specter of stoning gay people to death if Rushdoony's acolytes had their way. Yet Reconstructionism was still on Weyrich's mind. His letter is in some ways an admission that the Reconstructionists were, at least in part, right about the ills of American society. In some sense, Weyrich was confessing that his way didn't work. Electoral victories had not led to the re-Christianization of society. Liberalism was a Trojan horse smuggled into the Constitution, a congenital heart defect of the American republic. Perhaps the Reconstructionists had the right idea—to separate from mainstream institutions, plan a full-scale takeover of American society, and then launch their attack when the time came.

We know this because by 1999 the epicenter of Reconstructionism was no longer in Vallecito, California, at Rushdoony's compound. It was in Moscow, Idaho, in the burgeoning empire run by Doug Wilson. When Weyrich mentioned Idaho, he was, among other things, thinking of Doug Wilson—Pete Hegseth's future theological icon.

* * *

Just as mainstream media and legacy evangelicals were declaring Reconstructionism safely buried, it was being quietly revived—slowly, deliberately—in a small college town tucked into one of the least populous states in the country, gathering strength precisely because few were watching. In the 1980s, Doug Wilson cofounded *Credenda/Agenda*, a magazine whose writers adopted Rushdoony's theological worldview while eschewing his influence and refusing the labels "Reconstructionist" and "theonomist." A decade later, Wilson helped lead the charge to gather the magazine's authors and readers into a new denomination, the Communion of Reformed Evangelical Churches (CREC). Pete Hegseth's former church in Nashville is part of this denomination.[28]

Wilson and his colleagues maintained a "critical distance from the broader Christian Reconstructionist project," observes the Irish religion scholar Crawford Gribben, "precisely because their goals and presuppositions were in many ways so closely aligned with it."[29] As Gribben argues in *Survival and Resistance in Evangelical America: Christian Reconstruction in the Pacific Northwest*, Wilson revived Reconstruction by keeping it under the radar. His audiences were not the evangelical mainstream or American culture at large, but those sympathetic with the mission of patiently building Christendom 2.0 outward from its epicenter in Moscow and other satellites across the country.[30]

* * *

In some sense, Doug Wilson is everything Rushdoony was not. The latter was irritable and confrontational, the kind of man who offends you before you even meet him. His contrarian streak time and time again led to burned bridges with the likes of Billy Graham, Carl F. H. Henry—the editor of *Christianity Today*—and other luminaries in the evangelical world. In public, Rushdoony spoke with a scholar's cadence and a theologian's sensibility. Always a teacher, not an entertainer, his goal was to communicate the definitive truths of God's word, rather than to tell heartwarming stories or relate to the audience with personal vignettes.

In public, Wilson presents himself as a jovial pastor—a portly grandfather, with a frontier-core style and demeanor that toggles between hokey and hardcore. He cracks dad jokes constantly. His writings offer outdated cultural references and terms that are cringe to outsiders, but endearing to the highly churched audiences who love him. Wilson utilizes various forms of media to spread his message. Rushdoony was a prolific writer who mailed out a monthly newsletter for decades. He appeared on Christian television programs, but never became a branded personality like his contemporaries Jerry Falwell and Pat Robertson. By contrast, since the 1990s Wilson has been masterminding a media empire based in Moscow, Idaho—a publishing house, a podcast network, YouTube channels, live streams, and now Canon+, which is a streaming service akin to Paramount+ or HBO Max. Wilson's cultural awareness has enabled him to thread the needle between carrying on Rushdoony's Reconstructionist legacy and ensuring that he isn't canceled for being an extremist.

Wilson's theology aligns with Rushdoony's, but with a sense of caution and patience that sometimes felt absent in the heyday of Reconstructionism. Wilson calls himself a "kinder, gentler" Reconstructionist. In one breath he explains why God's law is unchanging and the only way to any semblance of human freedom—for believers and unbelievers alike—is to return the crown's rights to King Jesus. In the next he cautions that he isn't advocating for violence, or a revolution, or anything abrupt. There is time to take over the world. There is time to colonize the Earth for God. But if you start calling for it now, he warns, you'll introduce a "poison pill" that will scare everyone away.[31]

* * *

Despite constantly distancing himself from Rushdoony and the Reconstructionism of the late twentieth century, Wilson extends Rushdoony's theological framework in key ways. First, like many in the Reformed tradition, and certainly almost any Reconstructionist, Wilson argues that there is no such thing as neutrality when it comes to the public square. Like Rushdoony, he goes so far as to argue that "all societies are theocratic, with the only thing distinguishing them being the nature and attributes of the reigning theos."[32] The question is not if a society will worship a deity but which deity they will worship. Thus, secularism is not godless, but instead makes a deity out of human beings. The problem is that there is no anchor to such a society. Wilson concludes that in a Christian society—even a theonomic one—non-Christians would be more free, because such a society would recognize where the rights came from and who guarantees them (even though they would be unable to vote, practice a non-Christian religion in public, or have access to reproductive care and Medicare). What's more, they wouldn't have the right to marry unless they were heterosexual, or have Social Security, welfare programs, or perhaps even public schools. In this vein, Wilson advocates for what he calls "mere Christendom."

> I mean a network of nations bound together by a formal, public, civic acknowledgment of the Lordship of Jesus Christ, and the fundamental truth of the Apostles' Creed. I mean a public and formal recognition of the authority of Jesus Christ that repudiates the principles of secularism, and that avoids both hard sectarianism and easy latitudinarianism both.[33]

Wilson is calling for the creation of a Christian state in the United States—and in every nation across the globe.

He wants to abolish the separation of church and state in order to implement a model wherein "the magistrate has the responsibility to recognize her (the church), to convene synods and councils to seek her counsel, and to listen to her," Wilson writes. "The magistrate himself has the responsibility, as a public figure, in the discharge of his office, to believe in Jesus, Lord of Heaven and earth." Wilson is not afraid of critics, whether Christian or not, who decry the end of the American experiment as we know it. Things are so bad, he argues, "that the great secular experiment that is America appears to have already gone out behind the barn and shot itself."[34]

It may be hard to understand what is "mere" about Wilson's approach to Christendom. Though fashioned as a play on C. S. Lewis's *Mere Christianity,* Wilson's Christian nationalist agenda will seem to most like a dangerous imposition of Christianity on a diverse and unwitting public. Wilson views his agenda as Christian nationalism lite, because he doesn't want to enforce a denominational code on each state. So, if Virginia has a Presbyterian state and Minnesota is Lutheran, the loose federation of Christian governments can and should still operate. As long as the state abides by the Apostles' Creed, with no "funny business," Wilson is confident that a federal alliance will work. Of course, this excludes Jews, Muslims, Latter-day Saints, atheists, agnostics, and perhaps Catholics—you know, like 40 percent of Americans, or 135 million people.

However, in his view this isn't a toppling of the American ethos, or a call for a postconstitutional America. Like Rushdoony before him, Wilson sees it as a return to the Christian state once enacted by the Puritans and even the participants in the Constitutional Convention. "The First Amendment, rightly understood, does not prohibit a civil acknowledgment of the Lordship of Jesus. It prohibits the establishment of a particular denomination of Christians at the federal level as the national church."[35] Whenever possible, Wilson repeats the line that "nine of the first thirteen" states had ties to a Christian denomination. He conveniently leaves out the fact that by the 1830s those states voluntarily gave up those ties in order to set up state governments that mirrored the separation of church and state outlined in the Constitution. Wilson argues ridiculously that the Constitution's reference to the "year of our Lord 1789" is proof that God is part of our founding document, which seems like saying that if you sing a Christmas carol, you must be an orthodox Christian. He calls the American Revolution the "Presbyterian Revolt." "The fact that it was Christian meant that our republic was part of Christendom," Wilson writes of the American founding. "The fact that numerous Christian denominations were involved meant that we provided the beta-testing for a mere Christendom."[36]

When thinkers like Wilson make such grandiose statements, they whitewash a millennium's worth of Christian-on-Christian violence. Christendom was not a peaceful united regime that lasted centuries without disruption, but an ongoing intra-Christian battle for religious and state power. The colonists didn't intend to found the new republic as an extension of some continuous Christian civilization. They broke from a kingdom that wouldn't allow it to represent itself in its parliament or control the imports and exports of its communities.

Nonetheless, Wilson advocates for a return to the supposed purity of the colonies. What would a mere Christendom look like in the contemporary United States? Wilson outlines a vision in which religious minorities could live in the country without fear of punishment—as long as they accept that the public expression of their faith is not allowed.

> In this mere Christendom I am talking about (you know, the idyllic one, down the road), Muslims could come from other lands and live peaceably, they could buy and sell, write letters to the editor, own property, have that property protected by the cops, and worship Allah in their hearts and homes. What they could not do is argue that minarets have the same rights of public expression that church bells do. The public space would belong to Jesus.

Wilson wants to outlaw non-Christians from holding political office, and from building temples, synagogues, humanist spaces, or anything that is not a church. He may not dream of Franco's Spain, like Brent Bozell did. But he does seem to long for Calvin's Geneva, where dissenters were burned at the stake and power was concentrated in the hands of a few churchmen.

◆ ◆ ◆

While Wilson sells himself as a kind and gentle theonomist and less extreme than Rushdoony, there is one domain where he is as openly radical as his forebear: sex, marriage, and the family. If in public Wilson presents as a "a sort of gentle buffoon, a sort of endearing gramps," as Tia Levings, author of *A Well-Trained Wife: My Escape from Christian Patriarchy* calls him, behind the closed doors of his ministry he is a militant patriarchal pastor who has a record of protecting abusers.[37]

Wilson believes that God created men and women with different roles to play in the family, in the church, and in civil society. Echoing Rushdoony, he argues that "a man's head is Christ, and a woman's head is man." This means that any man "who abdicates his functional authority over his wife—one who capitulates to egalitarian feminism" is a heretic. His sin equals denying the Trinity.[38] Women have been given "strength" in the domestic realm as homemakers and mothers. Outside of the home, they are weak when it comes to leadership, politics, pastoral responsibilities, and "the important work of violence," as Wilson says in an argument against women serving in combat.[39] Thus, women should not be placed in roles of ecclesiastical, civil, or political leadership. He goes so far as to characterize the Nineteenth Amendment, which affords women the right to vote, as a matter not of extending suffrage to half the population, but of "taking it away from families."[40] Jared Longshore, the executive pastor of Wilson's church in Moscow, and Joe Rigney, another pastor on the church's staff, both express the desire to repeal the Nineteenth Amendment so that Americans would vote by household, with the man having the final say. Any single mothers or queer families left after Wilson's Christian purge would be unlikely to get a vote in such a system—or survive safely at all.

This retrograde approach to gender roles translates into a dangerous understanding of human sexuality. "A wife must meet her husband's sexual needs (1 Cor. 7:2–5)," Wilson writes in *Reforming Marriage*. "This involves more than just being 'willing' whenever 'he wants it'; it involves being a responsive lover."[41] In 2021, the writer Sarah Stankorb wrote a blockbuster piece of investigative journalism for *Vice* that revealed how Wilson's understanding of men's and women's roles has led to a culture of secrecy, fear, and abuse in and around his ministry. Stankorb points out that Wilson has written that "the sexual act cannot be made into an egalitarian pleasuring party." Instead, he argues that "a man penetrates, conquers, colonizes, plants," while a "woman receives, surrenders, accepts," and that "true authority and true submission are therefore an erotic necessity." One person in the church was told, according to Stankorb, that "a woman could be excommunicated from the church for refusal to have sex with her husband."[42]

More examples abound. Stankorb chronicles how Wilson wielded his influence in order to garner leniency for a man in his twenties who was abusing an underage girl, and how he officiated the wedding of Steven Sitler, a convicted child molester, against the wishes of the man's parole officer. "At Sitler's wedding, according to one guest, Wilson explained that sometimes people need to get married so the flesh can be contained," Stankorb writes. "Using a wife as a sexual decoy to distract Sitler from children didn't work. Later, a judge ruled Sitler must be chaperoned around his infant son, due to admitted sexual stimulation resulting from contact with the baby." In another case, the father of a teenage girl confessed to touching her inappropriately and watching her in the shower. When the girl asked Nancy Wilson, Doug Wilson's wife, for counsel, she was told "that her father hadn't done anything illegal. When [the teenager] would mention, for example, a hug where his hand strayed to her butt, Nancy Wilson suggested she give him the benefit of the doubt. 'That's the Christian thing to do,' she was told."[43]

* * *

The storefront building is not theirs. It's borrowed from a conservative think tank with ties to Mark Meadows, Trump's former chief of staff. Washington, DC, is replete with beautiful gothic churches and elegant colonial architecture. But this is a small office building next to a "My Eye Doctor." Yet in mid-July 2025 the church held its first service with members of the press and other notable figures in attendance. "Worship is warfare," Jared Longshore said from the pulpit.

"Standing at a grey lectern underneath an enormous American flag suspended across the ceiling, Jared Longshore prepares to address the crowd," writes Franziska Wild in *The Washingtonian*. "Dressed in a blue suit and striped tie with an auburn beard and professorial glasses, he looks like a policy wonk giving a speech at the Heritage Foundation. Political paraphernalia hangs on the walls: a plaque from the Republican National

Convention, a garishly yellow Gadsden flag, framed copies of the *New York Times* announcing conservative victories. It's a scene one might find at any conservative political fundraiser in DC."[44]

In a May 2025 letter, Doug Wilson explained why he and the team at Christ Church in Moscow were embarking on a "mission to Babylon" by planting a church in the heart of Washington, DC:

> So why are we doing this just now? The first reason is that we are reading providence in a particular way. With the change in administration, we believe that there will be many strategic opportunities with numerous evangelicals who will be present both in and around the Trump administration.[45]

One of the evangelicals who was present on the first Sunday that the new church opened its doors was Pete Hegseth. The leader of the American armed forces listened to the message about how "worship is warfare" by a church team who argue that the Nineteenth Amendment should be repealed, women should submit to men, wives are made to meet the sexual needs of their husbands, women should not serve in combat, trans people do not exist, any form of queerness is a sin, non-Christians should not be able to practice their religion in public, much less hold elected office, and that the goal of the church is to institute Christendom 2.0 in the United States and across the world.

As with the worship and prayer service he led at the Pentagon, Hegseth was there in order to revere "King Jesus," whom he and others in Wilson's orbit expect to conquer the world inch by inch in the coming age.

As Rushdoony faded from the spotlight and other prominent Reconstructionists became more extreme—and further ostracized—Doug Wilson patiently and methodically built an empire in Moscow—a distant outpost in the American northwest away from American Babylons like Los Angeles, New York, and especially DC. When historian Kristin Kobes Du Mez was writing *Jesus and John Wayne*, her enormously popular book on evangelical masculinity, some scholars wondered why Doug Wilson was included. In the 2010s, he was still so marginal that some of the leading scholars of American Christianity had not heard of him.[46] Wilson alternated militant calls for biblical masculinity and imperial Christianity with assurances that he was not an old-school Reconstructionist who wanted to stone people to death. His brand of dad-joke extremism provided cover for a violent worldview that is openly antidemocratic and anti-pluralist—the kind of Christianity that sees a republic based on the separation of church and state as a sin to repair.

Wilson's decision to launch Christ Church DC reflects how the extreme has become the mainstream in a matter of decades. The strain of Protestantism that proved too militant for Weyrich's and Falwell's Religious Right is now so popular—and so well-funded—that it has ventured from the far reaches of small-town Idaho into the heart of the nation's capital in order to take dominion of the world.

In August 2025, Wilson told CNN that sodomy should be a crime, that women should not vote, that there was "mutual affection" between masters and the people they enslaved, and that "women are the kinds of people that people come out of."[47] Pete Hegseth tweeted a link to the interview with the caption, "All of Christ for all of life."

✦ ✦ ✦

Like their Catholic counterparts, Rushdoony and Wilson prescribe a retrograde patriarchal theology centered on sacred violence and social control. It's hard to ignore the intuition that when men like this demand a faith as misogynistic, hierarchical, and cruel as this one, they are projecting onto God the type of despotic rule they want for themselves. These men need a God made in the image of a ruthless patriarch so that they can justify being ruthless patriarchs. In a way similar to Bozell and Weyrich, their anxiety in the face of social change bred a form of Christianity based more on nostalgia for ancient societies than on the teachings of the New Testament. They envision God's law as an eternal standard by which society must abide. But in doing so they remove any space for dissent, questioning, or internal debate. Any objection to Daddy's teachings represents an abomination against God the Father's immutable code. It may warm Wilson's heart to think of the Puritans as the godly exemplars of the American way. In reality, the Massachusetts Bay Colony was not characterized by tranquility but by terror. The Puritans perpetrated constant Christian-on-Christian violence, burning Quakers and independent women at the stake, viciously attacking indigenous people, and banishing the likes of Roger Williams for daring to disagree with their theocratic totalitarianism. History can be cute until you remember how much blood was spilled in the name of religious purity. For weak authoritarian dinosaurs like Wilson, these tales are cozy. For anyone sensible, they are blood-curdling.

Finally, the cost of Reconstructionist patriarchal hierarchy trickles down to anyone who is not a White male. Those who are exposed to their abuse—like the sexual assault victims from Wilson's church—are collateral damage in a system that provides no means of protecting them, because the earthly fathers must have full, unaccountable control over all things in the community. The sanctification of domination leads to the abuse of the innocent. This theology doesn't protect the vulnerable; it preys on them.

3

PETER THIEL'S TECHNO-MONARCHISM

The fate of our world may depend on the effort of a single person who builds or propagates the machinery of freedom that makes the world safe for capitalism.

—PETER THIEL

He looks like a brain trying to explode from its casing. The extruded vein, like a python, extends across his forehead, which is shiny with sweat. One would assume his resting state is tense rage. Every breath sounds like seething. Despite the guise of casualness—a fashionable T-shirt, a nonchalant mid-fade haircut, blue Dockers—there is nothing easy about this man. He looks, as George Packer once noted, "uncomfortable having a body."[1]

It's June 2025. Peter Thiel is sitting across from Ross Douthat, a conservative Catholic reporter from *The New York Times*, for a video podcast interview. Douthat asks him about the future of humanity.

What follows is clipped on social media endlessly, played tens of millions of times across the globe:

Douthat: I think you would prefer the human race to endure, right?

Thiel: Uh——

Douthat: You're hesitating.

Thiel: Well, I don't know. I would—I would——

Douthat: This is a long hesitation!

Thiel: There's so many questions implicit in this.

Douthat: Should the human race survive?

Thiel: Yes.

Douthat: OK

Thiel: *But I also would like us to radically solve these problems. And so it's always, I don't know, yeah . . .* [2]

This is a trademark of Thiel. Despite a mind built like a perpetually revving engine, he hesitates, hems and haws, when answering questions. It's as if he is calculating all the possible arguments for each side before coming out with his own answer. In the interim, everyone listening is treated to a filler-word salad.

Later in the interview, Douthat asks him about the Antichrist. This leads to another viral moment. Instead of hesitating, Thiel goes right into a script he's been reciting for years about who the candidates are for Antichrist, why warnings about Armageddon are a sign that the Antichrist is upon us, and how risk, rather than security, is the way to avoid existential collapse as a species. As much as one might be disgusted by Thiel's hesitation about the future of humanity, the more confusing question for many was about Thiel's religious worldview. Why was Peter Thiel, one of the most influential billionaires in the world—a man whose life is based on tech innovation and cold-hearted calculation—more ready to answer questions about the Antichrist, Armageddon, and the Bible than about the survival of humanity?

* * *

Thiel is known to the general public as the founder of PayPal and a Silicon Valley icon. He's the influential billionaire who was the first outside investor in Facebook, the guy who destroyed Gawker after they outed him, and the one who bankrolled JD Vance to the Senate in 2021. He was also the first major Silicon Valley figure to come out in support of Donald Trump in 2016.

Unlike Elon Musk, his longtime friend and rival, Thiel avoids the spotlight, at least in the flashy and often cringeworthy ways of his counterpart. Thiel appears in the shadows, on the edges of political and cultural life, showing just enough of himself to the masses to arouse intrigue and ire, but never succumbing to the temptation to become a worshipped brand like Musk. While Musk is holding a chainsaw on stage, Thiel is lecturing at the Oxford Union or giving a keynote at Harvard. Yet, while Musk entered a short-lived run as Donald Trump's "copresident" from January to May of 2025, becoming the figurehead of the Department of Government Efficiency (DOGE) and the teardown of the federal government, Thiel was the one wielding lasting power in the Oval Office and beyond. Thiel has direct connections to the vice president of the United States; the former acting director of the CDC, Jim O'Neill; the director of the Office of Science and Technology Policy, Michael Kratsios; the AI and crypto czar, David Sacks; and dozens of other officials in the Trump administration—from the Department of State, to the Department of Defense, the Department of Energy, and so on. He is the most influential non-elected, non-appointed person in the Trump government.

Moreover, his company Palantir has signed lucrative agreements with the Department of Homeland Security "to use artificial intelligence and data mining to identify, track, and deport suspected noncitizens." For its services, "ICE is paying Palantir $30 million for the platform."[3]

Thiel represents a Silicon Valley cohort of monarchists who openly criticize democracy as a defunct, exhausted, or downright foolish mode of governance. In religious terms, Thiel does not fit the mold of either the Protestant or the Catholic figures analyzed in the previous two chapters. Brent Bozell wanted a government integrated into the Church, and Paul Weyrich worked to make it a reality. R. J. Rushdoony wanted to reconstruct the American government according to biblical law, and Doug Wilson is in the process of carrying out that vision. Peter Thiel describes himself as religious, but not spiritual.[4] For him, religion provides a set of stories, histories, and symbols that illuminate how human societies function, even if he shies away from questions of metaphysics or the nature of God. His interest is in transforming governance—in the megapolitical structures that shape global society and the ways he can innovate new forms of human existence. Thiel does not envision such forms as possible under the guise of the current political order. So how do his constant reflections on the Antichrist, Armageddon, and the West fit into a broader conception of a monarchical future?

What is the gospel of Peter Thiel?

* * *

Peter Thiel was born in Frankfurt, Germany, in 1967. His father, Klaus, was an engineer for mining companies. As a child, Thiel lived in Germany, then in apartheid South Africa, and then in Cleveland, Ohio. His family settled for good in Foster City, California—a small town near Silicon Valley and Stanford University—when he was ten. Yet some observers of Thiel's life and work have described the imprint that his early years in South Africa impressed upon him. It was "an experience that, according to those close to him, cemented a belief that some people are simply meant to rule."[5] While he has denied supporting apartheid, Thiel's biographer Max Chafkin writes that when Thiel was confronted about his reported positive views of apartheid, he claimed "it works."[6]

Thiel was a gifted student: reclusive, intense, and focused. As a teenager he was exceptional in school and as a chess player. When he enrolled at Stanford in 1985, Thiel became known as a peculiar genius among a student body full of top-tier talent. According to his biographer, Thiel viewed his fellow students as debaucherous and unfocused. To the young Peter, Stanford felt like a nonstop festival of drinking, sex, and partying.

One of the reasons that college life might have seemed depraved to Thiel is his Christian upbringing. Thiel was raised Lutheran. He has a deep knowledge of the Bible and the history of the Reformation. Christianity is a lasting part of his identity and worldview, even if his beliefs and actions often appear Machiavellian to observers. "Mr. Thiel has long been an exception to the atheism and agnosticism of his peers," wrote Emma Goldberg in *The New York Times*. "He has said his Christian faith is at the center of his worldview, which he expounds upon with a heterodox approach."[7] Rod Dreher, author of *The Benedict Option*, characterizes Thiel's faith as "utterly sincere." Though he may not adhere to an orthodox theology, Thiel "really and truly does believe that we are likely living in the time of the Antichrist, and that we had all better take this seriously, learning to read the signs of the times, and not just brushing it off as a preoccupation of the dispensationalists of pop Evangelicalism."[8]

While Thiel's faith is puzzling, his intensity is apparent. From his school days to his time at Stanford, Thiel's peers have consistently described him as driven, competitive, and arrogant. He neither fit in socially, nor did he view such endeavors as worth his time. Yet, somewhere along the way Thiel began to transform. His persona morphed from an extraordinarily talented intellect determined to win the competition of life to a kind of rebel who was so smart that instead of vying for the top spot on the anthill, he would eventually build his own somewhere else. After graduating in 1989, Thiel went to Stanford Law School and then on to work for a finance firm in Manhattan. He got an interview for a clerkship with a Supreme Court justice. Yet, in the early 1990s Thiel left the only path he'd ever been on—one that assured him financial success and professional power—to strike out on his own. He explained in detail why his failure to land the Supreme Court clerkship proved pivotal to this in his 2016 commencement address at Hamilton College:

> This is sort of the top prize you can get as a lawyer. It was the absolute last stage of the competition. But I lost. At the time I was totally devastated. It seemed just like the end of the world. About a decade later, I ran into an old friend. Someone who had helped me prepare for the Supreme Court interview, whom I hadn't seen in years. His first words to me were not, you know, "Hi Peter" or "How are you doing?" But rather, "So, aren't you glad you didn't get that clerkship?" Because if I hadn't lost that last competition, we both knew that I never would have left the track laid down since middle school. I wouldn't have moved to California and cofounded a startup. I wouldn't have done anything new. Looking back at my ambition to become a lawyer, it looks less like a plan for the future and more like an alibi for the present. It was a way to explain to anyone who would ask—to my parents, to my peers, and most of all to myself—that there was no need to worry. I was perfectly on track. But it turned out in retrospect that my biggest problem was taking the track without thinking really hard about where it was going.[9]

Thiel had been destined to become an ultrasuccessful part of the white-collar guilds—a financier in New York, a lawyer at a top law firm in San Francisco, or a clerk for a Supreme Court Justice in DC. By exiting the entire ecosystem, he was at risk of losing everything he had achieved, but also saw an opportunity to do something singular, away from the groupthink herds of analysts, attorneys, and bureaucrats. "When I cofounded a technology startup, we took the opposite approach," Thiel says toward the end of the Hamilton commencement speech. "*We consciously set out to change the direction of the world.* Very definite, very big plans."[10] He was no longer a competitor. He was a founder.

In the way Thiel frames it, after a tumultuous few years in which he became the premier frenemy of Elon Musk, Thiel sold PayPal to eBay for more than a billion dollars. From there he became the first outside investor in Facebook and a mentor to Mark Zuckerberg. Two decades later, he is perhaps the most important figure in Silicon Valley—and quite simply the most connected person from Palo Alto to DC.

* * *

Peter Thiel has been discussing political theory, apocalypse, the Antichrist, Armageddon, and the Bible for two decades. His podcast appearances and class visits to universities like Harvard and Stanford provide glimmers of his worldview, but they are for the most part incomplete and unpolished. These venues do not demand that Thiel provide any real rigor or coherence to his thoughts. However, in 2004 Thiel wrote an essay titled "The Straussian Moment" for *Politics and Apocalypse*, a collection of academic essays.[11] In contrast to his talks, lectures, interviews, and op-eds, the essay stands out as the only piece that required Thiel to play by someone else's rules—and thus to refine his thoughts to some degree. Since the essay appeared alongside writing from renowned scholars on political theology, it was edited with the rigor of an academic text. The result is the decoder ring for Thiel's techno-theology.

The question Thiel entertained in 2004 was how the "West" should respond to the 9/11 attacks. According to Thiel, in light of bin Laden's attack on the World Trade Center, the Enlightenment model was no longer viable. The terrorist attacks brought a "religious" war that the United States neither wanted, nor was prepared for, but now must undertake. In response Thiel asks what political theory should be employed in order to ensure a world where religious terrorism is not allowed to descend into unlimited violence, but wherein the "West" realizes it's in a war with those who never put down their swords at the Peace of Westphalia—and sets out to destroy them by any means necessary. Paul Leslie summarizes this in a seminal essay at *Salmagundi* magazine:

> So "The Straussian Moment" is a post-9/11 political call-to-arms that is also Thiel's personal call-to-arms. The geopolitical "moment" overlays his existential crisis, marking the birth of Peter Thiel as a political player. The essay reads as an intellectually compelling but deeply conflicted attempt to respond to a world he perceives as broken. Thiel envisions a future shaped by figures willing to act unilaterally, sometimes in secret, and, when necessary, outside democratic norms to stabilize a world in crisis.[12]

In order to build a blueprint for that future, he turns first to the German political theorist and Nazi jurist Carl Schmitt—an authoritarian who despised democracy and multiculturalism, and who helped build the worldview of the Third Reich.

For Thiel, Schmitt reminds "the West" that "politics is the field of battle . . . in which humans are forced to choose between friends and enemies."[13] When we confront an enemy whose values are fundamentally different from our own, they force us "to confront the foundational questions about human nature anew."[14] This is Schmitt's infamous friend/enemy distinction. Instead of pretending that we can all get along, Thiel takes from Schmitt the lesson that "there are things that really matter," and history reveals that humans will never agree about those things. We have fundamental values that cannot be argued away by evidence or reason. Ultimate questions require ultimate answers. When we disagree on them, conflict is inevitable. The way forward is neither dialogue nor debate, but a battle leading to one group dominating the other.

Journalists and commentators have justifiably sounded the alarm over Thiel's apparent fondness for Schmitt in recent years.[15] Thiel's interest in Schmitt's work deserves close scrutiny because of Schmitt's role in the Nazi government and how his political theory closely aligned with the Nazi worldview. If any author quotes Schmitt approvingly, my antennae go up immediately. It's like if someone told you the KKK is just misunderstood or Mussolini actually had some good ideas. The bad news is that Thiel seems to accept Schmitt's premise that pluralism is not possible because our fundamental values will always create conflict. In practical terms, however, Thiel does not see Schmitt as the way forward in the post-Enlightenment world created by 9/11. "The incredibly drastic solutions favored by Schmitt in his dark musings have become impossible after

1945, in a world of nuclear weapons and limitless destruction through technology," Thiel writes. In other words, if we stop at Schmitt, we will all die in nuclear war. Thiel turns from the Nazi thinker not because his ideas are disgusting, but because they simply aren't practical in the modern world.

In order to move forward, he looks to the philosopher Leo Strauss, Schmitt's intellectual sparring partner. Strauss is one of the most debated political theorists of the twentieth century. He is a favorite of contemporary conservatives because he argued that there is a "natural right" to human nature and conduct—a timeless standard of good. In other words, there are criteria as to which societies are right and virtuous, and which are not. Presumably, Strauss could be used to argue that the American way, as flawed as it is, is superior to the Islamic terrorism of Osama bin Laden—and any "Islamic civilization" ever to exist. Strauss maintains that there is a universal "hierarchy of values" that should be pursued in human societies, and that the highest of these values were exemplified in the American founding. However, there is no universal means for achieving them. Strauss consistently points out in his writing that the peace, stability, and values wrought by the American founding were built on exclusion, espionage, and violence. In other words, sometimes one must betray the values of a moral society in order to build that society.

You can see in Strauss's work the moral quandary every CIA agent in a 1990s-era spy film faces: They must betray civil liberties and due process in order to protect a society based on civil liberties and due process. This paradox is both the basis for American society and the potential cause of its downfall. If the American public realizes that it is not really a "city on a hill," American society may not survive as a democracy. Thiel concludes his section on Strauss with a haunting quote from Oswald Spengler's *The Decline of the West*: "But for us, whom fate has placed in this culture and this moment of its development, in which money celebrates its final victories and its legacy, *Caesarism, quietly and inexorably approaches . . .*"[16]

The terrorist attacks on 9/11 showed "the West" not only that it could not remain neutral in a world full of pious passions, but that its own democratic society was built on violence and exclusion—the very values it would ostensibly be fighting against in the war against religious terrorism. Are we then relegated to Schmitt's limitless destruction or the rise of an American Caesar?

In order to find a third way, Thiel turns to Christianity—and his favorite college professor.

✦ ✦ ✦

When Thiel was an undergraduate at Stanford, he encountered René Girard, a French literary theorist and devout Catholic. It is safe to say that since then Girard has been the single most influential figure on Thiel's worldview. His biographer Max Chafkin observes that "the discovery of Girard seems to have awakened something new in him—if not a profound sense of personal zeal, then an awareness of the role that religion could play in his public identity."[17] It was as if Christianity became a rebellious story Thiel could adopt in order to set him apart from not only campus tomfoolery, but also the culture of "political correctness" and emphasis on diversity developing at Stanford—and on campuses around the country. Girard is the one who inspired Thiel to turn his faith into an "act of defiance."[18]

Drawing on Christian stalwarts like St. Augustine, Girard and Thiel see Christianity as more evolved than other religions since it doesn't try to return human beings to a mythical peace time, but instead always pushes humanity into the future. This isn't unique to Girard. Philosophers like Hegel argued for the superiority of the Abrahamic framework because it encapsulates the possibility of human evolution and development—prioritizing the achievements of the West over the "savagery" of non-European cultures. Yet, Girard's version struck Thiel because it accorded with views Thiel had already developed before his college years. A lifelong fan of *The Lord of the Rings*, Thiel's senior quote in his high school yearbook was: "The Great Adventure is what lies ahead / Today and tomorrow are yet to be said."

Years later he'd say that he'd memorized the entire passage, which continues, "The chances, the changes are all yours to make / The mold of your life is in your hands to break." As Chafkin says, "It would become, in a way, the motto of his life."[19]

Nearly four decades afterward, Thiel reiterated this idea in a 2024 interview with the economist and former *New York Times* columnist Tyler Cowen:

> I think there is some kind of a meaning to history. I think it has a certain type of linearity to it. Let's say the Judeo-Christian view of history as distinct from, let's say, the classical Greco-Roman one. I don't know if you can have a concept of history that's cyclical. If you look at Thucydides, where it's this great period of

> peace that leads to this great war between Athens and Sparta . . . but there's nothing particular in the history. None of the details matter in Thucydides. He makes up all the speeches and so on. And then you contrast us with something like of the Book of Daniel in the Bible, where it's a succession of four kingdoms, and it is a one-time World History, where everything that happens is unique, not to be repeated. There's a sense in which I would say the real first historian was Daniel, and Thucydides isn't even close.[20]

Inspired by a strange reading of Girard's philosophy, Thiel's theology is built on an existential crisis. In individual terms Thiel wants his life to matter. He doesn't think it can unless his actions are a unique manifestation of agency never to be repeated in some kind of cycle of time. On a collective level, he believes that the human species needs to see itself as moving ever forward if it is going to innovate beyond its primitive forms. The silver lining in this bizarre rendering of the Christian story is that we are not predestined to our fate. The bad news is that humans may lead themselves to radical destruction at the hands of their technological inventions. We are the creators of history, and could be its destroyers too.

If we ruin ourselves, it will be because of competition. For an investor and entrepreneur, Thiel is counterintuitively opposed to competition. In his 2014 book *Zero to One* he advises company founders to build their corporations such that there is no competition for their product. This comes directly from his reading of Girard. "All cultural institutions, beginning with the acquisition of language by children from their parents, require this sort of mimetic activity, and so it is not overly reductionist to describe human brains as gigantic imitation machines," Thiel writes.[21] Thiel credits Girard's mimetic theory with his decision to invest in Facebook. After all, social media is nothing more than endless replication of images, videos, and text. "Facebook first spread by word of mouth, and it's about word of mouth, so it's doubly mimetic," Thiel commented on the occasion of Girard's death. "Social media proved to be more important than it looked, because it's about our natures."[22]

Thiel is a monopolist who sees the endless striving to best one another as not only an inferior mode of living, but also as the source of human destruction. Mimesis inevitably leads to conflict as individuals and communities strive to vanquish their rivals. Humans are often ready to kill their neighbor in order to be like their neighbor, or at least have what their neighbor has. This leads to a familiar endpoint—the threat of unlimited violence. The reason Armageddon looms perpetually on the human horizon isn't because of Schmitt's friend/enemy distinction nor Strauss's conception of the immoral foundations of society, but human covetousness. We want what *they* have. We blame *them* for our problems. If *those people* would disappear, we would be happy and have what we want. If, as MAGA says, we could just get rid of all the immigrants, queer people, or "others," then our country would be great again.

Yet for Thiel the tragic silver lining in the case of human nature is that the "war of all against all" doesn't lead to unlimited violence, but "gradually drive[s] the combatants to gang up on one particular person."[23] I'm not sure this is the good news Thiel thinks it is. What he is proposing is that human conflict is really only resolved after a cathartic homicide of a person or group of persons breaks the spell of violent competition, leading everyone back to their senses.

Nonetheless, Thiel argues that in order to break the fever and reset the cycle, a scapegoat is needed—someone or something to blame for the me-vs.-you and us-vs.-them spells that plague communities, whose destruction will temporarily quell the state of competition. This could be a type of cultural outsider, a migrant group, or an aristocrat. But their killing is supposedly the reset button for societies embroiled in conflict. Once the blamed figure is killed, their death "helps to unite the community and bring about a limited peace for the survivors. That murder is the secret origin of all religious and political institutions, and is remembered and transfigured in the form of myth."[24] Society doesn't look away from the founding act of violence, but instead sacralizes it. A myth arises that the violence was necessary and justified. The slain scapegoat turns into a venerated figure—a god, saint, or spirit whose sacrifice is viewed as the door that opened the way for the group's peaceful coexistence.

That is, unless the scapegoat can delay the inevitable.

What if the person who is envied, hated, and copied by everyone else can postpone their sacrifice as a scapegoat? "One working theory is that monarchy originated this way," Thiel said in a lecture on René Girard at Stanford in 2012. "Kings became scapegoats who had not yet been killed. Every king was a living god. Every god was a murdered king."[25] Thiel invokes examples from the Aztecs, the ancient Egyptians, and the Zulu kingdom in order to support his thesis: Monarchy arose in human societies when "the scapegoat simply figured out how to maintain his power and indefinitely delay his execution."[26] The king is the transcendent figure elevated above the ordinary competition field of humanity. He has total power. He is both revered and hated. Everyone wants to kill him so that they can be him. But as the transcendent one, he has a unique power to found and refound how societies operate. If he can avoid murder, the king can do something most humans never dream of, much less achieve: push humanity forward through true innovation.

* * *

For Thiel, the Christian story's uniqueness stems from its linear conception of time, bestowing on humans the power to help create history, and revealing the path to transcending our copycat nature. Despite his heterodox approach to the faith, Thiel follows a standard conception of human fallenness. "And the closest thing you can say to nature is that people are fallen. That's the natural thing in a Christian sense, that you're messed up. And that's true."[27] From there, Thiel diverts from orthodox doctrine. In traditional Christian theology, Christ's redemption saves humanity from sin. In Thiel's heterodox rendering, Christ redeems humanity from mimesis. "The word 'nature' does not occur once in the Old Testament," Thiel told Ross Douthat in 2025. "And so there is a word in which, a sense in which, the way I understand the Judeo-Christian inspiration is it is about transcending nature. It is about overcoming things."[28] For Thiel, Jesus is the monarch whose murder led to human transcendence, liberating humanity from its mimetic shackles, freeing us—or at least a few tech kings—to innovate through technological tools. After Christ, the king is not only the one who is the living scapegoat, but is the rare innovator in a society of imitators. The True Original. The Non-Mimetic One. The King is the Founder. And technology is the means to salvation from the mimetic desire at the root of violence and rivalry.

* * *

In Thiel's techno-theology, the most important contemporary "kings" are the founders of tech startups—those who would take us to a new world. Tech founders, following Jesus's example, will save us. If we let them.

"Technology maps to miraculous supernatural creation, and globalization maps to naturalistic uniformitarian evolution," Thiel told George Packer in 2012. "Technology involves the creation of radically new things that have not existed, and globalization maps to the continual copying of things that already exist."[29]

Moreover, tech founders operate as monarchs within their organizations. "A startup is basically structured as a monarchy," Thiel says. "We don't call it that, of course. That would seem weirdly outdated, and anything that's not democracy makes people uncomfortable." In startup culture, there is no voting or representation. Even when a board is formed and the startup transforms into a "mature company," Thiel says, "it ends up somewhere between constitutional republic and monarchy."[30] Innovation requires the best ideas. That means allowing a godlike founder to reign as the unquestioned leader. "It is more tyrant than mob because it should be."[31] This is an argument that Thiel has made consistently over the last two decades: Democracy is not the best form of organization, because voting leads to the "lowest common denominator type results."[32]

For Thiel, the skepticism about democracy is biblical. He

argues that whereas the Greek philosophical tradition prioritizes a "community of wise people," the Hebrew and Christian scriptures teach us to follow a single great leader. "You know, for a biblical scholar, I would sort of ask the question, is there a single incidence in which the unanimity of the crowd is right?" Thiel posed this question in a 2023 interview at Stanford's Hoover Institution. "I think it's always wrong. Joseph is right. His brothers are wrong. The Tower of Babel, the global crowd is completely wrong. You know, Christ is abandoned . . . so, somehow, reason tells us to believe in the wisdom of crowds. Revelation tells us to be skeptical."[33] If Athens teaches us democracy, Jerusalem leads to Caesarism. Following the startup model and the teachings of the Bible, it seems Thiel's ideal form of governance is "a quasi-mythological structure where you have a king-like founder who can do more than a democratic ruler but who remains far from all-powerful."[34]

With this in mind, it's possible to follow the twisted theological path on which Thiel identifies the Antichrist as the leader of a totalitarian state who will stop all innovation in the name of everyone staying safe. His position has remained consistent, even if it has evolved slightly with the times: The Antichrist is the figure who promises to bring peace and protect the world from existential risk and limitless violence. In reality, however, the Antichrist does so in order to trap human beings in a safety-state wherein innovation and freedom are outlawed in favor of security. The Antichrist is the anti-monarch; the one who wants to keep humanity limited to the endless competition for more resources, more status, more real estate, and so on.

"The way the Antichrist would take over the world is you talk about Armageddon nonstop. You talk about existential risk nonstop, and this is what you need to regulate," Thiel says.[35]

Since the COVID pandemic, Thiel has identified those who are calling for a halt to innovation in the name of safety and human preservation as those who look and sound like the Antichrist. They are the ones promising to bring peace by telling the scary stories of the end of the world that will frighten the masses into submission to a one-world government. One of Thiel's favorite targets is Oxford professor Nick Bostrom, who warned of four major existential risks in a 2019 essay: AI, climate crises, nuclear war, and bioweapons.[36] In order to stave off Armageddon, Thiel says that Bostrom wants to restrict technological development, limit the diversity of thought to a state orthodoxy, implement preventive policing using advanced technology, and "establish effective Global governance."[37] For Thiel, these solutions point toward the rise of the Antichrist in the form of a "one-world totalitarian state."[38]

"The thing that has political resonance is: We need to stop science, we need to just say 'stop this,'" Thiel told Ross Douthat in a 2025 *New York Times* interview. "And this is where, in the seventeenth century, I can imagine a Dr. Strangelove, Edward Teller–type person taking over the world. In our world, it's far more likely to be Greta Thunberg." In other words, Thiel is more afraid of a nonviolent climate activist than the surveillance state he's helping to build through Palantir.

* * *

If we go back to the question Thiel took up after 9/11—the question of how to prevent limitless violence in a nuclear world beset by religious conflict and geopolitical strife—we now have his answer. It is not democracy. It is not liberalism. It is not a renewed commitment to institution building, global consensus, or peace talks. In Thiel's mind, democracy and liberalism are "exhausted."[39] The question is not whether democracy will survive, but what will come afterward. If 9/11 was a decisive blow to the American ethos, then the Trump presidencies have been a tearing down of the postwar consensus in favor of something yet to be determined.[40] Instead of looking for Girard's scapegoat, Thiel is configuring new forms of techno-monarchy. The choices seem to be a one-world government ruled by the likes of a Green Party hero like Greta Thunberg, who will squash all innovation and free thought in the name of existential safety, or a tech CEO who will use technology to lead humanity—or at least a small sector of it—into new forms of freedom, governance, and flourishing. "The usual narrative is that society should be organized to cater to and reward the people who play by the rules," Thiel said in 2012. "Perhaps we should focus more on the people who don't play by the rules. Maybe they are, in some key way, the most important. Maybe we should let them off the hook."[41]

Thiel's hope is not to be the good guy in a cosmic battle between good and evil. Much to the chagrin of the journalists who cover him, he is not a total Schmittian Nazi. However, he is also far from a champion of democracy, human rights, or equality. Unlike the Jesus of the Gospels, he shows no compassion for the marginalized, the poor, or the outcast. His Christianity is about the redemption of humanity—even if only a few humans survive to enjoy it. Thiel is a Founder, not a Hero. As such, his ultimate goal is not to ascend the top of the political pile, but to find an innovation beyond "the totalitarian and fundamentalist catastrophes to the unthinking demos that guides so-called 'social democracy.'"[42] This has led to his various investments in life-extension technologies and his interests in transhumanism, cyberspace, and autonomous network cities, as well as the development of surveillance technologies through his company Palantir (more on all of this later). As he said in an infamous essay over a decade ago, "I no longer believe that politics encompasses all possible futures of our world."[43] In ways resonant with Rushdoony, Wilson, Bozell, and Weyrich, Thiel's sights are not set on a renewal of the Pax Americana, but the escape from the current system—the innovation—that will lead to authentic human freedom:

> A better metaphor is that we are in a deadly race between politics and technology. The future will be much better or much worse, but the question of the future remains very open indeed. We do not know exactly how close this race is, but I suspect that it may be very close, even down to the wire. Unlike the world of politics, in the world of technology the choices of individuals may still be paramount.[44]

Yet, instead of a return to Christendom, he follows Jesus by looking to tech as the way to stave off Armageddon. "The fate of our world may depend on the effort of a single person who builds or propagates the machinery of freedom that makes the world safe for capitalism."[45] As George Packer noted in his *New Yorker* profile of Thiel, "There's no doubt who that is."[46]

* * *

Thiel's theology is a world apart from figures like Bozell or Rushdoony. But his political conclusions are stunningly similar. Like them, Thiel's anxiety over social change leads him to view democracy as a cause of, rather than a solution to, humanity's problems. While his techno-theology is ostensibly motivated by the desire to stave off limitless violence, his categorizing of figures interested in safety and security as the Antichrist means that only a single techno-monarch, acting without accountability or transparency, would have the courage and insight to lead Western civilization. Thiel may view the AI skeptics and Luddites in our midst as Antichrist figures, but the alternative he offers is a surveillance state in which a tech CEO has control over everyone else without their consent. His theology does nothing to fend off the idea that maybe the one talking the most about the Antichrist is the one who resembles it.

* * *

Thiel is an oligarch who holds common people with disdain. His theology reflects his contempt for the many in favor of the few and the One. The poor, the sick, migrants, and those most vulnerable to technological harm appear nowhere in his vision except as distractions—or as potential scapegoats. Somehow Thiel empties the Christian story of mercy and compassion. The salvation he envisions is only for the select few. It's like a tech-Calvinism fueled by eugenics. The Elect are the Founders. Atonement is for the kings. Everyone else deserves damnation. I don't think Thiel is the Antichrist, but I do think his theology is the most anti-Christian thing imaginable.

There is a simple democratic response to Thiel's anti-Christianism: Power without oversight becomes corrupt, exploitative, and violent. Freedom, at its most basic level, requires that those who govern us must answer to us. Monarchy may be simpler. Algorithmic governance may be less messy. Monarchs can ignore the pain, needs, and desires of their subjects. A king can privilege efficiency over equality, command over deliberation. But that is domination, not liberty—at least for everyone except the man on the throne. Democracy is slow, inefficient, often maddening. It is rarely simple or graceful. But it does something monarchy cannot: It binds us all to the same laws and standards. It is a story not of identical gifts or talents, but of equal power and treatment. I would rather live in a world where power is shared and officials can be challenged than one where a single megalomaniac with an Antichrist fetish wields the resources to dominate everyone else. History is crowded with would-be saviors convinced they were different from those who came before them. Peter Thiel may be a founder. He is not an exception.

4

A POSTLIBERAL CATHOLIC KINGDOM

> **I don't want to violently overthrow the government. I want something far more revolutionary than that.**
>
> —PATRICK DENEEN

Even though the men on stage are dressed in DC's unofficial menswear uniform—dark traditional suits emanating power and authority—the panel feels more like a family reunion than a wonky policy conversation. Kevin Roberts, leader of the Heritage Foundation and shepherd of Project 2025, sits in between then-Senator JD Vance (soon to be the candidate for vice president on a ticket with Donald Trump) on one side and the Notre Dame philosopher Patrick Deneen on the other. The fourth panelist, the author and Catholic convert Christine Emba, appears considerably younger than the three men, and is the only non-White person. Though she takes her turn in the speaking order, throughout the session Emba resembles a welcome visitor to a conversation the other three have carried on for years.

They are gathered in June 2023 at an event in Washington, DC, convened by the Intercollegiate Studies Institute, a conservative student group, to launch Patrick Deneen's book, *Regime Change,* which is the much anticipated follow-up to his bestselling *Why Liberalism Failed.* The audience is made up of earnest religious students and conservative DC wonks. Compared to Roberts's fireside chat with Dwarkesh Patel at the Silicon Valley Reboot 2024 conference a year later, the atmosphere appears natural and open. Deneen, Roberts, and Vance are at ease. Even if they disagree on certain points, they share the same governing worldview. They can argue safely, because everyone here is on the same team.[1]

Throughout the course of the panel, the three describe what America has lost, how to approach different segments of the American population about reclaiming the "soul" of the nation, and the need to see government as a vehicle for virtue cultivation rather than simply for economic gain. They don't all agree on tactics and diagnoses, but despite their quibbles, Deneen, Vance, and Roberts agree on a fundamental point: In order to save America, something transformational is in order. "I don't want to violently overthrow the government," Deneen says in response to a question about January 6 and whether or not his push for "regime change" might recall the violence of that day. "I want something far more revolutionary than that." This echoes a headline-making statement from Roberts a year later, just before the 2024 election. "We are in the process of a second American revolution," he tells Steve Bannon in the *War Room* podcast. "It will remain bloodless if the Left allows it to be."[2] Vance put it this way in 2021 in an interview with Jack Murphy: "We are in a late republican period. If we're going to push back against it, we have to get pretty wild, pretty far out there, and go in directions that a lot of conservatives right now are uncomfortable with."[3] But these are not originalists made in the image of Antonin Scalia. Their goal is not to restore the United States to the *Leave It to Beaver* era of the 1950s. Nor are they libertarians who simply want the government out of their way.

Deneen, Roberts, and Vance are "common good conservatives."[4] According to them, the role of government is to actively and forcefully structure society for the common good it was designed for by God. The state's raison d'être is not to maximize liberty or protect human rights, but to organize human communities according to the common good, which as Catholics they agree is the Highest Good outlined by the Creator—even if that good feels like coercion or manipulation to the masses. Despite the fact that what is good for you feels degrading, oppressive, or hurtful, those with authority and wisdom to implement the blueprint for human flourishing will do it anyway, knowing it's what's optimal for the one and the many.

They are "common good" conservatives because they want to replace the individual pursuit of life, liberty, and happiness with a collectivist religious vision. "The role of the government," writes political scientist Chelsea Ebin, "is not to preserve individual rights and manage competing interpretations of the good but to impose and enforce a singular conception of the good through the regulation of social relations."[5] In other words, the American experiment of liberal democracy should give way to the mandate of replicating God's vision for humanity on Earth through the power and force of the federal government. Thus, what they seek is a fundamental change to the structure and scope of the American government. In order to create a state designed for the common good of all humanity, America must shed the vestiges of liberalism. We must enter a *postliberal* era.

Common good conservatives like Deneen, Roberts, and Vance are postliberal because they believe that the country's woes can be traced to "errors made centuries ago by the American Founders and their ideological progenitors," writes the political scientist Damon Linker. "In place of our polity's commitment to individual rights, autonomy, and pluralism, the post-liberals aim to create a society unified around the common good, which is itself fixed on a theological vision of the Highest Good."[6] One way to think of the relationship between common good conservatism and postliberalism is that the latter is largely diagnostic, while the former is prescriptive—the antidote to our ailments and the resolution to our disorder. Together, the diagnosis and the prescription are bringing Paul Weyrich's and L. Brent Bozell Jr.'s radical Catholic projects into the twenty-first-century mainstream.

As we saw earlier, by the latter decades of his life, Paul Weyrich—creator of the Heritage Foundation and mastermind of the Moral Majority—concluded that "there is no moral majority" and that the way forward was to cultivate elites who could liquidate American institutions and influence the masses. He became enamored with Putin's illiberal restructuring of Russia as a kind of model for the US. Moreover, Brent Bozell envisioned a federal government designed for the common good precisely because it was a subsidiary of the Catholic Church; a temporal institution contoured for earthly human needs through replication of divine patterns and natural law.

Like Weyrich and Bozell in decades past, postliberal common good conservatism represents an explicit break with William F. Buckley's (and for that matter Ronald Reagan's) fusion of libertarian economics and Christian traditionalism. Instead, this model calls for a big, intrusive state that has the power—and gall—to enforce a Catholic vision of natural law on all Americans (even if they don't want it) through culture, policy, and taxation. While the main tenets of Bozell's radical Catholic vision were once outside the bounds of the American Right, under the banner of postliberal common good conservatism, his worldview is now seen as an "exciting new legal theory" that is all the rage in conservative legal circles and Federalist Society group chats.

"A new political vocabulary is emerging, too, with new watchwords—'integralism,' 'dyarchy,' and other ways of specifying the common good—of which one can find no precedent, or even in many cases awareness, in the fusionist writings of a decade ago," writes Kevin Gallagher in *American Affairs*. "Thus the decline of fusionist Catholicism has cleared space for the revival of ideas the fusionists sought actively to suppress. Instead of William F. Buckley and Richard John Neuhaus, young Catholics are reading Brent Bozell, William Marshner, and others who propose a discourse explaining why liberalism cannot resolve the crisis of politics that it engineered."[7] In other words, Bozell's Catholic integralism has gone from outré to trendy in a matter of decades.

The gathering of Deneen, Roberts, and Vance together on stage is like a reincarnation of mid-twentieth-century right-wing Catholic radicalism retrofitted for the Trump era and brought into the halls of DC power. Along with the constitutional law professor Adrian Vermeule, the cofounder of

Compact magazine Sohrab Ahmari, the editor of the conservative outlet *First Things* R. R. Reno, and others, Deneen is one of the heirs of Brent Bozell's Catholic intellectual project. He is part of a cadre of Catholic philosophers, theologians, and constitutional lawyers waging war on liberalism in the name of common good conservatism.

As the current head of the Heritage Foundation, Roberts echoes Weyrich's words and strategies by calling for a "second American revolution" and publishing a handbook for presidential leadership—Project 2025—based on the "family values" and imposing vision for the federal government Weyrich developed from the 1970s to the turn of the century.

JD Vance is a zealous Catholic convert and the presumed GOP leader-in-waiting who may just be the best chance at a postliberal common good conservative leader of the "free" world; the elected official on whom the dreams for an American Christendom are cast. While we will focus on Vance later, it is important to note here the significant intellectual influence both Patrick Deneen and Kevin Roberts have had on the vice president.

In their most extreme forms, postliberal common good conservatives represent a strain of American Catholicism determined to inspire and direct a second American revolution based on Catholic political theologies in which the state is a de facto subsidiary of the Church. No longer on the edges of the American Right, this movement sees this moment as its chance at a new form of conservatism—and a new beginning for the United States.

One of Brent Bozell's reasons for breaking with William F. Buckley and the *National Review* was his contention that there is no qualitative difference between American conservatism and American progressivism. Both, he argued, are forms of "liberalism," because they rely on the principles of individual choice—whether in the form of laissez-faire economics or the advancement of civil liberties. These arguments largely fell on deaf ears for decades as Buckley's influence reigned over the American Right.

However, the tides have shifted. Paul Weyrich's life and views reflect the evolving realization that the majority of Americans are not in favor of the retrograde social order religious traditionalists like he and Bozell offer. Thus, a free market will only lead to the majority of Americans choosing products, ways of life, and cultural symbols that go against the tide of re-Christianizing society—celebrating Pride Month at Target or spotting trans influencers on beer ads. Today, one can hear the echoes of Bozell's and Weyrich's positions in the work of prominent Catholic intellectuals. Patrick Deneen and other postliberals such as Sohrab Ahmari and Adrian Vermeule maintain that the conservative mainstream and the American Left are practically indistinguishable. "Both 'classical' and 'progressive' liberalism ground the advance of liberalism in individual liberation from the limitations of place, tradition, culture, and any unchosen relationship," writes Deneen in his enormously popular 2018 work *Why Liberalism Failed*. "Both traditions—for all their differences over means—can be counted as liberal because of this fundamental commitment to liberation of the individual and to the use of natural science, aided by the state, as a primary means for achieving practical liberation from nature's limitations."[8]

Sohrab Ahmari shares Deneen's view that American conservatism is in the main just another form of liberalism. Amari converted to Catholicism in 2016, and is now one of the most vocal and influential common good conservatives. He has written regularly for the *New York Post* and *First Things*, and in 2022 he started *Compact*, a magazine that "seeks a new political center devoted to the common good." In 2019, Ahmari picked a very public fight with *National Review* writer David French, using French as a totem of everything that is wrong with most Christian conservatives. "Though culturally conservative, French is a political liberal, which means that individual autonomy is his lodestar," Ahmari writes in "Against David French-ism." "He sees 'protecting individual liberty' as the main, if not sole, purpose of government." Amari's criticism recalls Bozell's and Weyrich's disdain for prioritizing economic choice over traditionalist values. For Ahmari, the problem with French's view—even if it is a caricature of French's position—is that "its ultimate aim is to secure for the individual will the widest possible berth to define what is true and good and beautiful, against the authority of tradition."[9]

Adrian Vermeule, a constitutional law professor at Harvard and also a Catholic convert, is the most celebrated intellectual force in the postliberal common good movement. Unlike Bozell, who never found a foothold in powerful American institutions, Vermeule is a towering figure in the field of constitutional law—who just so happens to be a Catholic integralist extremist. "What's even worse—and this is my thesis—is that most of the sub-movements on the American right that imagine themselves to be critical of liberalism are, objectively, its servants," Vermeule writes in an essay in *Compact*, the magazine founded by Sohrab Ahmari. "They serve the liberal order by practicing and, indeed, advocating, in one form or another, political quietism: the fundamental refusal to mount a political and public challenge to liberalism itself."[10] In Vermeule's view, "Conservatism, Inc." is nothing more than an economic behemoth with no concern for virtue, morality, or tradition. It is liberalism with a Judeo-Christian veneer.

For Deneen, Ahmari, and Vermeule, liberalism's treachery lies in its individualism. In *Why Liberalism Failed,* Deneen argues that liberalism is tyrannical. He calls it more insidious than either communism or fascism because while liberalism claims to be a neutral ideology that opens a fair playing field to all, in his estimation it "requires liberation from all forms of associations and relationships, from family to church, from schools to village and community, that exerted control over behavior through informal and habituated expectations and norms."[11] Instead of an opening to freedom of choice, Deneen views liberalism as a hungry ghost of emancipation from the individual's communal identity and commitment. It is a machete cutting through the jungle of any ethnic identity or religious practice or familial tradition. The liberal emphasis on human rights, cherished after World War II in the wake of Auschwitz and the rise of ruthless twentieth-century authoritarian regimes, means there is no mechanism to form "good" citizens. Rights trump virtue, and thus in Deneen's view "no truly hard choices [need] be made. There are only lifestyle options."[12] Deneen waxes poetic about a time before liberalism, but his nostalgia doesn't go to the 1950s.

His ideal past is somewhere in Christendom, before the Enlightenment and liberal theorists like Locke and Hobbes ruined everything. "Deneen's work begins with a reductive definition of liberalism that cherry-picks within liberal democracy's rich genealogy," writes political theorist Laura K. Field, author of *Furious Minds: The Making of the MAGA New Right*. "Then, as he sets out to answer the question posed by his title—i.e., to explain why it is that liberalism failed—Deneen tells a lopsided story that romanticizes the past and is decidedly dystopian about the present."[13] The answer is a return to a time when personal liberties were limited by a government with a singular and forceful vision of what is good for every person in the state.

Sohrab Ahmari agrees. He bemoans the modern emphasis on personal autonomy at the cost of forming a society around the Highest Good—even if it means curtailing individual freedoms. "Conservative liberals and libertarians share in this view of the highest good: The unfettered life is the best life. Most recognize the need for some limits, at least against freedoms that harm others. But the regulative ideal remains always operative: an ideal of ever-greater autonomy won through the removal of limits," Ahmari writes in his screed against David French. By contrast, he maintains, "Freedom requires a moral and religious horizon, not just in man's private sphere, not just at the level of culture and civil society, but also in his collective experience—that is, in the state and the political community."[14] One hears in these words the reverberations of Bozell's fondness for Spain and its public memorials, shrines, and liturgies to Christendom—a Catholic wonderland where the public square echoed with the hymns of the Church and assumed all were baptized.

Since liberalism prevents such public contours of religion, common good conservatives claim it replaces family, faith, and community with the tyranny of the state—in opposition to the Church. For Deneen, when the government sets policies or makes laws to ensure the rights and freedoms of all citizens are recognized and protected, it is an expansion of the regime. "'The Empire of Liberty' expands apace with an ever-enlarging sphere of state control."[15] For example, the legalizing of same-sex marriage and the right to a no-fault divorce signify not the protection of individuals from undue prejudice or the clearing of a space for them to exercise their inalienable rights, but the government acting as a "ratchet wrench, always in one direction, enlarging and expanding in response to civic grievances of distance and powerlessness."[16]

Likewise, Adrian Vermeule sees liberalism as an ideology designed from the beginning to destroy the Church. He likens liberalism's tyranny to a secular church, complete with its own rituals, liturgies, and festivals. "The problem is the relentless aggression of liberalism, driven by an internal mechanism that causes ever more radical demands for political conformism, particularly targeting the Church," he writes in "A Christian Strategy."[17] Liberalism's "cruel sacraments" are shaming and legal punishment, employed in conjunction with its "liturgical script," in which "liberalism ceaselessly and restlessly searches out new villains to play their assigned part." The onslaught of liberation, coupled with the mission to destroy Christianity, means that "yesterday the frontier was divorce, contraception, and abortion; then it became same-sex marriage; today it is transgenderism; tomorrow it may be polygamy, consensual adult incest, or who knows what."[18]

One of the effects of telling "a lopsided story that romanticizes the past and is decidedly dystopian about the present," as Field puts it, is to justify extreme action in the future. If the pre-Constitutional past was so splendid, and the present is so dire, then it follows that radical political steps will need to be taken in order to make America great for the first time.

In his feud with David French, Sohrab Ahmari once again ventriloquizes Paul Weyrich by arguing that the only way forward is "to fight the culture war with the aim of defeating the *enemy* and enjoying the spoils in the form of a public square re-ordered to the common good and ultimately the Highest Good."[19] Ahmari advocates using values to "enforce our order and our orthodoxy," with the mindset that "enmity is its own kind of moral duty." While Ahmari employs the language of enforcing order, other voices are more explicit about refounding the United States. In a 2020 column for *The American Conservative* titled "America Needs a New Founding," Matthew J. Peterson, the founder of the magazine *The American Mind*, puts it this way:

> The Left re-founded America. We are in need of statesmanship of the highest order to re-found it again. Conservatism must not merely make arguments, and reshape a bold new platform of policy—it must act on them, wielding "regime-level" power in the service of good political order to do so—or it will fail. We must lead a counter-revolution. Since this is not, by definition, "conservative," American conservatism may no longer be called "conservatism" if it chooses to rise to the occasion.[20]

Peterson's explicit call for a second American revolution brings into focus a key aspect of this strain of Catholic right-wing radicalism: It is not conservative in the sense that it wants to conserve bygone elements of the American ethos. It is a revolutionary religious ideology based on the idea that we need a new founding.

For Adrian Vermeule, the only way to affect that revolution is through Catholic integralism—the political theology espoused by Brent Bozell that seeks to integrate the state into the Church, with the former as a subsidiary entity in relation to the latter:

> The only intellectual movement on the American scene that is genuinely political is so-called integralism or, as I think a more accurate term, political Catholicism. . . . The political Catholic looks at the series of false alternatives offered by the localists, the free-marketers, the cheerleaders of martyrdom—national or local action? state or market? Rome or the catacombs?—and says, "Yes, both/and; I will take them all." The political Catholic wants to order the nation and its state to the natural and divine law, the tranquility of order, precisely because doing so is the best way to protect and shelter the localities in which genuinely human community, imbued with grace, can flourish.[21]

This is perhaps the clearest and most honest statement about the vision of common good conservatism. The goal is to order the state in accordance with "natural law," which comes from God. If one doesn't abide by that version of natural law, or believe in natural law at all, too bad. If one's identity as a gay person or nonbinary person or a single woman with no children is attacked, erased, or marginalized in the process, too bad. If unmarried and nonreligious citizens are relegated to a second class in the American public square? That's a sign that it's working.

"What is at stake is no less than authority, the full authority of a reasoned political order, composed of both temporal and spiritual powers in right relation to the natural and divine law, that would put a mere Rome to shame," Vermeule writes. "That limitless ambition is why liberalism finds a genuinely political Catholicism intolerable."[22] While ambition may be part of why Catholic integralism is viewed by many as incompatible with democracy, the more worrying aspect is the giving of authority to the Church as it relates to governance, policy, law, and individual freedoms.

From my perspective, liberalism has many flaws. There is an abundance of research on the loneliness epidemic and the way it leads to an individualist society without robust forms of community; how it prioritizes the freedom of the market in a manner that leads to the commodification of seemingly everything; the way it tends to protect the "right" to own property over all others. Scholars, activists, and community leaders have created a robust discourse on how liberalism creates the types of inequalities it is designed to eradicate. However, while imperfect, liberalism is also the philosophical framework that birthed the American experiment and the modern era of constitutional democracy. If you remember what came before the American and French revolutions, and before the Enlightenment, liberalism in some form appears a better choice than the European wars of religion wherein hundreds of thousands died in battle lines drawn between Catholics and Protestants or a medieval society where most forms of difference were suppressed by the Church. What we need are nuanced discussions about how to create conditions for human communal flourishing, not the wholesale imposition of a medieval worldview on the masses.

I would argue that a way forward is to find a new approach that prizes the dignity and rights of all people, regardless of their economic status, religious affiliation, ethnicity, gender, sex, or race, while also creating a more just, communal, and equitable system that accounts for the climate crisis and the onset of AI. But for Deneen, Vermeule, Ahmari, and other common good conservatives, the answer seems always to veer toward a state bent on controlling the lives of its citizens through virtue enforcement and moral policing. They have their sights set on the 1150s—something more like a papal state than anything else.

"The fabric of beliefs that gave rise to the nearly 250-year-old American constitutional experience may be nearing an end," Deneen writes in the introduction to *Why Liberalism Failed*. "We should rightly wonder whether America is not in the early days of its eternal life but rather approaching the end of the natural cycle of corruption and decay that limits the lifespan of all human creations."[23]

Liberalism for postliberals like Deneen is not a grand experiment in the course of human history that dared to envision a society in which all are equal according to the law and in which their inalienable rights are recognized, but rather a five-century diversion from the civilization built by Christians—Christendom. This is what makes their iteration of postliberalism a form of illiberalism. It is not an improvement upon the deficiencies of liberalism or a model that takes the errors in the liberal system into account while preserving its virtues, but instead one that seeks to replace it with a form of governance antithetical to the liberal foundations of human rights and individual choice.

These abstract theoretical gestures take concrete form in Adrian Vermeule's conception of "common good constitutionalism." Applying common good conservatism to American constitutional law, Vermeule defines law, following the medieval Catholic theologian and philosopher Thomas Aquinas, not as "maximizing individual autonomy or minimizing the abuse of power" but as ensuring "that the ruler has both the authority and the duty to rule well."[24]

Critics like law professor Kyron Huigens have noted that Vermeule's conception of American law and the Constitution are based on the idea that "law is a divine ordinance of reason."[25] In other words, according to Vermeule, American laws should be based on God's commands rather than human rights. Common good constitutionalism is just another way of doing "theistic natural law theory" based in a Catholic political theology going back to the Middle Ages.[26]

Given his theory's medieval origins, Vermeule doesn't see it as needing to reach any sort of bar raised by democracy. Instead, democracy must prove itself "valuable" to the common good.[27] This means that democracy is disposable if and when it no longer serves the divine ordinance of reason. If a different form of governance—such as an autocracy or other nonrepresentative model—can do better under this metric, it is preferred to one based on the will of the people. In an infamous essay for *The Atlantic* titled "Beyond Originalism," Vermeule makes the case that just authority in rulers can be exercised for the good of subjects, "if necessary even against the subjects' own perceptions of what is best for them—perceptions that may change over time anyway, as the law teaches, habituates, and re-forms them."[28] Inevitably, many American citizens would protest the stripping of their rights in the name of the common good at the hands of a president-turned-Caesar. After all, common good conservatives want to abolish gay marriage, cease healthcare for trans people, place limits on divorce, ban pornography, abolish abortion, and generally "legislate morality" according to Catholic natural law.

What of the citizenry, displeased with a government ordering their individual choices at every turn? Would non-Christians and the nonreligious have any sense of freedom from religion or religious freedom? Vermeule expects short-term dissatisfaction, but in the end, he trusts that all, or most, will come to understand that the government, in service of the Church, knows what is best for them, even when they don't know what is best for themselves. "Subjects will come to thank the ruler whose legal strictures, possibly first experienced as coercive, encourage subjects to form more authentic desires for the individual and common goods," Vermeule writes, "better habits, and beliefs that better track and promote communal wellbeing."[29] The common goods, derived from Catholic medieval political theology, must be enforced, since "the promotion of morality is a core and legitimate function of authority."[30] Put differently: If Americans can't behave themselves like good little boys and girls, then the Church will have to punish them by way of law and policy with the help of the government.

Given that democracy holds no sacred place in Vermeule's political vision, he argues that the ideal form of American governance, given the current constitutional restraints, would be "a powerful presidency ruling over a powerful bureaucracy, the latter acting through principles of administrative law's inner morality with a view to promoting solidarity and subsidiarity."[31] Vermeule's use of the word "subsidiarity" is key for understanding his ideal model of government. Ian Ward outlines the extremism of Vermeule's position:

> As it's traditionally understood in Catholic political thought, subsidiarity is a principle about the limits of government: It states that whenever possible, the more powerful authorities in a society should defer to less powerful authorities to perform responsibilities that either entity could legitimately carry out. But in Common Good Constitutionalism, Vermeule offers another reading of subsidiarity, according to which powerful public authorities have not only a right but a duty to step in when less powerful political authorities fail to protect the needs of the common good. . . . Taken together, these two arguments read an awful lot like a defense of a pseudo-constitutional dictatorship, or at the very least as a plausible legal justification for a right-wing coup.[32]

Ward's analysis tracks with Vermeule's position in his 2010 coauthored work *The Executive Unbound*, where he and Eric Posner go so far as to call the separation of powers "a historical curiosity." Against concerns that this view of the executive branch leads to a de facto dictatorship, Vermeule and Posner claim that politics and public opinion, coupled with concerns for propriety, will always prevent American presidents from overstepping their role into the domain of autocracy. In other words, Vermeule wants the president to have unbound power, but trusts—naively—that such power will never lead to autocracy because the president will care so much about their polling numbers and legacy. Shame and duty will keep them from overstepping their role—which is a laughable, embarrassing, and downright foolish position in light of Donald Trump's two presidencies.

In sum, one of the most accomplished authorities on constitutional law in the country argues that the executive branch of the federal government should have "potentially unlimited" power so that the state is ordered properly. Vermeule even quotes the Austrian theologian and jurist Johannes Messner, who claims that in cases when the morality of the people fails "even dictatorship may be compatible with the principle of subsidiarity."[33]

"They worship the executive," writes David Dyzenhaus, one of Vermeule's nemeses in the field of constitutional law, "but such worship depends on maintaining in power the person at the head of the executive who shares at least the most important tenets of their version of the 'common good.'"[34] In other words, one who recognizes that law descends from God's vision for society. "That requires not only freeing the executive from the constraints of the rule of law, both internationally and within the nation state. It also requires that democracy be hollowed out in order to ensure that periodic elections return the right person to power."[35]

Hollowing out democracy in order to empower an unbound executive seems like the worst possible idea when you have a man in the White House who uses the military on his own people, urges generals to shoot protesters, calls for the death of his political opponents, and begs state officials to "find" him votes so he will win the election. Having a king may sound great until he is the type of buffoon who sells a Bible with his name on it, falls asleep regularly in televised meetings, goes on unhinged social media rants in the middle of the night, destroys the East Wing of the White House, and fixates on taking over Greenland as a vanity project. Nonetheless, Vermeule argues that the Constitution can be shaped to remake

American law and society in line with God's natural law. If that requires the strong hand of a de facto autocrat, so be it.

In July of 2020 President Trump appointed Vermeule to the Council of the Administrative Conference of the United States, which is "an independent federal agency dedicated to improving the administrative process through consensus-driven applied research and providing nonpartisan expert advice and recommendations for federal agency procedures." Vermeule, who advocates for a political model wherein the United States government would be a subsidiary of the Catholic Church, was placed on an administrative board whose purpose is to advise the president on how the executive branch should work.

Patrick Deneen is a friend and intellectual conversation partner of Vice President JD Vance. At the book panel for Deneen's *Regime Change*, where Vance appeared with Kevin Roberts and Christine Emba, Vance praised Deneen for articulating the problems with the old conservatism and the challenges ahead if they are going to break the hold of the "uniparty." As distressing as it may be to realize that Vermeule and Deneen have this type of sway over top-level government officials, neither of them is the common good conservative with the most influence in Washington and the most incendiary vision for a second American revolution. That would be Kevin Roberts, leader of the Heritage Foundation and shepherd of Project 2025.

◆ ◆ ◆

Kevin Roberts was born and raised in Lafayette, Louisiana. Despite railing against identity politics and splintered racial and ethnic identities in his 2024 book *Dawn's Early Light*,

Roberts spends considerable time praising his Cajun heritage whenever the opportunity arises. Roberts first came into public view in 2015 when he became president of Wyoming Catholic College. Roberts refused all federal funding for the institution in order to "safeguard our mission from unwarranted federal involvement." He started calling himself a "cowboy Catholic," for the way he refused to play ball with the DC bureaucracy. After a stint at the Texas Public Policy Foundation, Roberts became president of the Heritage Foundation in 2021. At the time, the Heritage Foundation had seen executive turnover. Moreover, for a decade it had been losing its luster as the premier conservative policy think tank on Capitol Hill. A 2013 op-ed in *The Atlantic* proclaimed the "fall" of Heritage and how it was hurting the GOP's Obama-era strategy.[36]

Roberts stepped in with a plan to restore Heritage's place of influence in DC. One of his first moves was to build a grand strategy for the next conservative president of the United States. The result was the ninth iteration of its "Mandate for Leadership," which is a series of policy plans for conservative leaders. The most famous example is the one Heritage created for Ronald Reagan in 1981. When Reagan was elected, Heritage supplied him with an eleven-hundred-page handbook with two thousand policy ideas. "The foundation had a great hour when Ronald Reagan was elected president and found waiting for him three volumes of Heritage material designed to help him chart the nation's course in the right direction," said none other than William F. Buckley. "Sixty percent of the suggestions enjoined on the new president were acted upon."[37]

By 2023, the Heritage Foundation's Project 2025 was public: a 922-page plug-and-play manual for how the "next conservative president" could "cut through superficial distractions and focus on the moral and foundational challenges America faces in this moment of history."[38] In February 2025, weeks after Trump's second inauguration, one analysis "found dozens of cases where the president's early executive actions have aligned with portions of the 922-page policy agenda, including some instances with nearly verbatim language lifted from the report to the White House."[39] It is without a doubt the most influential strategy document on the second Trump administration's policies, budget, and appointments. There is no close second.

Like Deneen, Ahmari, and Vermeule, Roberts believes that liberalism is a treacherous ideology that has destroyed the foundations of American public life. In the contest for America's soul, he sees two sides: the Party of Destruction, which seeks to "abolish the existing order," and the "Party of Creation—those who defend the God-given natural order that is capable of generating flourishing and new life if we learn to live within it."[40] However, Roberts argues that in order to create America anew, it is time for conservatives to "fight fire with fire" by burning down the American institutions whose plague is destroying the American way of life: the FBI, every Ivy League university, the Boy Scouts of America, most Catholic educational institutions (which he considers too woke and liberal), the public school system, and the Bill and Melinda Gates Foundation, among others. He then names the "parasites" who are dismantling our society from within: "pantsuited girlboss advertising executives, Skittle-haired they/them activists, soy-faced pajama-clad work-from-home HR apparatchiks, Adderall-addicted dog mom diversity consultants, nasally voiced Ivy League regulatory lawyers, obese George Soros–funded police abolitionist district attorneys, hipster trust fund socialists . . ."[41]

Like other common good conservatives, he isn't nostalgic for a time when the United States was supposedly on solid Christian footing. In Roberts's view, the first American revolution was not novel. Instead, it was a continuation of Christendom—the civilization "built on top of the Roman order" designed to "keep an existing tradition of liberty and self-government alive."[42] He continues:

> The image of a pious statesman carrying the flame of civilization over the waters was a precious one to our classically educated Founding Fathers, so much so that the motto on the back of the Great Seal of the United States comes from Virgil: Novus ordo seclorum. That translates to "a new order of the ages," but to the Founders it evoked not "the birthday of a new world" (in Thomas Paine's words) but the renewal of civilization in the natural order of things. Later Christians believed that stanza from Virgil's Eclogues to prophesy the founding of a Christian civilization on top of the Roman order, carrying forward the flame of the West as Aeneas had.[43]

In this Christian revolutionary spirit Roberts argues that it is time for conservatives to "get over the old conservatism's reluctance to 'impose' its 'values' on others," "like a gardener pulling weeds to protect his crop."[44] In his public speeches and written work Roberts consistently maintains that the fusionism of the late twentieth century is no longer viable. What is needed is an imposition of the common good on the public square through policy, law, and taxation. Echoing Vermeule's medieval approach, he calls the common good "an eternal principle of a just polity."[45] Thus, he wants to use the federal government as a weapon for recreating a Christian civilization reminiscent of Constantine's Roman empire.

"The very reason the free market and free enterprise exist, and that our constitutional order guards them," Roberts wrote in 2022, "is to promote and embody the common good. This 'ordered liberty' is the fulcrum on which all the principles and ideals of the American Founding rest."[46] Like his philosophical and legal common good cohorts, Roberts does not believe in maximizing personal liberty as the purpose of government. "When the Founders spoke of 'pursuit of Happiness,'" Roberts writes in Project 2025, "what they meant might be understood today as in essence 'pursuit of Blessedness.' That is, an individual must be free to live as his Creator ordained—to flourish. *Our Constitution grants each of us the liberty to do not what we want, but what we ought.*"[47]

Like Paul Weyrich before him, Roberts focuses on influencing the president and other leaders in DC. He does not spend time in his writing or speeches arguing about the intricacies of libertarianism or the history of liberalism. Vermeule and Deneen write like academics whose jargon and polish make their extremism seem polite and mainstream. Roberts writes like a man trying to fight the page with his pen. The result is language that illustrates the exact type of relationship postliberal common good Catholics want between the Church and the state:

> Our deepest traditions about the purposes of government are reflected in the ancient ceremony for

> crowning England's kings, when the archbishop of Canterbury hands to his sovereign the Sword of State with these words: "With this sword do justice, stop the growth of iniquity, protect the holy Church of God and all people of goodwill, help and defend widows and orphans, restore the things that are gone to decay, maintain the things that are restored, punish and reform what is amiss, and confirm what is in good order.[48]

It is telling that Roberts uses the crowning of a king as the protector of the Church to explain the purpose of the United States government: a monarch taking the throne with the mission of defending the honor of God, rather than enacting the will of the people. There doesn't seem to be anything *less* American than this idea. After all, the American revolution was fought to gain autonomy from the very king Roberts references. How can you use the image of a king bowed to a church to illustrate the America you want, unless that's the America you want?

By the time L. Brent Bozell Jr. closed *Triumph*'s doors in 1976, he was a pariah. His politics were untouchable. His ideas were nuclear for the GOP and the American Right. Bozell's descent into alcoholism and mental illness provided an excuse for his former comrades to distance themselves from him and his legacy. During the last decade of Paul Weyrich's life, beginning in 2001, he had in some ways given up on the GOP. His last working years were spent cultivating relationships in Russia and Central Europe. The man who built the think tanks and institutions that are now essential organisms in the ecosystem of American conservatism became distant, and some would say ever more extreme.

Yet, sometimes what appears to be a dead end is simply a pathway that takes time to clear. In 1976, Bozell's ideas were considered far outside the Overton window, making him a pariah in conservative America. When Weyrich started touting the merits of Putin's leadership, he was ahead of his time. Most thought he had lost the plot.

That is no longer the case.

When Kevin Roberts, JD Vance, and Patrick Deneen gathered in 2023, in the heart of DC, they were advancing the legacy of those two men. As we shall see later, since his conversion to Catholicism in 2019 Vance has become a staple in postliberal common good Catholic settings. Deneen is a mentor. Roberts is a friend. Vance cites Bozell in his writings, and like Weyrich he talks about using the federal government to impose the right kind of family and marriage on American society. And he is just as revolutionary—and incendiary—as the rest of them. He concludes his foreword to Roberts's 2024 book *Dawn's Early Light* with this call to arms:

> The old conservative movement argued if you just got government out of the way, natural forces would resolve problems—we are no longer in this situation and must take a different approach. As Kevin Roberts writes, "It's fine to take a laissez-faire approach when you are in the safety of the sunshine. But when the twilight descends and you hear the wolves, you've got to circle the wagons and load the muskets." We are now all realizing that it's time to circle the wagons and

> load the muskets. In the fights that lay ahead, these ideas are an essential weapon.[49]

The revolution common good conservatives like Roberts, Deneen, and others seek is a reversion to a medieval governance model that would fundamentally alter the structure and scope of the American government. Their criticisms of liberalism and the separation of powers can be reduced to a simple truth: They view rights and consent as a problem, something that prevents elites who know what is best for everyone from imposing their vision through coercion and law. Yet, nostalgic old men like Deneen always neglect to mention that the homogenous societies they long for were built on the suppression and punishment of women, queer people, non-Christians, and dissenters. Difference was criminalized in the name of unity. Women were called witches and burned. Jews were accused of killing Jesus and murdered for it. Black people were viewed as less than human and enslaved. The Chinese were excluded. The Japanese were interned. The queer were hunted. Homogeneity comes at the cost of liberty. It is an enforced commonality that is anything but good.

In order to reckon with diversity and disagreement, Vermeule proposes giving an unbound executive near total control over the government. In his vision, the Supreme Leader would be granted full authority, armed with theological certainty and legal immunity. As flawed as liberalism may be, and as in need of rejuvenation and reform our public square is, when I read the proposals of men like Deneen, Vermeule, and Roberts I am reminded of why the idea of inalienable rights arose in the first place. When we grant that every human being has certain rights that cannot be violated or taken away—regardless of their heritage, creed, language, ethnicity, or gender—we grant them protection against the tyrannical men who would crush their lives in the name of whatever common good they believe is proper for all. Rights are not a revolt against natural law. They are a protection against unbound executives who would try to imprint their laws on our bodies without permission. They are a stalwart against the Caesars who want to define what is "natural" and "good" in a way that makes most of us an abomination or a heretic. They are a shield against holy crusaders who sanctify violence to flatten difference.

Postliberal Catholics don't want to just "own the libs." Their goal is to burn down the vestiges of liberalism even if Madisonian democracy is caught in the blaze and a king ends up atop the rubble. Their "good" is common only in the sense that men like them have been trying to force it on everyone else for millennia. We the People is the only obstacle in their way.

5

THEOCRATIC CAESARISM

> **I want Christians to have power, and with that power, I want it to be wielded righteously. What does that mean? It means crushing our enemies and rewarding our friends.**
>
> —JOEL WEBBON

> **You must learn what to hate.**
>
> —ANDREW ISKER

> **The Jews as a collective have largely operated at odds with the Old American way of life, rooted as it is in European Christendom.**
>
> —C. JAY ENGEL

In July 2017, Donald Trump invited more than a dozen faith leaders to the White House for meetings and prayer. It was a signal to all the conservative Christians who voted for him that he was going to keep his promise to fight for their interests and listen to their input on issues such as abortion, education, and religious liberty. The photos of the group praying for Trump are infamous. Everyone has their eyes closed in pious reverence. Those closest to him lay hands on his back and shoulders. With a few exceptions, the group is made up of White Christian male clergy—many of whom were skeptical of Trump as a candidate, but eventually came around to him as the one who could lead the country back to Christian glory. For Trump's religious supporters, the symbolism is clear: Trump is the kind of president who surrounds himself with Christian leaders who hold him and his administration in prayerful vigilance. Trump keeps his word to the Christians he credits with helping him get elected. He may not be a choirboy or a Sunday school teacher, but he is a president who prioritizes their kind of faith.

On March 20, 2025, just under eight years later, fifteen faith leaders gathered at the White House for a similar series of meetings with President Trump and administration officials, organized by the White House Faith Office. Eventually, the assembled leaders took a group photo, once again showing them laying hands on the president as they prayed for him. The photo is a re-creation—a sequel to the original taken in July 2017. It's exactly the same in structure and message, but some of the older members of the first group have been swapped out for younger ones. To the casual observer, almost nothing has changed. The photos reflect the fact that throughout his three presidential runs, Trump has garnered the overwhelming support of White Christians.

But if you examine the rosters of who attended in 2017 and

2025, it's possible to detect what's changed in the decade since Trump first announced his run for president. The two seemingly identical pictures tell the story of a radical escalation in mainstream White American Christianity. When Trump invited faith leaders to join him in 2017, the list included figures who represented the power and prestige of evangelical America going back to the Religious Right of the seventies and eighties: Ralph Reed, chairman of the Faith and Freedom Coalition; Tony Perkins, president of the Family Research Council; and Richard Land, president of the Southern Evangelical Seminary, among others. And of course, his first vice president was Mike Pence, a dyed-in-the-wool evangelical whose political pedigree is pitch perfect for the old-school Religious Right framework built by Paul Weyrich. These were baby boomers from the old guard—vestiges of the generation that opposed Jimmy Carter's administration, fought to get Reagan elected, and set their sights on overturning *Roe v. Wade*.

In 2025, Trump invited some of the same elder generation leaders who attended in 2017. But this time, he also invited more Gen Xers and millennial pastors and think-tank leaders whose cachet is with the extreme and imperial form of American Christianity that is now mainstream in the United States. Among them: David Rose, school board president at the Lake Havasu Unified School District in Lake Havasu City, Arizona, whom the *Daily Mail* describes as a "passionate advocate against DEI, 'grooming,' and biological males in women's sports."[1] And Owen Strachan, a well-known online provocateur who now works at the ultraconservative evangelical Dobson Institute (started by James Dobson of Focus on the Family fame).

However, the most notable attendee was William Wolfe,

who served in the first Trump administration as a State Department director and deputy assistant defense secretary. Before that, Wolfe worked at Heritage Action—the policy arm of the Heritage Foundation. Wolfe is an alumnus of Covenant College, a small Reformed school. In many ways, he is the embodiment of three important threads that run through the foregoing chapters: He is a former Defense Department official; he used to work at the Heritage Foundation; and he has ties to and a deep affinity for the Reformed theology of Doug Wilson.

Wolfe comes from a younger generation of Reformed leaders who view Wilson as the elder spokesman of a movement that is now ready for acceleration. Whereas Wilson has always been careful not to move too fast, lest he frighten mainstream evangelicals and American culture at large like Rushdoony once did, Wolfe and his comrades have no such inhibitions. This is clear in the 2023 "Statement on Christian Nationalism" for which Wolfe served as an editor. It was published online by a group of elected officials and abortion abolitionists as a defense of Christian nationalism and an outline of a Christian nationalist vision for the United States. One of the authors dubbed it "Project 2035."[2]

The statement resounds with themes from Rushdoony's and Wilson's theological projects, as well as those from other Reformed Protestant thinkers. It begins with a declaration that "Christ rules as supreme Lord and King of all creation, who has ordained civil magistrates with delegated authority to be under Him."[3] Later, the authors assert that all civil leaders—whether Christian or not—have a duty to ascribe to and enforce God's moral law. The Declaration also includes the statement that the civil government should not have any role in the education of children. "WE DENY that civil authorities are tasked with being the caretakers of citizens or educators of children, as these duties belong primarily to the Church and to families, respectively."[4] In other words, public schools should be abolished. Finally, the statement recalls Rushdoony's emphasis on "spheres," and the ways that Christian leaders in each domain of human life should have sovereignty over them in the name of the King of Kings, Jesus Christ. While the authors defend the separation of the church from the state, they argue that God and the state should never be separated. In other words, even if the church is not in control of the state, *churchmen should be*. Non-Christians cannot be given a place of leadership or authority, lest the government be given over to demonic forces.

While most of the statement is familiar to those who know the foundations of this brand of theology, one aspect sticks out.

> WE AFFIRM that a nation is not merely an idea, abstract principle, or ideology but tangibly defined by a particular body of people in a particular place. We affirm that a particular people are necessarily bound together by a shared culture, customs, history, and lineage while sharing common interests, virtues, languages, and worship. We affirm, in regards to "place" that a nation is definitively set by both its borders and times physically defined by God (Acts 17:26).[5]

This is a direct negation of the idea that the United States is a creedal nation. In place of an American ethos based on the affirmation of freedom, equality, representation, and the will of the people, those behind the Statement on Christian

Nationalism argue that the US is "a particular people . . . necessarily bound together by a shared culture, customs, history, and lineage while sharing common interests, virtues, languages, and worship." Real Americans are those who are a part of certain culture, religion, and history—shall we say "ethnicity"—those with the right lineage and language. In sum, the Statement on Christian Nationalism is a manifesto for Christian ethnonationalism based on the idea that the United States is rightfully a nation built by and for those of European heritage.

As one of the fifteen faith leaders invited to the White House in March 2025, Wolfe represents an influential set of young ethnonationalist theologians and pastors who not only believe that the United States was built for and by those of European descent, but who think that the only way to restore the country to greatness is through an autocrat fashioned in the model of a Julius Caesar. When Wolfe was invited to the White House, he brought with him a subculture full of anti-Semitic pastors and White nationalist theologians—men who believe that American Christian revival would be manifest in the mass deportation of foreign nationals and non-Christians; that women who get an abortion should be given the death penalty; and that the country should be ruled by a "Red Caesar" or "Christian prince," who will destroy democracy as we know it in order to institute a functional theocracy. These are the protégés of Doug Wilson. The grandsons of Rushdoony. And the new guard of American Protestantism.

* * *

On election night 2024, Wolfe spent hours on a live stream of the podcast *Contra Mundum*, which the hosts C. Jay Engel and Andrew Isker bill as the "number one Christian nationalist podcast in the world." Engel and Isker moved to Jackson County, Tennessee, in 2024 to lead a Christian nationalist takeover of the county. According to investigative reporter Phil Williams, the real estate component of the project is a joint venture between two related companies, "New Founding and RidgeRunner," which are led by investors Nate Fischer and Josh Abbotoy.[6] They envision communities like the one Isker and Engel are building as Christian network states wherein Christians can build self-governing communities filled with people who share the same values and ways of life. Abbotoy and Fischer also started *American Reformer,* an extremist Christian magazine where William Wolfe and C. Jay Engel publish their work.[7]

Before moving to Tennessee, Isker was best known for his 2023 book *The Boniface Option,* which is a disgusting anti-LGBT manifesto calling American Christians to holy war. Though Doug Wilson calls it "a good book,"[8] it is an example of how a work does not have to be serious in order to be popular. There is no sophistication to his writing or layers to Isker's message. His work is a straightforward call to White Christian nationalist hatred bathed in homophobia, xenophobia, misogyny, and anti-Semitism. If the worst jokes written on bathroom stalls in a junior high school bathroom had a love child with retrograde misogynistic theology, the result would be this book.

Isker is ordained in the CREC, the denomination cofounded by Doug Wilson. He graduated from a ministry associated with Wilson's church.[9] While he shares a theological background with Wilson, Isker has none of Wilson's carefulness when it comes to conquering the Earth for King Jesus. Instead of proclaiming, as Rushdoony and Wilson do, that Adam was created for dominion, Isker writes that "Adam was created for holy war," in order "to be a warrior priest. . . . God designed your body, your arms, your legs, your torso, your fingers, your mind, your soul, and your spirit for war."[10] For Isker, men—not human beings, but men—are called to holy violence against the enemies of God. He goes a step further from dominion over the world to hatred of it. "*You must learn what to hate,*" he writes in the first pages of *The Boniface Option*.[11] "Our parents were told to fill the earth and subdue it. The household is the basic unit of conquest."[12]

The Boniface Option is a play on a popular book published by Rod Dreher in 2017 titled *The Benedict Option*, in which Dreher argues that in light of the evilness of the world, Christians should gather into monastic alternative communities in order to protect themselves from the collapse of civilization. It is a call to retreat in order to conquer. Isker believes this is a cop-out. He takes inspiration from St. Boniface who, among other things, refused to back down from pagan rulers in eighth-century Germany. "The Benedict Option is not available to us; it is either the Boniface Option or destruction. You cannot run and hide from Trashworld. Our only option is to despise it and to fight back."[13]

For Isker, hatred and war are warranted because the world at large is a totalizing "globohomo" regime that "seeks to dominate every square inch of the planet."[14] Isker actually spends many pages explaining why the world is "fake and gay." By "fake" he means a setting in which human beings have been ripped from their natural environment (consisting of home, hearth, village, and church) in order to live in a consumerist tech nightmare. By "gay" he means:

> For the homosexual, insatiable desires must be pursued even knowing it will cost him his life. In economic terms, he is the ultimate high-time-preference man. He only lives in the present. There is no thought for the future. He is quite obviously incapable of pursuing offspring. He is willing to cut off any and all social relations that prevent him from pursuing his predilections. In short, the homosexual is both the apex consumer and the easiest personality to manipulate and lord over. Therefore the gayness of Trashworld is our rulers' social engineering of the population to create the exact same ethos of the homosexual in everyone, regardless of their sexual tastes. They want you to be spiritually homosexual whether or not they can make you actually homosexual. They want everyone uprooted and alone. They want you to be only concerned with satisfying your immediate desires. They do not want you to care about the future. They do not want you to have children. They want your entire purpose in life to be "Consume today, for tomorrow we die."[15]

In sum, this creates the "globohomo" regime, the only answer to which is "a Christianity that is equally aggressive and expansionary."[16]

According to Isker, that form of Christianity would send queer people "through the woodchipper."[17] He comes to the razor's edge of declaring his enemies less than human: "There is nothing meaningful we hold in common with them from which we can form mutual understanding."[18] As a result, he advises his flock that instead of trying to evangelize to them, like the Apostle Paul did to the Greeks in the book of Acts, "you must do what Jesus did when opposing those who are incapable of acting in good faith—you hold them in derision. That is Christlike."[19] In other words, war is the only option since there is no possibility of working together, living peacefully in the same civil space, or finding common ground. It is a battle for domination and survival.

When it comes to strategizing about how to overcome the evil forces facing God's holy warriors, Isker leans on a common theme among his cadre of extremist Protestant leaders: "We must physically move closer to those who share the same loves and hates we do. Your children need a people to belong to, they need a tribe, they need bonds of friendship even stronger than blood."[20] The answer is creating homogenous Christian communities that can overcome the pluralism and diversity of the United States. In place of persuasion, dialogue, or even prayer, the principal strategy is to gather en masse to overpower all those who are deserving of derision and hatred. "A group of ten to twelve men, who would die for one another is a thing that is more powerful than an entire division of conscripts. With such a group churches can be planted that can conquer entire cities."[21] Isker gestures at something here that C. Jay Engel, his partner in ministry and podcasting, develops more expansively in his political writing: The way to victory is outright ethnonationalism based on one people displacing and/or dominating all others in order to make the United States into a godly nation.

Engel's writing appears more complex than Isker's in the sense that he draws on political theorists and theologians to advance his ideas. However, the message is almost identical. If Isker sounds like a teenage boy murmuring slurs from the corner of gym class—a human equivalent of the *Simpsons* character Nelson Muntz—then Engel tries to justify Christian hatred by couching these ideas in political theory drawn from the Nazi jurist and infamous political theorist Carl Schmitt.[22] And, yes, if you are keeping tally, Engel is the third figure—after Peter Thiel and Adrian Vermeule—in this book to engage directly with Schmitt. The movements to crown an American Caesar are marinated in ideas the Third Reich embraced.

Following Schmitt, according to Engel, Christians are called to show "a love for their own," because the Church and the civil sphere are separate realms with different rules and practices. Politics, or what Engel calls the "civil kingdom," precedes the Kingdom of God. In other words, while Christians are on Earth their political loyalties, based in "families, kin groups, and nations," take precedence over the Kingdom of God.[23] Your friends may be White nationalist Proud Boys, neo-Nazis in Patriot Front, or the KKK. But if you share an ethnicity and heritage, and if they are united in their hatred of your enemies, then they are good "friends" who will help the White Christian do battle against their foes, like the Southeast Asian Christian across the street or the Hindu teacher at your kid's school. Not all of your "friends" on Earth will be part of the Kingdom of God in heaven. For Engel that's just fine. In the Civil Kingdom, you must destroy your enemies, mete out justice, and protect the clan by every means necessary. Christians are thus called to conflict based on their loyalties to families and kin, not baptismal status. If this means teaming up with neo-Nazi militias, so be it.

And who are the enemies at the gates? Engel is clear. Those who oppose "Heritage Americans" like himself. "We live in a world where the state has been weaponized against Heritage

America and there should be nothing holding us back from exercising whatever power is necessary to confront enemies both public and private," Engel writes in "Why I Am Not a Libertarian."[24] Anyone who threatens "my heritage, the customs I want to uphold, and the traditions I want recovered" are his enemies—Christ's love be damned. According to Engel, "Heritage Americans" are "those who are ethno-culturally tied to the ethos and spirit of the United States prior to its definitional transformation into a Propositional Nation after World War II." While Engel "includes" Black people "from the Old South" and Native Americans in this definition, he is clear that in his definition of Heritage Americans people from those groups play a different role in American society:

> It affirms however the domination and pre-eminence of the European derived peoples, their institutions, and their way of life. Heritage America is centered around the experiences and norms of Anglo-Protestants. It was their customs, their instincts, their priorities, their norms, their struggles, their perspectives, that set the tone and vision of Heritage America. Anything outside of that either assimilated or was killed off.[25]

In other moments, Engel labels the Jewish religion as "blasphemous" and "anti-Christian." According to the Bible, he says, there are no more Jews. "It's only Christians and non-Christians."[26] Engel views Jews as opposed to Heritage America. "The Jews as a collective have largely operated at odds with the Old American way of life, rooted as it is in European Christendom," he wrote on X on November 9, 2024 (a few days after Trump was elected the second time).[27] "The Jewish leaders really brought about the coming of the twentieth century; which was a rebuke of the Old Order."[28]

In sum, Engel's political theology is a justification of the supremacy of White male Anglo Protestants in the United States. It is ethnonationalism bathed in Christian jargon. Christian life on Earth is not a matter of loving your enemies or practicing the Golden Rule, at least not outside of personal relations. Instead, it is "to adopt a counter-revolutionary consciousness" in order to "defend your family and your people against other groups agitating for domination."[29] The Christian call is to the will to power in the name of White Anglo Protestant heritage.

Remember: William Wolfe, one of the fifteen faith leaders invited to the White House for meetings and prayer with President Trump in March 2025, chose to spend significant time on election night 2024 appearing on Isker and Engel's podcast. Wolfe also spoke at *American Reformer*'s private conference alongside Isker and Engel in 2024. He interacts with them often on social media and other podcasts. These are his colleagues and comrades in the fight for a Christian nation. And they are far from the only Christian ethnonationalists with influence in our government and in the public square.

* * *

On election night 2024, Isker and Engel invited a roundtable of guests to sit in on the *Contra Mundum* podcast live stream. In addition to William Wolfe, they were joined by Stephen Wolfe (no relation), a former postdoctoral scholar at Princeton and a Christian political theorist. Stephen Wolfe is the author of *The Case for Christian Nationalism*, which was published by Canon Press—Doug Wilson's publishing house. The book has had "tremendous influence" in Reformed Protestant circles.[30] Wolfe has appeared on Wilson's various platforms and is a rising star in the extended Wilson-verse. For most of 2022, his book was debated and celebrated by Reformed pastors, theologians, and seminarians. In comparison to Isker's and Engel's, Wolfe's work appears theologically nuanced and academically rigorous. He writes in a methodical style, calling on evidence from John Calvin, Thomas Aquinas, St. Augustine, and other Christian luminaries at every turn. However, despite the scholastic sheen of Wolfe's writing, he advances the same dangerous Christian ethnonationalism as Isker and Engel.

Wolfe fashions himself a political theorist, not a theologian. Yet, his political theory is based on a bizarre construal of the state of nature. Whereas Hobbes and Rousseau—two figureheads of modern liberalism and social contract theory—understood the state of nature as the condition of individuals prior to political society, Wolfe instead imagines the state of nature through a fantastical reading of the first three chapters of Genesis.

Like Rushdoony, Wilson, Isker, and Engel, Stephen Wolfe believes that men—not humans, but men—were created to take dominion over the planet. Wolfe likens it to ownership of a land that is an image of self-mastery and control.[31] However, Wolfe goes farther than any of his cohorts in imagining what life on Earth would have been like if Adam and Eve had not sinned—and what this means for human civilization today—because he bases his entire political theory on a set of extrapolations from a hypothetical condition with basis neither in the Bible nor history.

According to Wolfe, even if humans had not sinned in the Garden of Eden, they would have still grouped themselves into various communities across the globe. "Adam's progeny would have formed many nations on earth," Wolfe reasons. "And thus the formation of nations is part of God's design and intention for man."[32] These communities, or nations, would develop different customs, practices, and traditions—just as different people groups do now in the postlapsarian (i.e., post–Garden of Eden) context. Wolfe never explains how he knows how humans would have communally organized themselves in the event that Adam and Eve had not succumbed to the temptations of the serpent in Genesis 3. He chalks up his reasoning to natural principles that are evident to anyone construing an argument based on the scant and mythological evidence in an ancient creation narrative.[33] Reading the first chapters of Genesis in a literal way requires intellectual gymnastics. But Wolfe takes it to an absurdist register by claiming that he knows the alternative reality we all would have experienced if the most consequential event in biblical history—the first sin by Adam and Eve—had never taken place.

Nevertheless, he concludes that "the formation of nations is not a product of the fall; it is natural to man as man."[34] In other words, in the scenario where Adam and Eve resist the temptation, the world would still be organized into nations, based on shared language and customs, administered by a civil government. "Neither is civil government introduced by the fall," Wolfe asserts, "for civil government would have been necessary for unfallen people to coordinate action for the common good."[35] Wolfe goes so far as to claim that even in an "unfallen" world, men would have led the household and the civil government, and they would need to prepare themselves for violence because predators, such as "serpents," "fallen angels," and—potentially—sinful men, would roam across the land.[36] It's an argument for the Second Amendment to apply to the second chapter of Genesis. Christian nationalists like Wolfe are so interested in being violent men with guns that they want to make sure that everyone knows that there would have been dragons for them to slay even if there was no sin in the world.

With this imaginary story of human origins and human nature in place, Wolfe is able to advance the real concern of his book:

> Since grace restores nature and natural law contains all the moral principles concerning social relations, the Gospel does not alter the priority and inequality of loves amongst those relations. A Christian should love his children over other children, his parents over other parents, his kin over other kin, his nation over other nations. The instincts that lead one to these unequal loves are reliable.[37]

Wolfe's argument and conclusion go something like this: Even if humans had not fallen into sin, they would have created separate nations with warriors patrolling their borders. Those nations would have distinct ways of life that we can call "ethnicities." Given that even prelapsarian (i.e., pre-sin) human beings were designed to create particular communities based on in-group/out-group distinctions, it is natural for humans to live in homogenous ethnic enclaves where they share language, religion, blood relations, and daily practices. In fact, it is not only natural for them to do so, but it is ordered by God for them to develop such societies based on the way God designed human nature.

For Wolfe, nations and nationalism are part of God's

design. Christians do not have a different mission or calling from Adam. Even if Christ's redemption saved them from sin, it did not change their calling to dominate the Earth by setting up distinct ethnically pure nations. God created humans to love their own—those who are like them—more than others. God's plan is for humans to cultivate and defend their own "volk" in order to protect the homeland they have mastered. "The human instinct to socialize and dwell with similar people is universal," Wolfe argues. "Though for many today, especially Westerners, this instinct is understood as evil or pathological."[38] Intermarriage, according to Wolfe, is almost always a sin based on the idea that such unions mix two ethnicities and cultures.[39] Moreover, national exclusion is a function of God's design. Mass deportation is justified—and in some sense commanded—by God's plan for human societies. Even if those deported are Christian, it is for the benefit of all humans, since civic fellowship is not the same as spiritual fellowship.[40] There may be people of different ethnicities in heaven, but they are not meant to live together on Earth.

Wolfe's Christian ethnonationalism leads him to a stunning conclusion about the status of White Anglo-Saxon Protestants in the United States: "There's no distant place that we call home. We have nowhere else to go. But this is our home. This is our native land. *We are Native Americans,* born of those who didn't immigrate, but who settled here."[41] Wolfe means exactly what he says: White people are the real Native Americans. They are not immigrants. They are settlers who made a civilization where there wasn't one, which of course is a dehumanizing insult to all the indigenous tribes who were on this land thousands of years before Europeans even imagined it. Speaking about those who are not WASPs, Wolfe said in a podcast interview that it should be "permissible for Christians to deem certain groups to have positions that are detrimental to the fundamental features of society and to rescind their political equality."[42]

Joel Webbon agrees. Another follower of Stephen Wolfe's Christian ethnonationalism and protégé of Doug Wilson, Webbon often appears with C. Jay Engel and Andrew Isker on podcasts and at conferences. Stephen Wolfe calls Webbon a "great man." Webbon, who is a pastor and provocateur based in Austin—with hundreds of thousands of followers on social media—outlines the practical applications of Wolfe's, Isker's, and Engel's worldview. When asked recently what a revival in the United States would look like, Webbon answered that "it would look like millions of people being deported. It would look like mothers getting death row for murdering their children."[43] When asked about the presence of non-Christian and non-White people in the United States, Webbon argued that their presence is a sign of judgment on America.

"Throughout scripture, the idea of full-blown invasions from foreign peoples who worship foreign gods, it is never, in scripture, spoken of as a blessing of liberty. It is always spoken of as a judgment," Webbon stated on his podcast in 2024.[44]

"I believe that America is under God's judgment. And I don't think that the forms or the expressions of God's judgment merely lie with Drag Queen Story Hour, but that they also include the fact that my neighborhood is thirty percent Hindu."[45]

How would Christians rule if they gained power? In addition to ensuring that women can't vote and non-Christians can't practice their religion publicly, Webbon outlines his vision thusly: "I want Christians to have power, and with that power,

I want it to be wielded righteously. What does that mean? It means crushing our enemies and rewarding our friends." The enemies? Immigrants. Non-Christians. Autonomous women. Queer folks. Anyone who is not a White Anglo native-born patriarchal Christian.

* * *

Unsurprisingly, Christian ethnonationalists don't view democracy as the way to implement their vision of society, especially in the contemporary United States, which is no longer a White Christian–majority nation and will soon be majority-minority. Instead, they unanimously call for a monarch of some sort to save the ailing republic from its wayward state. On election night, William Wolfe—the pastor and former Trump administration official who was one of fifteen faith leaders invited to the White House in March 2025—proclaimed that Trump should go "full red Caesar mandate" in his second term.[46] In 2024, Joel Webbon said that "the Constitution, it's not suited for governing degenerates." In order to regenerate society, Webbon argues, "you need a Caesar type . . . I don't think constitutioning even harder is going to get us out of our current mess."[47] For his part, C. Jay Engel, the pastor and podcast host who is fond of the Nazi theorist Carl Schmitt, has claimed several times on social media that an "American Franco" is inevitable.

"The use of Protestant Franco—or Appalachian Pinochet—shall be to crush the Administrative State, to liquidate the DC bureaucracy," Engel wrote on X in October 2023. "And then to release the captivity of localities on the periphery. Power shall be exercised against Power, in solidarity with Old American sentiments."[48]

Among them, the one who has most fully worked out his vision for a "theocratic Caesarism" is Stephen Wolfe, the author of *The Case for Christian Nationalism*. For Wolfe, the ideal form of governance is by a "Christian prince," whose "executive power and personal eminence in relation to the people" make him "one whom the people can look upon as father or protectorate of the country."[49] We see here an idea that runs through nearly every thinker, leader, and politician covered in this book: In order to save the people from themselves, they need a father figure who will set in order the disobedient children and unruly women of the national household. Whether it is Brent Bozell, Paul Weyrich, R. J. Rushdoony, Doug Wilson, or Peter Thiel, they all think we need a Big Daddy who will spank the children and control the women in order to get the national household back to how it was intended to be.

As in the model Christian nationalist home, the "will of the people" is not the Christian prince's principal concern. Instead, "the people's collective will expresses consent to be ordered . . . Hence, a prince is not bound to any specific dictates of the people (though certainly these should be taken seriously when expressed clearly); he is bound to what is good, namely, the moral law of God."[50] The Christian prince, in other words, is a representative of the King. "Civil power being original to God," Wolfe writes. "The prince mediates God's divine civil rule."[51] This is a monarchy based on God as king and an earthly executive who carries out his will. The Christian prince is a "master in the Master's universe."[52] Thus, it's no surprise that Wolfe sees the role as "the most excellent office, exceeding even that of the church minister, for it is most like God."[53] Wolfe goes so far as to call him "a sort of national god," who is "the mediator of divine rule for this nation and as one with divinely granted power to direct them in their national completeness."[54] In addition to creating laws that encourage Christian practice—such as Sabbath rest policies, punishments for blasphemy, and outlawing the practice of non-Christian religion—the prince's general vocation is to enforce hierarchy, maintain ethnic exclusivity, and develop a masculine society that resists any form of "gynocracy."[55]

◆ ◆ ◆

The central claim made by the juvenile heirs of Wilson and Rushdoony is that the Gospel is fundamentally about the clan. They argue that God's command to humanity was not only to subdue the Earth, but to do so through distinct ethnic communities, where love for one's own people reflects love for God. For Isker, Engel, Webbon, and Stephen Wolfe, the primary responsibility of God's people is to purify their nation. They ground this duty in what they describe as the natural design of human nature, which they believe is oriented toward ethnic grouping and nation-building. In their view, this mandate comes before—and in practice outweighs—the Kingdom of God as preached by Jesus. Instead of a gospel based on the idea that Christians are called to build God's invisible Kingdom on Earth through charity, inclusion, and selflessness, these thinkers advocate a gospel based on hatred. They have an aversion for diversity of any kind. This is Christian nationalism distilled into White ethnonationalism based on a vision of the United States as a Protestant and White community. It is a justification for prioritizing the love of those like you and the removal or marginalization of those not like you through a divine imperative.

◆ ◆ ◆

Unfortunately, this brand of theology has a long and dark history in the United States. In her groundbreaking work, *Gospel According to the Klan,* historian Kelly J. Baker reveals how the most prominent iteration of the Klu Klux Klan, or KKK, the version that began in 1915, was at its heart a Protestant organization. Klan members saw themselves as carrying on a legacy and set of traditions based in love for God as love for country. In the midst of a wave of immigration of Catholic Europeans, the freeing of Southern Black Americans from enslavement, a changing economy, and concerns about national identity, such "love" was expressed through a hatred for Jews, Catholics, immigrants, and Black people. "The Klan told a story of the importance of white Protestants from the nation's founding until the 1920s, and their artifacts—the robes, the fiery cross, and the American flag—materialized the order's commitment to Protestantism, white supremacy, and 100% Americanism," Baker writes. "The Klan wanted a homogenous, white, Protestant America, free from the corrupting influences of 'diversity,' whether political, religious, or racial."[56]

White Protestants were, in their eyes, the only real Americans. Everyone else was subject to death, imprisonment, subjugation, or deportation. While there are distinctions to be made, it is often hard to find a de facto difference between the rhetoric of these hateful men and the KKK of the 1920s. The latter organization had great success recruiting White Protestants frightened by the country's increasing religious and racial diversity to its ranks. By the mid-1920s an estimated four million Americans were members of the Klan. They spread the gospel of White purity through the Gospel of Christ. For millions of Americans, the two were one and the same. If you're thinking that the popularity of White Christian ethnonationalism can't happen here, the reality is that it already did.

Whether or not the current generation of Christian ethnonationalists will have the same success is yet to be seen. In 1915 the White supremacist film *The Birth of a Nation* was screened by President Woodrow Wilson at the White House. The film is credited as one of the inspirations for the KKK's formal reboot later that year. In 2025, William Wolfe was invited to the White House in what was a resurrection of MAGA Nation in Trump's second term. It's not the same thing. But it's not that different, either.

6
TECHNO-FEUDALISM

> **An executive "under law" is not an executive at all. We are living in the Babylonian captivity of Article II, which can only be ended by a radical and unconditional act of executive restoration—an American reassertion of the ancient English rule that "the king is above the law."**
>
> —CURTIS YARVIN

The Epic of Gilgamesh is the oldest surviving literary work in human history. Nearly four thousand years old, the ancient Babylonian tale tells the story of Gilgamesh, an innovative warrior who grew up thinking he was better than everyone else. He uses a new technology to develop the city of Uruk, over which he is king. Gilgamesh has no regard for other people, and so he rules without empathy, waging sexual violence on the women in the city and treating the men as his natural inferiors. He eventually forms a friendship with Enkidu, with whom he destroys sacred forests and overruns holy places. They flout the limitations of humanity and test the gods, defeating demons and rejecting divine favor. Independent. All-powerful. Singular. Gilgamesh and Enkidu appear unstoppable, until Enkidu dies at the hands of a god-sent curse.

Overcome by grief, Gilgamesh leaves the city he built in order to find the cure to mortality. After an arduous journey, he meets the immortal man Utnapishtim, the only human to survive the Great Flood that overtook the Earth. Utnapishtim directs Gilgamesh to dive deep into the sea in order to retrieve a root that will cure his finitude. However, after retrieving it Gilgamesh is overcome by fatigue and falls asleep. A snake sneaks up on him. When he wakes, the root is gone. Gilgamesh makes the journey back to Uruk, stopping before he reaches the walled city to view the place he built, "having learned that, though he is mighty and famous, he will be equal in death with all other human beings."[1]

Our most ancient epic centers on a king who does everything possible to transcend his species in order to be a royal god unhindered by mortality, physical limitation, or human relationship, only to realize that finitude is a fate that must be accepted. It is the basis of human solidarity, the foundation of our being-together. Raging against it is a pathway to misery and ruin. Trying to become not just a king, but a transcendent monarch, leads not to beatitude, but to defeat and isolation. Even after four thousand years, these lessons are hard to learn.

◆ ◆ ◆

Peter Thiel is a billionaire monarchist theologian who has spent two decades sizing up our democracy in order to figure out a way to topple it. Through his enormous wealth, political grooming of elites, and platforming of antidemocratic philosophers, Thiel has fused national security and monarchist theory into a single governing project. However, there is seemingly a contradiction at the heart of Thiel's political mission. Thiel's most important business venture since 9/11 is Palantir, a data mining company that sorts enormous amounts of information in order to surveil individuals and track criminal or terrorist threats in real time. Palantir is now worth $386 billion; the stock has grown 1,700 percent in value since it debuted on the market in 2020.[2] From the beginning, Thiel, Palantir's CEO Alex Karp, and other key figures in the company have positioned Palantir as a nation-building endeavor whose twin missions are to make billions of dollars and to ensure that the United States remains the preeminent military power on the planet. This is Thiel's on-the-ground response to 9/11: a panoptical surveillance company designed to prevent terrorist attacks against the US and its allies.

Yet Thiel has also spent the last two decades cultivating projects designed to surpass the nation-state in favor of techno-feudalism. In 2008 he cofounded the Seasteading Institute with Patri Friedman, grandson of the highly influential libertarian economist Milton Friedman, an organization dedicated to building independent human communities on the ocean. This *Waterworld* fantasy for rich people imagined a way out of living under the auspices of the nation-state. While seasteading is no longer in fashion, Thiel and Friedman haven't given up their dream of escape. Thiel is now a principal investor in Friedman's company Pronomos, which supports the creation of network cities in independent economic zones across the world. These cities are meant to be autonomous territories outside the jurisdiction of the countries out of which they are carved.

Perhaps the clearest indication of Thiel's political worldview is not in his investments, but in his art. In a November 2023 feature in *The Atlantic*, Barton Gellman describes the sculpture Thiel commissioned for his new home in Los Angeles: It is a map of Thiel's worldview featuring a hero molded "in the aesthetic of Dungeons & Dragons, thick with monsters and knights and castles . . ." Thiel is at the center of the piece, waging battle on a lion and dragon with a longbow. "The lion is labeled 'Fair Elections.' The dragon is labeled 'Democracy,'" Gellman writes. "The Thiel figure is trying to kill them."[3]

Thiel is also an investor in Tlon, the startup founded by his friend Curtis Yarvin, the dissident provocateur who openly calls for the end of democracy in favor of a monarchical government. Yarvin has risen from an obscure blogger writing under the name Mencius Moldbug to a mainstream "intellectual" who has the ear of the vice president and others in the Trump White House. Yarvin's monarchism is more radical than Thiel's Girardian version. When Thiel began appealing to monarchy two decades ago, it was considered idiosyncratic at best and startling at worst. Now Yarvin is profiled in *The New York Times*, *The Atlantic*, and *The New Yorker* as one of the most avant-garde voices of the tech Right.

From the outside, Thiel seems to be helping build the nation, while also working to escape—and perhaps destroy—it. He is a "patriot" driving the marriage between statecraft and Silicon Valley innovation. But his time and money are spent looking for ways to transcend his *patria* for a new kind of human community. He is reinvigorating American national power through Palantir while creating the conditions for serving as the founder-king of a startup city. He is a defender of the "West," and the liberal democracies therein, who openly wonders if monarchy wouldn't be a better model of governance than one fueled by We the People.

Yet, for Thiel, there is a bizarre coherence to the two seemingly discordant projects. If the ultimate goal is to save humanity—or at least a few humans—by escaping politics through technology, he needs the safety and security required to develop the requisite parts. You can't build a moon rocket from the trenches. Thus, together Alex Karp (CEO of Palantir) and Curtis Yarvin represent how Thiel's techno-theology has become the basis for a postliberal vision of the West based on surveillance, violence, and the usurping of liberty and rights in the name of order. You might be tempted to write off Thiel's theory *and* application as nothing more than a contradictory rigamarole manufactured by a billionaire with too much money and power for his own good. But Thiel is one of the most influential people on the planet.

Even if he is reenacting the first half of the Epic of Gilgamesh before our eyes, we don't have the luxury of dismissing his machinations as the tinkering of a weird technocrat. When his project is untangled, there is a strange internal coherence to it, but it appears even more grotesque than before. Most importantly: Thiel may have more power and influence over the short-term direction of the United States than any of the other figures explored in this book. Dismissing his ideas as the quack fiddling of a modern-day Howard Hughes is not an option. Thiel has plans that will affect all of us.

• • •

There was an office, but no engineers or code. It was an idea in a box. In 2003, the same period when Thiel was writing "The Straussian Moment," he had a vision for a company that could sort through enormous sets of data in order to identify national security threats. He named it Palantir, after the magical stones from Tolkien's *The Lord of the Rings*. In Tolkien's fantasy world, the *palantíri* enable powerful figures to see things happening in a distant place. They could be used for surveillance over Middle Earth. But they were also tools of evil in the hands of bad actors interested in dominating others. Alex Karp, Palantir's CEO, describes the company's overarching ambition as "saving the Shire."[4] There is little evidence that either he or Thiel realize that Palantir could be interpreted as a tool of Sauron, or the Antichrist for that matter.

Palantir uses various software programs in order to collect and sort enormous datasets in order to track people in real time:

> In the last five years Palantir has become the go-to company for mining massive data sets for intelligence and law enforcement applications, with a slick software interface and coders who parachute into clients' headquarters to customize its programs. Palantir turns messy swamps of information into intuitively visualized maps, histograms and link charts. Give its so-called "forward-deployed engineers" a few days to crawl, tag and integrate every scrap of a customer's data, and Palantir can elucidate problems as disparate as terrorism, disaster response and human trafficking.[5]

In the summer of 2025, Palantir signed a $38 million contract with the Department of Homeland Security, even though tech workers had long protested DHS's use of Palantir's software to "track the immigration status and whereabouts of people entering the US by collecting large amounts of data on them."[6] Palantir officials have claimed that its software is not involved with the wing of ICE that oversees detention and deportation of undocumented immigrants. Yet, in 2017, ICE officials reportedly used "Palantir's Investigative Case Management software to target the parents and other relatives of unaccompanied minors crossing the border—a precursor to the Trump administration's family separation policy."[7] This software is capable of providing immigration officials with info on an individual's "schooling, family relationships, employment information, phone records, immigration history, foreign exchange program status, personal connections, biometric traits, criminal records, and home and work addresses."[8] In May 2025, the Trump administration began the process of adopting Palantir software at the Social Security Administration, IRS, and Health and Human Services. This means that "creating detailed portraits of Americans based on government data is not just a pipe dream," but an imminent reality.[9]

To many, such a reality represents a dystopian nightmare haunted by a surveillance state void of any sense of freedom. How can you have a democracy when the government is tracking your every movement? How can we claim to be free if the Tech Deep State has a super database on every American that includes biometrics, location data, and health histories? Yet to Peter Thiel this is the answer to the question he asked a quarter century ago in the wake of 9/11. Creating a global panopticon may destroy individual liberty, but who cares if it thwarts rogue attacks and illegal border crossings? In his view, sacrificing the dignity of ordinary citizens is worth it in order for men like him to be safe—and transcendent.

* * *

I argued earlier that Thiel's 2004 essay "The Straussian Moment" is the decoder ring for understanding his political theology. It is the one work in Thiel's oeuvre where he shows his cards and reveals how he understands human nature in full. The essay is the key not only to understanding Thiel's gospel, but also to seeing how the political contradictions in Thiel's life have a strange internal rationality.

In "The Straussian Moment," Thiel spends considerable time pondering if and how the political philosophy of Leo Strauss might provide answers to the question of how to protect the West from Islamic terrorism in the wake of 9/11. Thiel concludes that Strauss's diagnosis of human nature and politics is useful, but incomplete. This is why he ultimately turns to René Girard to fill out the picture. However, he does not think Strauss is entirely wrong. For Thiel, Strauss is a philosophical stage on the way to the whole picture of human history and human futures. While Strauss's approach may not offer the full view of what's possible, it's useful in wartime. When you are under attack, your concerns narrow to survival, safety, and protection.

Strauss is helpful because he recognizes that in order to protect a good and moral society—one based on order, right, and law—it is sometimes necessary to engage in actions that contradict those foundational values. In other words, if you want a city on a hill, you have to be willing at times to use any means necessary to protect it—even if those means are repugnant to the enlightened citizens of your homeland. "Strauss also reminds us of the exceptional framework needed to supplement the American regime," Thiel writes. He then quotes Strauss himself: "The most just society cannot survive without 'intelligence,' i.e., espionage," even though "espionage is impossible without a suspension of certain rules of natural right."[10] In order to have a "good" society, sometimes you can't be the good guy in the fight; sometimes you have to cease pursuing what is right in the name of the good of protecting your people—even if they don't like it.

Like Strauss, Thiel believes the only way to protect the city on a hill, founded on natural right and freedom of thought, is to engage in illiberal tactics and brutal warfare outside the legitimate channels of the liberal democracy in which you live:

> Just as there appears to be something shaky and problematic about a theoretical framework that is not subject to the give and take of open debate, so there appears to be something subversive and immoral about a political framework that operates outside the checks and balances of representative democracy as described in high school textbooks; but if American liberalism is decisively incomplete, then its critique is no longer quite so decisive.[11]

From Thiel's perspective, Strauss is a key wartime voice because he argues for the moral superiority of the West and makes no pretenses about the tactics needed to defend "our" way of life against "inferior" cultures. Thiel finds in Strauss a set of resources for a nationalistic, pro-Western, and at times antidemocratic philosophy—one that is implemented in the name of defending the Western values of free thought and free markets, even if actions and movement are constantly surveilled.

* * *

A quarter century ago, Thiel joined with his friend from law school, Alex Karp, and others, to found Palantir. Karp became the CEO. When Thiel and Karp met at Stanford Law, neither of them was sure he wanted to be a lawyer. They spent those years arguing endlessly over politics, philosophy, and the future of the world. Karp brought to the table a talent for raising funds. However, he had no background in tech. He can't code or design products. He had never been part of a startup and didn't know the ins and outs of Silicon Valley tech culture before Thiel tapped him for the job. He grew up in a neo-Marxist household with a Black mother and a Jewish father. He describes himself as a progressive "racially ambiguous dyslexic."[12] After graduating from Stanford Law, he moved to Germany in order to pursue a PhD in social philosophy at Goethe University. In his talks, Karp often cites the likes of Heinrich Heine and Goethe to unsuspecting tech audiences. In 2020, Karp donated to the Biden campaign.

On the surface, Karp seems like the least likely candidate to head Thiel's most important venture of the twenty-first century. Politically and professionally Karp is Thiel's antithesis. To this day, Karp isn't sure why Thiel chose him.[13] But within the grand scheme of Thiel's worldview—read through "The Straussian Moment"—he makes perfect sense.

In February 2025, Karp and Nicholas Zamiska published *The Technological Republic*. Claiming that 90 percent of the book's ideas came from him, Karp says plainly that the work is an articulation of the theory behind Palantir.[14] Page after page, the reader is hammered with the thesis that the "software industry should rebuild its relationship with government and redirect its effort and attention to constructing the technology and artificial intelligence capabilities that will address the most pressing challenges that we collectively face."[15] For Karp, Palantir is a "national project" that expresses American values and identity, while preserving "the enduring yet fragile geopolitical advantage that the United States and its allies in Europe and elsewhere have retained over their adversaries."[16] The call to action is for Silicon Valley to take part in the normative work of ensuring that the superiority of the US is both extended and protected. "We should return to that tradition of close collaboration between the technology industry and the government," Karp argues. "It is that combination of a pursuit of innovation with the objectives of the nation that will not only advance our welfare but safeguard the legitimacy of the democratic project itself."[17]

In order to explain American exceptionalism, Karp, the self-proclaimed progressive and ostensible political inverse of Peter Thiel, turns time and time again to right-wing theorists. Karp calls the American Left "a caged animal" that is "unable to offer an affirmative vision of a virtuous or moral life, whose content it long ago stripped away to the bare essentials."[18] He labels "woke" a destructive pagan religion.[19] Karp then references Roger Kimball, the right-wing critic and author, who encourages Americans to take heart in the "nobility" of our way of life.[20] At other times, Karp cites neoconservatives such as Allan Bloom, Roger Scruton, and Samuel Huntington in order to bolster his case for the superiority of the West. The writer Jack McCordick summarizes this trend: "If there is a single pattern of thought that defines *The Technological Republic,* it is that of a wavering liberal, hair-splitting his way toward civilizational chauvinism."[21]

To top it off, Karp and Zamiska draw on Leo Strauss himself in the final pages of the book to seal the argument. "It was this 'indifference to any goal, or of aimlessness and drifting,' as Strauss put it, that is the seed of our current nihilism as a culture." In order to build the technological republic Karp and Zamiska envision, "a rich and thriving and raucously creative communal experiment—not merely the bacchanal of permissive egalitarianism of which Strauss warned—will require an embrace of value, virtue, and culture, the very things that the present generation was taught to abhor."[22]

Karp's nationalistic chauvinism goes like this: America, as the superpower of the West, is the preeminent human society on Earth. All cultures are not equal. Some are less "civilized," advanced, humane, or moral. Ours is at the top of the hierarchy. We should reinstate our values and virtues, abandoning multiculturalism, pluralism, and globalism in order to build a cohesive national identity. In the past few decades, "the right was pursued while the good was abandoned," Karp argues.[23] In other words, Karp wants us to pursue the good of the United States without concern for what is right for anyone else. Instead of concerning ourselves with universal human rights or climate justice, the US will limit its scope to national profit and power. In order to do that, we need to reinvigorate our religious orthodoxies. Karp quotes the godfather of neoconservatism in order to make his case. "As Irving Kristol, who founded the *National Interest* in 1985, has written, 'The delicate task that faces our civilization today is not to reform the secular, rationalist orthodoxy,' but rather 'to breathe new life into the older, now largely comatose, religious orthodoxies.'"[24]

What makes the US so superior to other nations? And who will fill in the American national project with the specificities of the religious orthodoxies Karp sees as key to our greatness?

A clear takeaway from *The Technological Republic* is that American, and by extension Western, superiority is based not on elevated morality or democratic virtue, but on our ability to kill our enemies. In other words, for all the talk of American values and virtue, Karp's understanding of American greatness rests on the ability to hurt other people: "Americans are the most loving, God-fearing, fair, least discriminatory people on the planet," Karp argues, with no recognition of the skyrocketing numbers of Americans who are nonreligious or of the history of enslavement, Jim Crow, redlining, and other forms of racial, sexual, and gender prejudice in our history. There are many reasons to be proud of who we are as Americans, but Karp whitewashes history in order to justify a violent future. "And they want to know that if you're waking up and thinking about harming American citizens or if American citizens are taken hostage and kept in dungeons, or if you're a foreign power sending fentanyl to poison our people," Karp continues. "Something really bad is going to happen to you and your friends and your cousins and your bank account and your mistress and whoever was involved."[25]

The legacy of the tech industry's entanglement with American statecraft is the atomic bomb. For Karp, the Manhattan Project is the blueprint for how Silicon Valley should envision its role in the American project. "What really makes America great, the book claims, is not so much its system of government, nor its vaunted ideals and values, but its software industry," writes Jack McCordick in an incisive essay at *The New Republic*. "And, wouldn't you know it: The most important software companies are the ones whose products, as Karp has put it, 'power the West to its obvious, innate superiority' and 'bring violence and death to our enemies.'"[26]

McCordick goes on to point out that in a 2025 earnings report, Karp quoted Samuel Huntington, the author of *The Clash of Civilizations,* directly in explaining the global dominance of the West: "The rise of the West was not made possible 'by the superiority of its ideas or values or religion . . . but rather by its superiority in applying organized violence.'"[27] Karp argues for taking pride in Western values by funneling financial and human capital to military dominance with no regard for larger human problems. This is "a remarkably impoverished vision of what the United States should stand for at this moment in history," writes William D. Hartung at *The Nation,* "when non-military challenges like disease, climate change, racial and economic injustice, resurgent authoritarianism, and growing neofascist movements pose greater dangers than traditional military threats."[28] In the Palantir worldview, as long as we can kill more effectively, we will be the superior culture.

Moreover, the call to revive religious orthodoxies in the context of a politics based on American dominance and military power opens the door for pacts with the religious extremists examined earlier. The alliance between Christian bigots and technocrats like Karp is tenuous. The delicate alignment of their values and worldview could disintegrate in the near future. However, Karp's mission to revive Western supremacy provides common ground with White Christian ethnonationalists like Andrew Isker, C. Jay Engel, William Wolfe, and Stephen Wolfe.

Karp is also aligned with another towering Silicon Valley luminary—Elon Musk. Musk does not identify as a Christian in any robust sense. While he sometimes posts on X about the symbiotic relationship between "the West" and Christianity, his rhetoric rarely veers toward the themes of God, church, or Christ. But Musk's tweets often center on defending and renewing "Western Civilization." In a podcast interview, Musk told Joe Rogan that empathy is the fundamental weakness of Western civilization. He later claimed that an excess of empathy for other groups is a suicide gene built into the West. On November 5, 2025, the right-wing author Gad Saad tweeted: "American exceptionalism . . . has yielded the greatest society that the world has ever known. Suicidal empathy is going to destroy it because Western tolerance is its fatal Achilles tendon." Musk concurred in a quote tweet that reads "Western Civilization is doomed, unless the core weakness of suicidal empathy is recognized and actions are taken that are hard, but necessary for survival."[29] A month later, someone with the handle @rothmus posted on X:

> Diversity and multiculturalism were always code for whites becoming minorities in every single country, city, and small village. A West ruled by foreigners

> who despise it in collusion with domestic enemies who equally abhor it, its institutions occupied, its morality inverted, intellectually subdued, occupied by ballots, invaded without an army, shamed into submission, and mustered no resistance. We are witnessing the historical suicide of a civilization. The West will change. But change isn't always for the better. The third worldist shitholization of the West is here.

The same day Musk—*an immigrant from Africa*—amplified the sentiment with this response to the post: "The doom of Western Civilization must be averted!"[30] Musk's whining about civilizational decline, which echoes Karp's Western chauvinism, seems like less a rally around a shared way of life than a pathway to oligarchical control over a society that is more economically unequal by the day. The man who will be the world's first trillionaire sees empathy as a bug to be eliminated in the name of order and efficiency.

* * *

Overall, Karp's American exceptionalism plays a key role in Thiel's overarching political theology—and provides an ideological reinforcement to fellow Silicon Valley technocrats like Musk. It is as if Thiel was able to manufacture a philosopher to articulate his interpretation in "The Straussian Moment" in real life: Palantir exists as the application of the theory that technologists should work hand in hand with the American government in order to defend this country and its allies as the preeminent human societies in the world. Following Thiel's reading of Strauss, Palantir is willing to spy on people and kill our enemies in order to make sure that Americans are safe and prosperous—even if it means living in a dystopian surveillance state.

Moreover, Karp's self-identification as a political progressive intellectual presents a helpful misdirection from the imperial ideology behind Palantir's software—and Thiel's fondness for monarchism. In "The Straussian Moment," Thiel points to Leo Strauss's advice that philosophers conceal their true views within layers of philosophical indirection, to avoid the fate of Socrates—executed by the Athenian authorities for corrupting the youth. Thiel reflects in particular on Strauss's warning that philosophers should hide their authentic understandings of human nature from those in power: "It would be enough for the attentive reader, but not enough for the invariably less intelligent government censors."[31]

Alex Karp is in a real sense the Philosophical Indirector in Chief. His supposed centrist ethos, coupled with his wacky philosopher persona, enables him to espouse a neoconservative ethnocentric nationalism that belies any sense of pluralism or global cooperation. He is a philosopher of *good repute* authorized to articulate political views of *ill repute*. Karp seems, in other words, an inversion of the Straussian ruse—his persona engineered to trick the censors of political correctness and "cancel culture" into thinking that the head of Palantir is a liberal Biden supporter who shouldn't scare them like Peter Thiel does.

To escape a nation, sometimes you have to build one. For Thiel, the nation-building project embodied by Palantir is necessary for creating the conditions for his nation-transcending visions of the future. Palantir is the protection from limitless violence *against* the West. Networked cities and techno-feudalism represent the potential innovations—the technological answers to run-of-the-mill human politics. But those aren't possible, in Thiel's view, if our public square is under threat from foreign terrorists or "invaded" by undocumented immigrants. It's like Maslow's hierarchy of needs for creating your own monarchical utopia—you can't have the innovative future without the safe and secure present (and billions of dollars). Security becomes the nonnegotiable first level, one defined so widely that it justifies totalitarian surveillance and ruthless violence. This foundation provides the base support to build the next rung: a technocratic kingdom where a Gilgameshian CEO rules without accountability or dissent.

* * *

In 1997, the conspiracy theorist and Newsmax trustee James Dale Davidson and the investor and editor Sir William Rees-Mogg wrote a tech manifesto titled *The Sovereign Individual: Mastering the Transition to the Information Age*. The work is a field manual that prepares elites for the revolutionary changes that information technology will bring. The authors argue that the "new revolution" will liberate individuals "at the expense of the twentieth-century nation-state."[32] In their view, the "civic myths of the twentieth-century nation-state" are rapidly eroding, revealing that this form of governance is "exhausted."[33] The Information Age will see the passing of the nation-state in favor of a techno-feudal future in which, "in hundreds, and ultimately in the millions, individuals will escape the shackles of politics. As they do, they will transform the character of governments, shrinking the realm of compulsion and widening the scope of private control over resources."[34] Citizens will become customers. Governments will resemble monopolistic companies. Bureaucrats, prime ministers, councils, and tax agencies will lose their power. While not everyone—or even close to everyone—will benefit from the "liberating" nature of this global governance structure, the few who do will "operate like the gods of myth in the same physical environment as the ordinary, subject citizen, but in a separate realm politically." These gods among us "will redesign governments and reconfigure economies in the new millennium. The full implications of this change are all but unimaginable."[35]

In 2014, Peter Thiel called *The Sovereign Individual* the most influential book he'd ever read.[36] In his preface to the 2020 edition, he explained that after two decades the import of the work is in its vision of the new human age ahead of us. Rees-Mogg and Davidson are not afraid to approach megapolitical questions that go beyond the framework of the postwar consensus, the UN, the EU, and the dominance of the US in order to envision a future beyond the nation-state. "In truth, the great conflict over our megapolitical future is only just beginning," Thiel writes. "Reading *The Sovereign Individual* in 2020 is a way to think carefully about the future that your own actions will help to create. It is an opportunity not to be wasted."[37] Thiel is not alone in his praise for *The Sovereign Individual*. His friend and fellow billionaire Marc Andreessen calls it "the most thought-provoking book on the unfolding nature of the 21st Century that I've yet read."[38] Tech magnate Balaji Srinivasan has also drawn on the book heavily in his talks and writing.[39]

Thiel's interest in a postdemocratic world isn't limited to

The Sovereign Individual. A few years after its publication, Thiel became enamored with the political vision of Curtis Yarvin, who rose to niche online prominence under the name Mencius Moldbug. Though Thiel seems to have discovered Yarvin's work in the mid-aughts, the two first met in 2009 after Thiel gave a speech at the Cato Institute where he outlined a kind of postlibertarian vision for escaping the failed politics of liberal democracy. Thiel sketched an ideology of escape that mirrored his Girardian vision of tech founders as monarchs—figures who break free from the cycle of mimesis, resisting imitation in favor of invention and the world-altering "miracles" of technology. But there was another strain of influence in Thiel's lecture, one that felt more contemporary than either Girard's mimetic theory or the prophecies of *The Sovereign Individual*. Thiel's turn away from libertarianism to an explicitly postdemocratic vision of the future was evidently filtered through the core ideas in Yarvin's early writings. Beyond their friendship, Thiel has also invested in Yarvin's startup Tlon. Some have dubbed Yarvin the philosopher of Thiel's court; Thiel even gifted him a portrait with the title "Philosopher" emblazoned on it.

* * *

Yarvin began writing his blog *Unqualified Reservations* in 2007. It soon became a cult favorite among Silicon Valley dissidents. The blog reads like the musings of a computer programmer with too much time on his hands: "The other day I was tinkering around in my garage and I decided to build a new ideology."[40] Yarvin's writing is full of neologisms, obscure quips, and snark. He is a know-it-all who seems to think that the fundamental problems of the human condition could be solved if a rational genius like him was simply allowed to clear the deck and start over. He calls for the end of the United States and the global order in favor of a neofeudal system made up of thousands of tiny sovereign states. And he castigates the media and universities as the "Cathedral" that maintains an information monopoly, and thus is able to warp reality to its universalist ideology. *Unqualified Reservations* became a strange meeting site for disaffected right-wing techies thankful that someone was saying publicly what they'd thought privately for years: Democracy was inefficient and inferior to monarchy.

Yarvin calls his political model formalism: "The basic idea of formalism is just that the main problem in human affairs is violence," he writes. "The goal is to design a way for humans to interact, on a planet of remarkably limited size, without violence."[41] Compared to organized violence, Yarvin argues that "all other problems—Poverty, Global Warming, Moral Decay, etc., etc., etc.—are basically insignificant." Yarvin is a computer programmer who spent most of his early adult life either coding or online in early versions of internet communities. Like many in his Silicon Valley audience, he has no interest in beauty, virtue, tradition, or spirituality.[42] There is a sense reading his early work that Yarvin is not a person whose politics take account of the desires, vulnerabilities, and needs of embodied humans. For him, human society is not a matter of competing values, pieties, and passions, but an "engineering problem."[43] Thus, "any solution that solves the problem is acceptable. Any solution that does not solve the problem is not acceptable."[44] In sum, formalism is founded on the premise of engineering a society free from violence and disorder by any means possible, even if it means curtailing civil liberties or doing away with democracy altogether. For Yarvin, democracy is a terrible form of governance for many reasons, but the main one is that it prioritizes representation, rights, and freedom over security and order.

In his early work, Yarvin is aware that calling for the end of democracy in favor of a formalist security state will set off alarms. However, he explains, we don't actually live in a democracy—or even the outlines of one—now. Yarvin claims that by paying taxes to the government, American citizens are "corporate serfs." By extension, the government "is nothing but a corporation. That is, it is a formal structure by which a group of individuals agree to act collectively to achieve some result."[45] Once again, Yarvin takes no consideration of human life beyond engineering. For him, the values celebrated in the American founding—the will of the people, elected representation, the guarantee of certain inalienable rights—are little more than "ancient mystical horseradish."[46] The government is a business, pure and simple:

> It is not a mystic trust consigned to us by the generations. It is not the repository of our hopes and fears, the voice of conscience and the avenging sword of justice. It is just a big old company that holds a huge pile of assets, has no clear idea of what it's trying to do with them, and is thrashing around like a ten-gallon shark in a five-gallon bucket, red ink spouting from each of its bazillion gills.[47]

The solution is to economize the government. Party politics and elections mean nothing if the corporation is not streamlined and made profitable. This will lead to the highest levels of security and order, even if it means the erasure of democracy and representation. "I don't think it's too crazy to say that all options—including restructuring and liquidation—should be on the table," Yarvin says.[48]

If formalism is a diagnosis, then Yarvin's solution is a corporate monarchy. In line with *The Sovereign Individual*, Yarvin proposes the idea of a "patchwork" global order marked by "a global spiderweb of tens, even hundreds, of thousands of sovereign and independent mini-countries, each governed by its own joint-stock corporation without regard to the residents' opinions."[49] Citizens would be property of the joint-stock company. They wouldn't technically be owned by the state, since they would have the choice to leave at any time for another patch. This is Yarvin's all "exit" and no "voice" model of civic status: Individuals would have no say in how their government is run, but could ostensibly leave anytime to find a new patch in which to live. The state would be led by a monarch modeled after a CEO, who, along with a board of directors, would have unilateral control over the territory.

Despite all the attention given to Curtis Yarvin by Thiel, Elon Musk, *The New York Times, The New Yorker*, JD Vance, and countless others over the last two decades, almost none of his vision for corporate monarchy is novel. He openly admits to the influence of the Austrian school, a controversial group of anarcho-capitalists who believe democracy is a deficient form of governance. Yarvin arrived at his most important conclusions about the optimal structure of human governance from the likes of the ultra-right-wing economists Murray Rothbard, Hans-Hermann Hoppe, and Ludwig von Mises:

> Then Hoppe points out: we can see the premodern international order as a spontaneous order! It's actually the ultimate in libertarianism: states are competing sovereign corporations. Above them, there is no government at all—a global anarcho-libertarian paradise of armed 'sovcorps.' Yet strangely, in this ultra-libertarian model, states are not libertarian at all! A nation is a land and its settled people. The sovcorp owns both—because who else would? So the state, not as in Anglo-American limited-government theory, but as in Continental sovereignty theory, is absolute.[50]

This passage is key for understanding Yarvin's role as the mouthpiece of a certain faction of the American Right. Those who identified as libertarian, like Peter Thiel did for decades, fought for limited government, low taxes, and isolationist foreign policy on the grounds that true freedom comes when the state doesn't interfere with individual liberty. However, Yarvin realized in the mid-aughts that libertarianism wasn't winning and never would. Instead of trying to convince the masses that a minuscule representative government is best for human flourishing, Yarvin concluded that if democracy and representation could be taken out of the picture, then an absolute state run by a rational CEO and his trusted advisors is a more preferable—and realistic—option than the Goldwater-Buckley-Koch vision for laissez-faire capitalism.

"Hoppe argues that, unlike democratically elected officials, a monarch has a long-term incentive to safeguard his subjects and the state, because both belong to him," writes Ava Kofman in an illuminating *New Yorker* profile of Yarvin. "Anyone familiar with the history of dictatorships might find this idea disingenuous. Not Yarvin."[51]

Yarvin assumes that the long-term "ownership" of subjects and state will lead the rational actor at the top of the hierarchy to implement an incentive structure that will benefit all stakeholders. Even beyond the subservience and lack of human dignity involved in such arrangements, there is no reckoning with the grotesque histories and cruelty involved when one human has "owned" another human. Yarvin is bringing up the cruelest form of human relationship, the one fraught with the most sadistic and exploitative elements seen in the history of our species, and blithely suggests trying it again would be fine.

Moreover, Yarvin takes no account of the historical autocrats who have acted irrationally, selfishly, cruelly, and oppressively in order not only to maintain control of what they have, but also to increase their power. When asked about these scenarios, Yarvin whisks them away, claiming that there will be no need for international conflict or megalomaniacal rulers in a global system of autonomous sovereign corporations. He is so incensed by the state of America that instead of the invisible hand of the market, Yarvin wants the crushing grip of a monarch who will eliminate disorder and violence, even if it means citizens of the state are "owned" by their "sovcorp." "Any well-run Patchwork realm is congenitally dedicated to the good old Marxist ideal of exploitation," Yarvin writes in an infamous passage. "It has no intrinsic sympathy for the aged, the crippled, the deformed, the useless. Into the biodiesel vats with them!"[52] In ways that echo Nazi ideology, he expresses the idea that "useless" individuals should be turned into fuel for the superior races. In one interview, Yarvin made the vile racist comment that the "church Blacks" should control the "ghetto Blacks" until the latter can control themselves. (His girlfriend considered it a win when she got him to stop saying the N-word in her presence.) In his early writings he advanced the idea that biology is a determining factor in intelligence, retrofitting eugenicist ideas in twenty-first-century terms. In sum, Yarvin is not only a monarchist, but a eugenicist racist who flippantly (he maintains, jokingly) suggests that the elderly and the disabled should be burned in ovens.

While at times Yarvin argues that the goal of governance is human flourishing, he seems to have no conception of what that is beyond the absence of violence and the profitability of the company who owns the people and land of its "patch." His vision is sophomoric—the musings of a chronically online former quiz champion who thinks that citing one historical source or a Wikipedia page is enough to win an argument about the American founding or the nature of democracy. When you drill down into the heart of Yarvin's writings, you find a simplistic and fanciful reflection on human nature by a person with a severely limited experience with actual human beings. He sounds like the pompous engineer, sitting in the back of a political science class, chiming in every chance possible to inform the professor that all the analysis of human nature is unnecessary. If one simply allowed the programmers to take over, they could eliminate the bugs in our system—solving the problems of the good life and human difference in the matter of an afternoon. However, those "bugs" are the elderly who need government assistance, those with disabilities, people struggling with addiction, and folks who haven't been given a fair shot due to some aspect of their identity. When people are treated as glitches, cruelty soon follows.

The shallowness of Yarvin's proposals hasn't stopped the powerful from listening. Yarvin is friends with Michael Anton, the former Claremont Institute fellow—and author of "The Flight 93 Election"—who was director of policy planning at the State Department. Marc Andreessen, the billionaire founder of Netscape and the investment firm Andreessen Horowitz, cites Yarvin's influence and work in interviews. In 2021, JD Vance publicly mentioned Yarvin by name, recalling the latter's idea that the next conservative president should fire all government employees. Yarvin was invited to Trump's second inauguration, and since Trump re-entered the White House dozens of articles have been published about how Yarvin's ideas are "coursing" through Washington, DC, as the lifeblood of the new administration's governing ideals.[53]

However, the most public manifestation of Yarvin's ideology came in the form of Elon Musk's implementation of DOGE early in Trump's second term. In a clear echo of Yarvin's ideas, in 2020 Musk told *The Wall Street Journal* that the government is simply "a corporation." When he took the helm of DOGE early in 2025, Musk began implementing a "hard reboot" of the government following Yarvin's blueprint.[54] Musk's DOGE lieutenants openly claim Yarvin as their greatest philosophical inspiration for gutting federal agencies, laying off workers, and destroying the social safety net. One DOGE team member told *The Washington Post* that Yarvin represents "the most crisp articulation" of what DOGE is trying to achieve. Another said that "it's an open secret that everyone in policymaking roles has read Yarvin" and that they are using his theory "to empower people on the ground to actually do stuff—even if they can't admit it publicly."[55] The DOGE team was infamously composed of young, inexperienced men, including a teenager who went by the moniker "Big Balls." In sum, Musk's DOGE underlings—some of whom are not old enough to buy beer—operationalized Yarvin's antidemocratic fantasy in order to create something akin to a corporate executive branch. That work was both vicious and futile. Experts believe that the abrupt end to programs at USAID led to approximately four hundred thousand deaths globally. Moreover, DOGE's efforts saved the federal government a minuscule amount of funds. Musk didn't rid DC of fraud, waste, and abuse. He enacted the shallow musings of an online troll with predictable results: death, destruction, and inefficiency.

The adoption of Yarvin's ideas isn't limited to Elon Musk's run at DOGE. They have been seemingly sanctioned throughout Trump's second term.

In 2024, Yarvin laid out a slate of proposals for the post-Biden era. First, Yarvin called for "a radical and unconditional act of executive restoration."[56] He claimed that "an executive 'under law'" is not an executive. What we need is "an American reassertion of the ancient English rule that 'the king is above the law.'"[57] In February 2025, just weeks into his second term, Trump posted an infamous Napoleon quote to Truth Social: "He who saves his Country does not violate any Law."[58] A few days later, Trump signed an executive order that established him, the president, as the sole interpreter of the law within the executive branch:

> The President and the Attorney General, subject to the President's supervision and control, shall provide authoritative interpretations of law for the executive branch. The President and the Attorney General's

> opinions on questions of law are controlling on all employees in the conduct of their official duties. No employee of the executive branch acting in their official capacity may advance an interpretation of the law as the position of the United States that contravenes the President or the Attorney General's opinion on a matter of law, including but not limited to the issuance of regulations, guidance, and positions advanced in litigation, unless authorized to do so by the President or in writing by the Attorney General.[59]

In other words, Trump's will is equal to the law.

Yarvin also suggests that the president must claim plenary power in order to save the nation from ruin. "To escape the sickening, ever-growing coils of DC's Gordian knot, American voters have only one realistic option," Yarvin writes. "They need to elect a President who clearly states his intention and preparedness to take over the entire American government, assuming *plenary power*—not just in response to any specific event or emergency, but *immediately* upon his inauguration (when his democratic authority is at its strongest)."[60]

In October 2025, Stephen Miller, senior adviser to the president and the man many consider to be the shadow leader of the executive branch, said on television that the president has "plenary power." In a bizarre moment, he then froze, refused to speak further, and the interview was cut short. Miller's strange admission wasn't the only evidence for the belief in the executive's absolute authority. Trump's administration has repeatedly called on Article II of the Constitution to explain Trump's heterodox actions. In February 2025, Trump officials referenced Article II in order to maintain "the president's authority over almost all regulatory agencies that were created by Congress to act independently, or semi-independently, from the president." Frank Bowman, a scholar of constitutional and criminal law, characterized the order as a step toward "an open declaration of dictatorship."[61]

In order to restore executive power, Yarvin argues that the president must "claim the powers of a conquering enemy general. For these powers to make sense, he needs to *govern* like a conquering enemy general—using *direct command of the police* to maintain public stability as he spins up a totally new executive branch, run like a startup with startup-quality people."[62] In the summer of 2025, Trump sent the National Guard to Los Angeles in order to support the Immigration and Customs Enforcement (ICE) agency's operations throughout the city. "We knew that we were part of the experiment to see how much the American people would tolerate," Mayor of Los Angeles Karen Bass testified at a congressional hearing in November 2025. "The fear that blanketed this city is difficult to describe, frankly, because it's so hard to believe it actually happened."[63] The Trump administration continued to deploy ICE around the country to undertake operations designed for the mass deportation of undocumented immigrants. Yet hundreds of documented migrants and American citizens were detained during the raids. Soon after sending the National Guard to Los Angeles, Trump occupied Washington, DC, with hundreds of troops who spent most of their time walking the streets and picking up trash.

In September, ICE turned its attention to Chicago, where in one instance ICE officers rappelled from Black Hawk helicopters into an apartment building:

> Shortly after midnight on Sept. 30, some 300 agents from Border Patrol, the FBI and other agencies stormed the 130-unit apartment complex. SWAT teams rappelled from a helicopter, knocked down doors and hurled flash-bang grenades. They arrested 37 immigrants, most of them Venezuelans, who authorities say were in the country illegally. Agents also zip-tied and, for several hours, detained many U.S. citizens.[64]

Residents were forced outside into the frigid cold. Children were zip-tied in the middle of the night. Despite dozens of arrests, and a claim that two dangerous gang members were detained in the raid, "Federal prosecutors have not filed criminal charges against anyone who was arrested. Nor have they revealed any evidence showing that two immigrants arrested in the building belonged to the Tren de Aragua gang, or even provided their names."[65]

Behind the chaos of Trump's immigration enforcement is a set of intersecting influences—from Stephen Miller's rabid xenophobia to the Heritage Foundation's nine-hundred-page manifesto on executive power. However, if one wanted to at least try to follow Yarvin's advice on how to turn the executive branch of the federal government into a monarchy, these actions would be exactly the kinds of moves one would make.

✦ ✦ ✦

While Karp and Yarvin are independent intellectual forces, their rise and normalization in American culture signal the translation of Thiel's idiosyncratic techno-theology into accepted political discourse. They are powerful figures, wielding the financial resources and intellectual capital needed to command the attention of officials at the highest levels of government. Given their stature and influence, their ideas cannot be ignored. Remarkably, a monarchist and a civilizational chauvinist now rank among the most influential political theorists of our moment.

Their visions of Western civilization—and of the future path of the United States—are distinct. Karp eschews pluralism and cultural coherence in the name of a violent defense of Western superiority. His foreign policy seems to be as close to Schmitt's friend/enemy distinction as that of any figure examined here. He sees the United States as the preeminent force of a Western civilization based on a Judeo-Christian foundation. For his part, Yarvin doesn't want a return to American glory. He wants to liquidate the American republic in order to reinstate monarchy. This would include the end of liberalism, human rights, and the freedoms promised in our Bill of Rights. The People would no longer have a voice in their government. Their only right would be to leave if they so chose. Instead of marching to the voting booth, our only choice would be to march into the arms of another owner-king. Karp is paving the way for the government to be able to spy on its own citizens through a super database. Yarvin is providing practical strategies for turning the world's oldest democracy into a monarchy. Both are postliberal voices extending certain aspects of Peter Thiel's techno-theology.

If we return to the question of how Thiel's efforts to build the nation and his interest in theorists who want to destroy it have any coherence, you could argue that Palantir is a step on the path to monarchy. A state that tracks its citizens' biometrics and movement in real time would not seem to be a democracy in an important sense. If you wanted to "own" your citizens, such tracking would be a key tool in suppressing dissent. Palantir's work thus far has been characterized as defending the superiority of the West. But it's not hard to see how it could be turned against the foundational principles that for many of us make the United States and other liberal democracies decent places to live: free and fair elections, civil liberties, the protection of human rights, the rule of law, and the ultimate rule of the will of the people.

* * *

On the whole, what these men offer is not courage in the face of geopolitical change, but fear. They are afraid of the rest of us. Of the difference, pluralism, and messiness of embodied human life in the real world. None of these men has a robust theory of human dignity, no sense of what human life means beyond order and efficiency. They want to eliminate the need to persuade the people so that they can command them. Democracy was not invented in spite of people like Thiel, Karp, and Yarvin. Democracy is a response to men like them—those who think they are smarter than the rest of us, who think we need them more than we need ourselves, who would crush our rights and autonomy in the name of order, who would spy on us in the name of safety. Beyond their theories of governance and innovation, the foundation of their shared worldview is the notion that they are innovators of singular genius. Their core belief is that they are unique creators of new worlds and a new humanity. In reality, they are retreads—tired archetypes—of the characters, like Gilgamesh, who since time immemorial have been convinced that if we just gave them all the power, resources, and authority, they could solve the human condition.

Democracy may feel chaotic and broken. Liberalism may seem mired in bureaucratic drudgery. But I'd rather work as hard as possible to find a path forward with We the People than hand the keys to the kingdom to St. Peter and his megalomaniacal disciples. I don't want to hack human nature. I don't want a shortcut to utopia. I want to work, struggle, and progress in a community of shared power. I want to flourish through solidarity, not escape, in order to make a future that matters precisely because it is our own.

7

THE THREADS OF THE POSTLIBERAL ALLIANCE

> Either the suicidal empathy of Western civilization ends or Western civilization will end.
>
> —ELON MUSK

> The United States of America is the last stand of Western civilization. It lives or dies here. Let's hope it lives.
>
> —SAMO BURJA

> The fight for Western Civilization has begun—and Americanism will prevail.
>
> —US DEPARTMENT OF LABOR

I converted to evangelical Christianity in 1995, in May of my eighth-grade year. In a matter of months, I transformed from an unchurched punk kid to a devoted disciple. That period was my spiritual boot camp. I immersed myself in Bible studies, prayer groups, radio sermons, and any youth group event possible. My off hours were spent reading scripture. My time with friends was spent telling them how much they needed Jesus.

One of the questions that gets tossed around often in evangelical circles is the matter of salvation. Will anyone who isn't a "real Christian" be saved? What about those in the world who've never heard the Gospel? What about those who lived before Jesus came to Earth? What about other Christians who got many things wrong, but still believed in the same God—like Catholics? Some of my elders in the church said that there was no way Catholics could go to heaven. They claimed that Catholics "worship Mary," make idols out of saints, and place the Pope on the same level as holy scripture. Blasphemy, outright blasphemy, I was told. Others—perhaps those with Catholic kin—were less harsh. Some Catholics, those with a living faith, not the ones who had been baptized and then forgot about true devotion, they would be in heaven. But only them.

In addition to the question of salvation, another issue preoccupied my teenage evangelical brain: the end of the world. When would Jesus return? How would we know it was really him? How much time did I have to convert the people I loved in order to make sure they would be with me for eternity? I read the book of Revelation over and over in order to understand the symbolism and prophecies about the eschaton. My peers and I devoured the bestselling *Left Behind* books, which are a fictional depiction of the rapture and its aftermath, in order to grasp the ways that politics and culture would succumb to the

Antichrist in the tumultuous years before Jesus returned. We watched movies and listened to sermons about how it would all happen suddenly, like "a thief in the night," coming without notice.

One of the theories we heard often was that the Antichrist would institute a one-world government. It would be the apotheosis of communism, with all remnants of capitalist ingenuity and individual expression snuffed out in favor of a conformist totalitarian regime. God would be outlawed. In many ways, our conception of the Antichrist was almost identical to Peter Thiel's—with one striking difference. We were taught that the way that Christians would be forced into demonic submission to the evil one would be through technology, not in spite of it. The most common rumor was that every person would be assigned a bar code, which would be tattooed on their body. This would be how you would pay for groceries, go through security lines, and identify yourself to authorities. The Christians who resisted, well, they would be the ones persecuted by the demonic regime.

Technology was as suspect as the Catholic Church; something that not only might help usher in the Great Tribulation before Christ's return, but that was making traditional forms of family and morality less viable. Wasn't it the media—delivered through cable television and this new thing called the World Wide Web—that was distracting young minds from walking with God? Wasn't it technology, and the advent of beepers and cell phones, that kept us from centering our lives on family, faith, and nation? It was hard in those days to imagine technology—and the grand masters behind it—as anything but our enemy in the culture wars.

I bring all this up as someone who has both lived inside

the culture of American evangelicalism—and once accepted its biases and prejudices against all kinds of other religious and political groups—and as a scholar who has studied American religion for two decades. The deep resonances among the Protestant, Catholic, and technocratic movements I've traced in the foregoing chapters are as surprising to me as anyone. It would be mistaken to view this as a set of relationships marked by reciprocal confidence or common perspective. Deep suspicions remain across the triumvirate. There is a tacit assumption that the struggle is over which group will prevail and crown the American Caesar. They have not coalesced into an unrecognizable illiberal blob. However, we've reached a place where their diagnoses of our "civilizational decline" and their proposed solutions overlap significantly.

Despite differences in tactics and approach, they share a set of commitments that shape their political worldviews. All three movements view liberalism as the poison pill of Western culture, and in turn advance a postlibertarian politics that rejects individual freedom in place of hierarchical control. They treat democracy with open disdain—a weak form of government that lets women, children, and the biologically inferior run amok. In its stead, they prefer a patriarchal autocratic leader who can rule without accountability or transparency. Underlying all of these commitments is a belief in Western supremacy, which provides a civilizational justification for excision, subjugation, and violence. Taken together, these ideas form a coherent ideological foundation among the disparate religious and quasi-religious groups analyzed here.

✦ ✦ ✦

My teenage years corresponded to that peculiar decade in American history right after the Cold War but before the new millennium and 9/11. Our generational anthem was Nirvana's "Smells Like Teen Spirit." In my mind, Kurt Cobain's raspy voice belting out "Here we are now, entertain us" still represents the spirit of those years. We were no longer in an existential battle against the Soviet Union. My generation didn't do atomic bomb drills underneath the desk. We didn't have a Big Bad Other, opposition to whom generated American spirit or collective effervescence. Like the rest of the country, we wondered who we were at a time when it seemed that, in Fukuyama's terms, history had ended and there were no more bad guys for capitalist democracy to defeat.

As Nicole Hemmer shows in *Partisans,* her insightful analysis of how the 1990s set the stage for twenty-first-century political polarization, it was in this moment of victorious malaise that the postwar consensus began to dissolve. Without the threat of nuclear war or the ideological battle of democracy versus communism, many on the American Right began to look inward and question the collective wisdom of the liberal order. It was a moment where external safety allowed for internal strife without concern for existential disaster. One of the legacies of this moment in US history was a castigation of liberalism as the root of American decline. Protestant and Catholic voices constructed revisionist histories that told a story of liberalism, going back to the New Deal, or even as far as the American founding, as the Trojan horse planted within the city on a hill. These histories weren't new. Bozell and Rushdoony, along with other dissident voices, had been trying to find audiences for them well before the fall of the Berlin Wall in 1989. They caricatured conservatives and liberals as basically on the same team, fighting over just how fast economic and cultural change should happen, but agreeing on almost everything else. In this story, FDR and William F. Buckley are both enemies of real Americans, because they prioritize human rights over Truth and the Good.

Their version of the story claims that liberalism prioritizes individual rights over any sense of the common good. After World War II, the United States emerged as the world's superpower, charged with spreading democracy as far as it could in order to defeat communism. This led to two betrayals of the American ethos. Secularism took root, as Americans supposedly began to think they no longer needed God in order to thrive. And the American empire spread so far and wide, taking the gospel of democracy to Central Europe and Latin America, that the elites forgot about the real Americans at home.

"Illiberal thought, at its core, is an ideological reaction against perceived liberal domination and hegemony in politics, economics, culture, and society," argues the political theorist Julian Waller. "And its solutions involve the use of state power, the rejection of autonomous individualism (both in economics and in society), and deep suspicion of existing institutions—in some cases extending to the political regime itself."[1]

Postliberalism is the common thread among the figures in the foregoing pages. Paul Weyrich and Connie Marshner worked for decades to make the heterosexual nuclear family, rather than the free individual, the "bedrock of civilization." Patrick Deneen, the Catholic philosopher of anti-liberalism, maintains that liberalism is worse than both fascism and communism. For Christian ethnonationalists like Stephen Wolfe and C. Jay Engel, as well as technocrats like Alex Karp, liberalism claims that all cultures are equal, thereby destroying the basis for normative judgments about good and evil, right and wrong, and cultural superiority and barbarism. We spend so much time accommodating other cultures, they maintain, that we have forgotten that ours is the superior one. R. R. Reno, the postliberal Catholic editor of the conservative magazine *First Things*, summarizes it this way:

> Economic globalization shreds the social contract. Identity politics disintegrates civic bonds. A uniquely Western anti-Western multiculturalism deprives people of their cultural inheritance. Mass migration reshapes the social landscape. Courtship, marriage, and family no longer form our moral imaginations. Borders are porous, even the one that separates men from women.[2]

For nearly all of the Protestants, Catholics, and technocrats examined here, liberalism opened the door for multiculturalism and the "invasion" of the United States by documented and undocumented immigrants. The liberal "open border" policy destroyed "our" common way of life, desecrating the shared fabric of the greatest country on Earth.

In sum, liberalism is the scapegoat for all the perceived problems in Western civilization, and thus the shared enemy of the three distinct movements under analysis here.

◆ ◆ ◆

Across all three movements the same shift is clear: libertarianism giving way to monarchy, dictatorship, or a functional equivalent. Beyond the ideological disaster of liberalism is the economic and political failure of libertarianism. If, as Deneen says, liberalism "turns the human individual into a being with rights, but no imperative to be good or virtuous," then libertarianism's prescription of small government and lack of regulation is little help in the battle for the American soul. Brent Bozell was the pioneer on this path.

"If freedom is the 'first principle' in politics, virtue is, at best, the second one," writes Bozell. If personal liberty is the foundation of the economic order, then "virtue" is unenforceable. "God desires—for its own sake—a human order that conforms to the transcendent order," Bozell argues, "and therefore He measures virtue by the extent to which human action existentially reflects divine norms."[3] If individual freedom supplants virtue, then society is based on the primacy of human choice, rather than on the purpose of reflecting God's will. For traditionalists, whether Protestant or Catholic, there is a sense that a libertarian approach, which prioritizes commerce rather than virtue, destines the decline of public Christianity in the United States. JD Vance credits Bozell for helping him see the ineptitude of libertarianism:

> Brent Bozell dismantled this argument years ago: we are concerned with people behaving well, and if cultural (and legal) pressures encourage them to do it, that's just fine. . . . While we might praise the meritorious worker who finds his way to church despite working a 12-hour shift on Sunday, the average traditionalist will (correctly) want to make a life of virtue easier, and not harder. So close the damn businesses on Sunday. Commercial freedom will suffer. Moral behavior will not, and our society will be much the better for it.[4]

R. J. Rushdoony often praised the merits of libertarianism, because he believed that the biblical model of government was based on local feudal states unencumbered by a centralized authority. He worked for a libertarian think tank and associated closely with Robert Welch, the libertarian founder of the John Birch Society. Brent Bozell cut his teeth with leaders and thinkers such as Barry Goldwater, Russell Kirk, and his friend and brother-in-law William F. Buckley. These were the men who forged the fusionist ideology that attempted to merge traditionalist Christian values with the libertarian ideals of small government, minuscule taxes, and unregulated commerce. From the time he read Ayn Rand as a teenager, Peter Thiel identified as a libertarian who believed that true freedom was possible only apart from the government. His friend and interlocutor Curtis Yarvin praises libertarianism as the only viable intellectual pathway to human freedom, but eventually turned to Hoppe and the Austrian school after realizing that even if libertarians were right, they would never win political power in the US.

Yarvin's realization is the one that key figures in all three movements came to independently: The electoral tides, coupled with the expansion of the federal government over the last century, mean that an ideology committed to limited government will never be potent enough to "save our civilization" from moral degeneracy and foreign invaders. Buckleyite and Reaganite fusionism is unviable, as Peter Thiel articulated in his infamous 2009 speech "The Education of a Libertarian":

> I remain committed to the faith of my teenage years: to authentic human freedom as a precondition for the highest good. I stand against confiscatory taxes, totalitarian

> collectives, and the ideology of the inevitability of the death of every individual. For all these reasons, I still call myself "libertarian." But I must confess that over the last two decades, I have changed radically on the question of how to achieve these goals. Most importantly, I no longer believe that freedom and democracy are compatible.[5]

From here, Thiel takes the political leap that Bozell, William Wolfe, C. Jay Engel, Curtis Yarvin, Adrian Vermeule, and other figures also made: The strategy should not be to fight for the invisible hand to be free to control the markets, but to give power to a strongman with a heavy hand who will organize not only the markets, but all of society. "We live in a world where the state has been weaponized against Heritage America," Engel writes. "And there should be nothing holding us back from exercising whatever power is necessary to confront enemies both public and private."[6] The state is a weapon to be expanded, not a necessary evil to be reduced.

Thus it is no longer accurate to label figures like Thiel or Yarvin, much less Doug Wilson or Patrick Deneen or Adrian Vermeule, as libertarians. When you advocate for a government that seeks to impose religion on its citizens, to install a tech CEO who will "own" the land and the people, to mass deport tens of millions of people, or to regulate morality, virtue, and tradition in the public square, you are the opposite of a small-government conservative.

* * *

The theologians, technocrats, pastors, and intellectuals I've examined in these pages generally made the postlibertarian turn because they all came to believe not only that libertarianism wasn't a viable political pathway to power, but also because of another important realization: Democracy is the problem, not the solution. Whether it is Peter Thiel or Joel Webbon, Kevin Roberts or Curtis Yarvin, they share the belief that most people are unable to govern themselves without descending into moral degeneracy and economic ruin. Democratic egalitarianism must be abolished. Theonomy, aristo-populism, integralism, or corporate dictatorship must be instituted in order to save the people from themselves. They want a second American founding, another revolution, or a transformed world order that is not a return to what was, but the beginning of something else. Despite their differences, they all agree: Americans need an external authority to tell them how to live, under fear of punishment, if we are to have a well-ordered society. Gender norms must be enforced. Women must be controlled. Reproduction should be prioritized. Non-Christians and non-"Westerners" should be deported, punished, or forced to assimilate. Immigration needs to stop. And men need to be unquestioned leaders always and everywhere.

Moreover, ending democracy as we know it will foreclose the supposed grave danger that the masses, who are increasingly non-White and non-Christian, pose to "real Americans." The group who identifies this explicitly is the White Christian ethnonationalists. They argue that the presence of non-White and non-Christian people in the US is an existential threat to the country. The country they envision is for "heritage Americans" only. In their mind, if non-White and non-Christian people continue to have influence over the culture, politics, and economics of this country, the "American" way of life will be destroyed. "Christians don't have to tolerate degeneracy," argues Joel Webbon, "and degenerates absolutely must tolerate righteousness or they need to go to jail, or leave the country."[7] This is of course an iteration of White Replacement Theory, something that reactionary Catholics like Kevin Roberts and JD Vance have peddled in various forms.

Patrick Deneen's tone is notably softer. He does not traffic in conspiratorial or fantastical versions of White Replacement Theory. Still, he argues that liberalism's failures require a more restrictive immigration regime and the reintroduction of tariffs as tools for preserving national cohesion and economic stability. He is a localist and a populist. In a statement signed by Deneen and fellow common good Catholics, immigration is deemed a threat to "our countrymen":

> We oppose attempts to displace American citizens. Advancing the common good requires standing with, rather than abandoning, our countrymen. They are our fellow citizens, not interchangeable economic units. And as Americans we owe each other a distinct allegiance and must put each other first.[8]

Curtis Yarvin, who spent much of his childhood living overseas, and Peter Thiel, an immigrant born in Germany, also argue that multiculturalism is a bug, not a feature, of our society, that some people are biologically inferior to others, and that since the 1920s—when women got the vote—a functioning democracy has been impossible. "Since 1920, the vast increase in welfare beneficiaries and the extension of the franchise to women—two constituencies that are notoriously tough for libertarians," Thiel said in 2009, "have rendered the notion of 'capitalist democracy' into an oxymoron."[9]

For Yarvin, democracy is a terrible idea for many reasons:

> One conclusion of formalism is that democracy is—as most writers before the 19th century agreed—an ineffective and destructive system of government. The concept of democracy without politics makes no sense at all, and as we've seen, politics and war are a continuum. Democratic politics is best understood as a sort of symbolic violence, like deciding who wins the battle by how many troops they brought.[10]

Yarvin makes no mention of the fact that across the world population, education levels have transformed for almost every demographic. Moreover, the "writers" he alludes to were all men of privileged social standing who might have seen democracy as a threat to their social monopoly.

Nonetheless, Yarvin argues that democracy is so destructive because it offers equality and political inclusion to "inferior" types of people. When asked by the journalist Ava Kofman how to rectify problems in urban settings, Yarvin gave this response:

> Unless we can totally reengineer DNA to change what a human being is, there are many people who should not live in a modern way but in a traditional way. . . . And that is a level of revolution that is so far beyond anything the Trump-Vance regime is doing.[11]

When you want to turn citizens into "tenants," believe that Black people were better off before the Civil War led to the end of slavery, and argue that most of the people around you are the problem, democracy—the model that gives the power to the masses—is viewed as the root cause that must be overcome. "It is very difficult to argue that the War of Secession [the Civil War] made anyone's life more pleasant, including that of freed slaves," Yarvin wrote in his blog, *Gray Mirror*.[12]

* * *

To understand how Christian Reconstructionists, reactionary Catholics, and technocrats see the American masses, Western Christian supremacy is a more useful framework than Christian nationalism. The two are not incompatible. Rather, the former represents a kind of extreme antidemocratic iteration of the latter. If Christian nationalism exists on a spectrum ranging from those who will only vote for "Christian candidates" to those who want the church to have veto power over the government, then Western Christian supremacy lies at the radical intolerant end of that spectrum.

Christian nationalists have long desired to return to a period such as the 1950s when White Christian men reigned as the undisputed political, economic, and cultural authorities in the American public square.

Yet, as we've examined in the work of Brent Bozell, Doug Wilson, Peter Thiel, Adrian Vermeule, and a variety of other figures, the mission now isn't reform; it's a deliberate march back to a premodern hierarchy where democracy disappears, militant patriarchy reemerges, and Europeans reclaim civilizational supremacy. For the likes of Wilson, Rushdoony, and

Stephen Wolfe the ideal state is something like Calvin's Geneva or the theocracy of the Massachusetts Bay Colony; for Bozell, Roberts, and Vermeule it is medieval Catholic Christendom; for Engel and Isker it is a collective mix. Nearly all the figures examined here link Christian society to something they call "Western Civilization," which folds in ideals and histories from Greek and Roman sources, medieval and Reformation theology, and European colonialism, all in order to create a vision of the archetypal American society. C. Jay Engel sums this view succinctly:

> Western Civilization is a grand mixture of Greek myth and philosophy, Roman civics and political order, and a Christian metaphysic and teleology. Christianity depended upon the world of antiquity; that is, God in His providence brought about Christ at a specific moment in the historical drama so as to take advantage of the civilizational contributions of cultures that had come before. This means not only that God used the Deep Past to build up a cultural foundation, but He also used it to bring about the historical destruction of major powers and people groups. Thus, our Heritage stretches back to Homer, forward to Aristotle, onward to Charlemagne, and forward and Westward from there.[13]

Similarly, Vermeule's "common good constitutionalism" is based on the idea of recovering the "classical" legal tradition that is rooted in Roman and medieval sources. For Kevin Roberts, the first American revolution was an encapsulation of

Roman civilization and Christendom, calling it a "renewal of civilization in the natural order of things." For his part, Palantir CEO Alex Karp believes in the West's "innate superiority": "We have a consistently pro-Western view that the West has a superior way of living and organizing itself, especially if we live up to our aspirations," he told *The New York Times* in 2025.[14]

This clash of civilizations ideology is textbook Western supremacy. In their extensive research on populisms across the globe, scholars Ihsan Yilmaz and Nicholas Morieson define this as an ideology that classifies people by civilization, drawing sharp boundaries between "the people," "elites," and "others." In this framework, "the people" are portrayed as good and authentic precisely because they belong to a civilization deemed pure and virtuous.[15] Religion plays a key role in how such populists define their civilization as superior to others, which people count as the real citizens of their land, and why foreigners from other religious-cultural contexts are existential threats to their way of life. In its most extreme form, civilizational populism views non-European immigrants as unassimilable to American Christian culture.

The movements we've traced here have popularized a civilizationist worldview that doesn't stop at simply privileging Christians above all others in the United States. Instead, Protestants like Stephen Wolfe, Andrew Isker, and Engel, along with Catholics like Roberts and Vermeule, not to mention technocrats like Alex Karp, are mainstreaming the idea that "people of different civilizations possess incompatible ethical and moral frameworks." Civilizational populists want to "create societies in which religious minorities are viewed as intolerable existential threats."[16] It's no coincidence that leading lights from all three movements take inspiration from Carl Schmitt, the Nazi jurist and progenitor of the friend/enemy distinction. In this case, the "enemies" are those who are unassimilable to the West.

Rushdoony, Wilson, and Stephen Wolfe claim that Europe's longer Christian history has allowed the Gospel to shape European and European-American culture more fully, yielding superior beauty, virtue, and transcendence compared to African or Asian cultures—a conclusion built on dubious history. While they resist charges of racism by claiming that the superiority of cultures is not a matter of biology but of history, the elements of Christian supremacy are clear and present. They go beyond many of their fellow Christian nationalists by claiming that American society is superior to others because European Christian heritage is superior to all other forms. Real Americans are thus those who are a part of a certain "ethnicity." Stephen Wolfe said in a podcast interview that it should be "permissible for Christians to deem certain groups to have positions that are detrimental to the fundamental features of society and to rescind their political equality."[17]

It is one (bad) idea to claim that Christians should hold an elevated status in the United States. It is another to argue that non-Christians and non-White immigrants are civilizationally incompatible with the American way of life and thus pose an existential threat to its citizens. Those who hold these views are not only racist and xenophobic, they are historically ignorant. Every major wave of immigrants—European Catholics and Jews; Middle Eastern Muslims; Asian Buddhists, Hindus, and Sikhs—has at some point been labeled "civilizationally incompatible" with US culture. Each time, those claims proved wrong as immigrants integrated with, contributed to, and strengthened our core institutions. American economic growth, scientific innovation, military strength, and cultural influence have been supercharged by immigration. Diversity has expanded American capacity rather than eroded it. Framing non-Christian or non-White immigrants as threats relies less on data than on fear. The only way to make the argument is on anxious bias, not evidence or history.

Western supremacy also provides a lens for understanding how thinkers like Yarvin, Karp, and other technocrats—such as Elon Musk—who identify neither as Christians nor as even religious, fit into a larger nexus of those claiming to rescue Western society from liberal ruin. Rather than trying to force tech monarchists into a Christian nationalist paradigm, the Western supremacist approach wraps them into a fold of those who believe that Western civilization is being denigrated by traitorous elites and inferior invaders. Yarvin, who comes from the tech industry—which is filled with immigrants in the US on work visas—rages against the invasion of immigrants and the elites in Ivy League universities and legacy media outlets who have sold out the country. This is rich coming from a guy whose industry is led by and pushed forward through the insight, hard work, and genius of the immigrants at Apple, Google, and so many iconic Silicon Valley companies. Nonetheless, he advocates for "a total shutdown of international relations, including security guarantees, foreign aid, and mass immigration, and a return to the nineteenth-century policy of neutrality."[18] In his early writings under the pseudonym Mencius Moldbug, he proposed "the liquidation of democracy, the Constitution and the rule of law, and the transfer of absolute power to a mysterious figure known only as the Receiver," who will "transfer 'decivilized populations' to 'secure relocation facilities' where they will be assigned to 'mandatory apprenticeships.'"[19]

⁂

Western supremacy in the United States isn't new. Remember how many times Donald Trump (a non-churchgoer) asked Barack Obama (a regular churchgoer) to show his birth certificate? When he did, Trump and millions of others wouldn't accept it as real. Obama's achievements and record were irrelevant, because a multiracial man with an African father who Trump claimed was Muslim would never be American in his eyes. The birther conspiracy was a Western supremacist lie—a framing of the first Black president as religiously and culturally alien to the "real people" of the United States. What made Obama a Western supremacist's worst nightmare was that the "inferior invader" became the elite par excellence—the president of the United States.

Overall, Western supremacy justifies radical antidemocratic approaches to rescuing the West from external and internal threats.

⁂

One of the hallmarks of twentieth-century evangelicalism was a preoccupation with the apocalypse. While Christians, including evangelicals, have always disagreed about the nature and timing of Christ's return, one of the predominant eschatological frameworks in American Christianity has been the idea that Christ may return at any moment, calling home all believers and leaving everyone else stranded during a time of great tribulation caused by the ascendance of the Antichrist. After this tribulation period, Christ and his followers will return to Earth, instituting a thousand-year reign of peace. A "premillennial" approach to the end times, this envisions Christ's return as taking place before the millennial period.

This is the eschatology I adopted as an evangelical. My teenage years were spent in tense expectation of Christ's coming. I lay awake many nights wondering if I would have time to convert my Japanese American Buddhist dad, or to get my White Southern mom to see the importance of re-committing herself to Christ. As a Christian living in what felt like an increasingly godless world, I saw myself as swimming upstream in a culture headed for calamity. My goal was not to convert the culture or redeem Western civilization, but to save as many as possible before it was too late.

Times change. That includes the end times. During the last two decades a different approach to eschatology has taken hold among American Protestants. R. J. Rushdoony, Doug Wilson, and many of their spiritual progeny are "postmillennialists." They believe that Christ will descend to Earth only after Christians have created the thousand-year millennium of peace through their efforts to colonize the planet for God. While on the surface the minutiae of eschatological arguments among evangelical Christians may seem like a jaunt too far into the theological weeds, there are grand political consequences to the shift from premillennial to postmillennial theologies. The latter view Christians as the crusading force that will usher in the Kingdom of God on Earth through a Herculean effort to capture every aspect of human society for King Jesus, as Rushdoony outlines:

> Postmillennialism makes clear that Christians not only have a task of soul-saving, but also of school, home, church, business, state, vocation-saving, a calling to bring everything into captivity to Christ the King. Postmillennialism restores the law to its place as the way of sanctification and a plan for conquest. Postmillennialism takes seriously the lordship of Christ. He is not only Head of the Church, but the King of Kings and Lord of Lords. This means that He is Ruler of all nations and Lord over all authorities in every area, and all things are to be put under Christ in time as well as eternity.[20]

In essence, postmillennialism is the license for a new crusade. Christians are not called to save individuals. They aren't swimming upstream in a godless world, hoping to save as many as possible before it's too late. Their task is the "conquest" of every domain of human society. When they say "King Jesus," they mean placing Jesus on the national throne as the autocratic ruler of both Heaven and Earth.

Rather than fulfilling the Great Commission by converting souls, the mission is to colonize every nation through force, imposition, and if need be, violence. There remains an eschatological expectation of the end of the world. But instead of envisioning it as the sudden return of Christ, it is now imagined by postmillennial Reconstructionists as a race against the destruction of civilization at the hands of the demonic forces influencing the woke leftists trying to destroy any remnant of Western virtue. Reconstructionists see themselves as the heroes in a cosmic struggle versus evil.

So do many of their tech counterparts. Peter Thiel's techno-theology is based on the premise of not allowing the Antichrist to thwart the miracle of human innovation, which he considers analogous to God's creation of all things. In Thiel's mind, there is a "race" between politics and technology that may come down to a single person who can deliver Western society from demonic ruin. Silicon Valley's apocalyptic fears aren't limited to Thiel. Theorists have observed a coherence among a variety of tech-based movements based on their "techno-utopian" vision of the future. Such utopianism "anticipates a time when advanced technologies enable humanity to accomplish things like: producing radical abundance, reengineering ourselves, becoming immortal, colonizing the universe and creating a sprawling 'post-human' civilization among the stars full of trillions and trillions of people," writes the theorist Émile Torres.[21]

Whereas Christian Reconstructionists see themselves as creating the realm of King Jesus on Earth, techno-utopians often refer to their AI projects as the creation of an omnipotent God-like force. "AI's knowledge should be all-encompassing and as far-reaching as possible," says xAI, Elon Musk's artificial intelligence company, in its mission statement. "I feel that the four big AI CEOs in the U.S. are modern-day prophets with four different versions of the Gospel," observes the MIT scientist Max Tegmark, "and they're all telling the same basic story that this is so dangerous and so scary that I have to do it and nobody else."[22]

Though their Protestant counterparts likely do not appreciate the notion of "creating God" as an artificial intelligence, both groups agree that it is up to a select few to save humanity from itself. Peter Thiel's investments in seasteading, network cities, cryogenics, and other megapolitical ventures are just one example of a Silicon Valley culture that believes tech Founders are the superheroes of our time. Way back in 2023, one AI engineer claimed that he and his cohorts are "making God."[23] "The world cannot be saved by caped crusaders with great strength and the power of flight," writes a computer programmer under the name lukeprog, echoing Peter Thiel's techno-theology. "No, the world must be saved by mathematicians, computer scientists, and philosophers."[24]

There is a deep cosmic sense to the race to build an all-knowing AI in order that human beings can live in a painless and peaceful state forever. It may not be spiritual, but it is religious. "They invented a new, secular religion," argues Torres. For tech-optimists "'heaven' is something we create ourselves, in this world." As in Christianity, "the few who are lucky enough will resurrect." It won't be via the blood of Christ, but through cryogenization and mind uploading.[25]

Admittedly, postliberal Catholics are less invested in the end times than their Protestant or technocrat counterparts. However, there is a sense of civilizational urgency among them—the feeling that unless tectonic political transformation happens, all might be lost. "It's fine to take a laissez-faire approach when you are in the safety of the sunshine," says Kevin Roberts. But not "when the twilight descends."[26]

✦ ✦ ✦

For those embroiled in an apocalyptic civilizational battle against evil, the next logical step after calling for the end of democracy is to envision a different system. All three of these movements are illiberal, antidemocratic, and against free markets. They oppose economic and social systems that recognize individuals as having inalienable rights or economic freedom, as those concepts are commonly understood in the United States. "That is, an individual must be free to live as his Creator ordained—to flourish," Kevin Roberts says in Project 2025. "*Our Constitution grants each of us the liberty to do not what we want, but what we ought.*"[27]

Thus, in different ways and through various theologies and philosophies, those profiled here conclude that what will restore the United States and the world to its proper order is the institution of some kind of single leader who will overturn the will of the masses in the name of the real "people," imposing the order and structure that a monarch, tech CEO, or representative of King Jesus will impose on everyone else, restricting their freedom in the name of doing what's best for them. All three movements are clear that a few people are clear-eyed enough and capable to structure society for the rest of us. This takes different forms among the Protestants, Catholics, and technocrats, but there is a common through-line: The strong rule of one, with the help of the few, will rectify the disorder, degeneracy, and inefficiency of the many. Stephen Wolfe wants a Christian prince. Adrian Vermeule wants an "unbound executive."

"Subjects will come to thank the ruler whose legal strictures, possibly first experienced as coercive, encourage subjects to form more authentic desires for the individual and common goods," Vermeule writes, "better habits, and beliefs that better track and promote communal well being."[28]

Curtis Yarvin openly calls for monarchism. Patrick Deneen prescribes an aristo-populism, but is also sympathetic to

Vermeule's position that an imperial president who rules as a de facto autocrat is needed to set things right. Christian ethnonationalists like C. Jay Engel and William Wolfe dream of a Red Caesar, Appalachian Pinochet, or Protestant Franco who will rule over the US as a Christian strongman. Way back in the 1960s, Brent Bozell fell in love with Franco's Spain precisely because it was an autocracy that gave exclusive public right to Catholicism.

Reconstructionists like R. J. Rushdoony or Doug Wilson may claim that they've never called for a monarchy, but instead simply want God to reign in this country as he should. Yet, even if they don't want an American king or Caesar, their visions for "King Jesus" to rule over the US would create a de facto theocracy in which one, or a few, would have near total power over the rest of us. In these kinds of models, the religious and political leaders who represent the King on Earth end up being the de facto autocrats and oligarchs. If one person has the sole right to interpret the absentee leader's decisions and desires, then that person holds all the authority. The call for King Jesus to reign is an antidemocratic vision that threatens any semblance of a multicultural, pluralist, multireligious, multiracial society. It is the usurping of the Will of the People for the Rule of the King (implemented by whoever represents him on Earth).

When I was an evangelical, we praised religious freedom because it recognized that people could not be coerced into Christian faith. Even if the dominant culture were Christian, what matters is a spiritual rebirth, not a lukewarm conformity. We recognized Christ as the King of the heavens and Earth, but that didn't mean spiritually terrorizing nonbelievers. It meant reaching out to them, persuading them, demonstrating to them the way to the Messiah. Now, the prevailing model seats Jesus on the throne of the United States as a stern, unforgiving monarch who will punish those who don't recognize his authority—and the authority of the men (and only men) who represent him.

* * *

Given the course of Trump's second term, it would be natural to surmise that the figures I've profiled view Trump as the answer to America's democracy problem. Some Christians do in fact view Trump as a messianic figure. As religion scholar Matthew D. Taylor chronicles in his detailed work *The Violent Take It by Force*, many leaders in the New Apostolic Reformation, a movement made up of independent charismatic Christians who believe in present-day prophecy and apostolic authority, see Trump as a figure chosen by God to create the context for a great American revival. Many from this movement have been elevated to positions of authority in Trump's administration.

The Protestant Reconstructionists, reactionary Catholics, and technocrats in this work take a more measured approach to Trump's role in history. For the most part, they view Trump as the Great Disruptor—the leader willing to break the crumbling American machine, reveal its rot, and open the pathway for something new. Some of them, particularly the baby boomers, see Trump's second term as a relative success. Speaking to a Hungarian journalist, Patrick Deneen proclaimed the first six months of Trump's second term as "quite extraordinary," given what he has done in foreign policy, immigration, and economic reform.[29] However, he also pivoted soon thereafter to the fact that Trump's time is almost up—and that the real question is if JD Vance will succeed him in the White House.

Doug Wilson agrees that Trump has been a blessing to people in his camp. Early in Trump's second term, he said that "it's been Christmas every morning."[30] Yet Wilson was also critical of Trump's appointment of Paula White-Cain to head the White House Faith Office. Wilson, an ultrapatriarchal theologian who believes that Americans should vote as households—and women should not have the right to vote—is naturally opposed to the leadership of women.

Peter Thiel soured on Trump long ago. Thiel was the first Silicon Valley luminary to support Trump in 2016. He thought Trump would upset the Democrat-Republican binary and open pathways for innovation in tech, economics, and culture. "There are a lot of things I got wrong," Peter Thiel told Barton Gellman in a 2023 interview, after explaining he wouldn't be donating to Trump's campaign in 2024. Thiel also refused to participate in the 2020 fundraising cycle. "It was crazier than I thought. It was more dangerous than I thought," he said, reflecting on Trump's first term. "They couldn't get the most basic pieces of the government to work. So that was—I think that part was maybe worse than even my low expectations."[31]

Thiel's friend Curtis Yarvin sees Trump as the figure who "exposed the system's farcical, brittle condition, revealing the absurdity of it all, because it was already broken to begin with." For Yarvin, Trump is neither an angel nor a demon, but a useful destroyer. "That is the genuine nature of Trump. You cannot truly understand him by simply demonizing him, nor can you understand him by sanctifying him. You can only grasp his essence if you comprehend how this entire comedy functions."[32]

However, less than a year into Trump's second term, Yarvin, like Thiel, became fed up with the Trump administration. "The second Trump revolution, like the first, is failing," Yarvin admitted. "It is failing because it deserves to fail. It is failing because it spends all its time patting itself on the back. It is failing because its true mission, which neither it nor (still less) its supporters understand, is still as far beyond its reach as algebra is beyond a cat."[33] Yarvin seems to think the administration hasn't gone far enough in its attempts to destroy administrative agencies, cripple universities, and silence the press.

Protestant Reconstructionists share his disappointment, but on different grounds. In a November 2025 interview, Fox News's Laura Ingraham asked Trump if he would suspend the H-1B visa program that allows skilled foreign workers to enter the country.

Trump: You have to bring in talent.

Ingraham: We have plenty of talent.

Trump: No, you don't.

Ingraham: We don't have talented people here?[34]

The program is especially popular in Silicon Valley, where major tech firms hire large numbers of engineers and other workers, many of them from South Asia.

Trump's pronouncement about the lack of talented American labor set off millennial Christian ethnonationalists like Joel Webbon and C. Jay Engel: "It's long past time to admit that Donald Trump is NOT our guy. He was merely the 'precursor' to another. MAGA is DEAD," Webbon said in a post on X soon after the interview. "America First is ASCENDANT. This is the new litmus test: If someone refuses to say this, they're not on the team."[35]

Responding to his friend, C. Jay Engel wrote: "This is always what he was. Some of us have been saying this from the beginning. The point of Trump is to radicalize, to buy time, to give access to a few who can get in, and to show the Right the futility of electoral means of political change."[36] He later posted that the Trump administration doesn't realize that "we would rather go through economic hell than continue forward down the path of replacement migration."[37]

Postliberal theologian Brian McCall, editor of *Catholic Family News*, a traditionalist Catholic magazine, seems to agree with Webbon and Engel, even if he articulates it in milder terms: "But are we putting a Band-Aid on something that doesn't have the whole real solution? And that doesn't mean I'm saying go vote for Joe Biden or anything like that [chuckles] clearly. . . . Maybe we need to do this [support Trump] as a short-term measure now, but we need to have larger strategic thinking than that."[38]

The younger set of Reconstructionists, traditional Catholics, and tech dissidents are less confident in Trump than their elders. Whereas Wilson and Deneen see real results, Yarvin, Webbon, Engel, and McCall are already set to move on to the figure who can actually deliver something like their vision for a new American founding. For the Gen X and millennial voices in these movements there is an appreciation for the fact that

Trump has torn apart the postwar consensus, and thereby opened new vistas for America's future. However, he is not viewed as a visionary who has the plan or wherewithal to carry the nation forward into a new version of itself.

That mantle falls to his vice president, JD Vance.

8

JD VANCE: CROWN PRINCE OF POSTLIBERAL AMERICA

I think that what Trump should do, if I was giving him one piece of advice: Fire every single mid-level bureaucrat, every civil servant in the administrative state, replace them with our people. And when the courts stop you, stand before the country, and say . . . the chief justice has made his ruling. Now let him enforce it.

—JD VANCE

The thing that I admire about Vance and that's really remarkable about him as a leader is that he contains within him all kinds of Americans. His ability to connect with flyover Americans in the world that he came from is great, but the other thing that's neat about him is that he went to Yale Law School, and so he is a fluent speaker of the language of *The New York Times*, which

> you cannot say about Donald Trump. And . . . it's utterly essential for anything like an American monarchy to be the president of *all* Americans.[1]

This is the tech monarchist Curtis Yarvin praising JD Vance effusively in *The New York Times* two days before Trump's second inauguration. When asked about Vance's views on democracy, Yarvin responded:

> It depends what you mean by democracy. The problem is when people equate democracy with good government. I would say that what JD Vance believes is that governments should serve the common good. I think that people like JD and people in the broader intellectual scene around him would all agree on that principle. Now, I don't know what you mean by "democracy" in this context. What I do know is that if democracy is against the common good, it's bad, and if it's for the common good, it's good.[2]

Yarvin's comments are a prism for understanding Vance's popularity among key leaders in the three movements profiled in the previous chapters. For Yarvin, Vance contains multitudes. He is, contrary to common wisdom, a man whose public persona is more versatile than Trump's. When asked about Vance's perspective on democracy, Yarvin turns to the common good. As we uncovered here, the common good doesn't necessarily mean the will of the people. It's the vision of a properly ordered society imposed on citizens, even if it goes against the majority's desire. Vance's familiarity with and receptiveness to these ideological approaches to American governance has made him the vanguard of the new postliberal political class.

* * *

It may be difficult to imagine a future in which Catholics, Protestants, and tech monarchists work together in order to achieve a shared vision. History proves that once such groups reach any point of general success, there is likely to be violent disagreement on the details of leadership and policy, including whose man gets to sit on the throne (and where the throne is located, and so on). There are already key divergences among them.

First, there is the obvious discord between Protestants and Catholics, a five-hundred-year family feud that has its own American history of exclusion and persecution. Then there is the fact that many of the Silicon Valley monarchists, like Curtis Yarvin and Alex Karp, are not orthodox Christians, something that can be accommodated in the big tent of Western supremacy but is nonetheless a dividing issue. There are other cleavage points—an integralist model based on the integration of the government into the Catholic Church is at odds with a vision of a tech founder as the head of a government corporation that owns both its land and its people. Additionally, where the Silicon Valley set favors the immigration of skilled labor to fill jobs in the tech industry, both Reconstructionist Protestants and reactionary Catholics generally view such trends as part of a scheme to edge out native-born American workers from well-paying jobs.

However, at least for now, they are bound together ideologically by a foundational opposition to liberal democracy, their shared enemy. You might expect Donald Trump to be the repository of their collective dreams—a Jungian archetype of postconstitutional American rule. However, despite the fact that Trump has won two of the last three presidential elections, key figures in these worlds see him as a beginning, not an end. Beyond Trump, there is a figure who represents the bridge to the refounding of America—the man standing to his right: the self-proclaimed hillbilly turned Ivy Leaguer, turned Silicon Valley investor, turned one-term senator and vice president. In the eyes of many of the men examined in these pages, Vance is the crown prince of the MAGA movement; the one they hope someday will implement a vision even more radical than Trump's MAGA populism.

* * *

In July of 2016, Donald Trump announced Mike Pence as his running mate. The choice was seen as an olive branch to the insiders of the Republican Party who appreciated Pence as a classical conservative with rock solid right-wing policy views. Pence also represented a salvo for White evangelicals still unsure of voting for Trump. "I'm a Christian, a conservative, and a Republican—in that order," Pence proclaimed in his acceptance speech. As Richard Land, former president of the Southern Baptist Convention's Ethics and Religious Liberty Commission, told *The Atlantic,* "Mike Pence is the 24-karat-gold model of what we want in an evangelical politician. I don't know anyone who's more consistent in bringing his evangelical Christian worldview to public policy."[3]

Critics railed against Pence's record on abortion rights, his opposition to gay marriage, and his response to an AIDS crisis in Indiana while he was governor. Yet, regardless of who you asked, one thing was clear: Mike Pence was chosen to represent white evangelicals and their allies in the White House.

Neither he nor the rest of us may have realized it at the time, but when Pence accepted the nomination for vice president in 2016, he was a vestige of a dying movement: conservative fusionism. Articulated most influentially by *National Review* founder William F. Buckley, fusionism had its golden age in the Reagan era. As I outlined in chapters 1 and 4, fusionism is a political philosophy that coheres libertarian ideals—including small government, minuscule regulatory policies, and low taxes—with a religious identity based on "family values," an aggressive national defense, and America's "destiny under God," as Reagan said in a 1981 address to the Conservative Political Action Conference (CPAC).

The awkward reality of the Trump-Pence pairing, aside from their wildly different personae, is that from the beginning Trump promised more government in the form of laws banning Muslims from the country (something Pence opposed) and aggressive immigration policies, not to mention an isolationist approach to foreign policy contrary to Reagan's (and Pence's) calls for American leadership throughout the world. From the beginning, Trumpism has been about more government at home and less abroad—the mirror opposite of Pence's Reaganite approach.

In July 2024, Trump announced JD Vance as his running mate for the upcoming election. Vance, a first-term senator from Ohio, was largely seen as a choice bolstering Trump's outsider image—a young Midwestern firebrand who would bring

Silicon Valley money and youthful energy to the ticket. What went largely unnoticed at the time was that Vance is a more radical religious politician than Pence, despite the latter being hailed as the "Christian" candidate.

Unlike Pence, Vance is a confounding political figure. He is known as the author of *Hillbilly Elegy*, and thus a self-proclaimed representative of Appalachia who supposedly stands for those forgotten by globalism and coastal elites. However, before running for office, Vance made millions as a Silicon Valley venture capitalist. He also was a vehement Never Trumper in 2016.

"I go back and forth between thinking Trump is a cynical asshole like Nixon who wouldn't be that bad (and might even prove useful) or that he's America's Hitler," Vance texted his friend Josh McLaurin in 2016. "How's that for discouraging?"[4]

The easy conclusion is that Vance is an opportunist who changes his policies and positions according to what benefits him. Yet, there is another way to understand Vance's Silicon Valley influences, his conversion to Trumpism, and his hatred for American elites: Vance adheres to postliberal Western supremacism and is deeply invested in the ideas coming from integralists, reactionary Catholics, tech dissidents, and American nationalists. The very forces profiled in the foregoing pages shape his political worldview. He represents their shining hope; and they remain his ideological inspiration.

* * *

Vance is unabashedly a Peter Thiel acolyte. Their relationship goes well beyond politics. Vance met Thiel in 2011, when the latter gave a lecture at Yale Law, something Vance calls "the most significant moment of my time at Yale Law School."[5] In this first meeting, Thiel passed on the knowledge he had gained from René Girard about rivalry, sacrifice, and Christianity. The way Vance tells it, Thiel enabled him to see that the competition for prestigious clerkships and career prizes was simply a meaningless game of imitation in the form of competition. Thiel opened up a possibility model for Vance in more ways than one. First, he was an intellectual Christian, something Vance hadn't considered viable. In Vance's eyes, Thiel was "possibly the smartest person I'd ever met, but he was a Christian."[6]

From there, Thiel imparted to his future protégé the wisdom in Girard's understanding of Christ as the founder/scapegoat: "To Girard, the Christian story contains a crucial difference—a difference that reveals something 'hidden since the foundation of the world,'" Vance wrote in *The Lamp*, a Catholic literary magazine. "In the Christian telling, the ultimate scapegoat has not wronged the civilization; the civilization has wronged him."[7] It's clear that Girard's Christology inspired a conservative political response in Vance, who concludes that "Christ is the scapegoat who reveals our imperfections, and forces us to look at our own flaws rather than blame our society's chosen victims."[8] Christianity inspires individuals to look inward to their own failing, rather than to put the onus on their circumstances or systematic marginalization. So far, this is standard twentieth-century libertarianism. But like Thiel, Vance takes from Girard the lesson that the recipient of the "rage and violence of the crowd" is an undeserving scapegoat like Christ. Victimhood, in other words, is next to godliness; a sign of virtue rather than moral iniquity.

Vance's development of this idea burst into view in the first week of February 2025, just weeks after his swearing in as vice president. Elon Musk's DOGE team had just received the resignation of Marko Elez, a twenty-five-year-old engineer who promoted eugenics and racism on social media, including making the statement "normalize Indian hate." JD Vance is married to Usha Vance (born Usha Bala Chilukuri), a woman of Indian heritage. They have three children, with a fourth on the way. Vance inserted himself into the conversation about Elez's firing in a social media rant where he said that some of the posts were "regrettable" but that the engineer should be brought back to DOGE and only fired if he was bad at his job.

"I obviously disagree with some of Elez's posts, but I don't think stupid social media activity should ruin a kid's life," Vance wrote on X. "We shouldn't reward journalists who try to destroy people. Ever. So I say bring him back. If he's a bad dude or a terrible member of the team, fire him for that."

Congressman Ro Khanna, who is of South Asian descent, challenged Vance on X:

> **Ro Khanna:** Are you going to tell him to apologize for saying "Normalize Indian hate" before this re-hire? Just asking for the sake of both of our kids.
>
> **JD Vance:** For the sake of both of our kids? Grow up. Racist trolls on the internet, while offensive, don't threaten my kids. You know what does? A culture that denies grace to people who make mistakes. A culture that encourages congressmen to act like whiny children. I cannot overstate how much I loathe this emotional blackmail pretending to be concern. My kids, God willing, will be risk takers. They won't think constantly about whether a flippant comment or a wrong viewpoint will follow them around for the

> rest of their lives. They will tell stupid jokes. They will develop views that they later think are wrong or even gross. I made mistakes as a kid, and thank God I grew up in a culture that encouraged me to grow and learn and feel remorse when I screwed up and offer grace when others did.[9]

Vance turns Elez's "victimhood" at the hands of those who oppose racism into the virtue of being a "risk taker" in the process of growing up and making mistakes.

In an even more disturbing incident from October 2025, Vance downplayed the seriousness of a leaked group chat from young Republican leaders and elected officials. In the texts, men mostly in their late twenties and early thirties make anti-Semitic jokes. One even says, "I love Hitler." "The reality is that kids do stupid things, especially young boys," Vance said of the grown men, most of whom have been legal adults for over a decade. "They tell edgy, offensive jokes. That's what kids do. And I really don't want us to grow up in a country where a kid telling a stupid joke—telling a very offensive, stupid joke—is cause to ruin their lives."[10] It's not clear when Vance thinks conservative male officials become old enough to be held accountable for expressing admiration for Hitler or advocating for putting Jews to death. What remains clear: He has learned much from Peter Thiel about how to turn perpetrators into victims that must be let off the hook.

* * *

Peter Thiel isn't the only person in Silicon Valley who has shaped Vance's politics. During a 2021 appearance on the Jack Murphy podcast, Vance named Curtis Yarvin as an influence and then reiterated one of his more popular ideas. "So there's this guy Curtis Yarvin who has written about these things," Vance said. "I think that what Trump should do, if I was giving him one piece of advice: Fire every single mid-level bureaucrat, every civil servant in the administrative state, replace them with our people. And when the courts stop you, stand before the country and say . . . the chief justice has made his ruling. Now let him enforce it."[11]

This is Vance parroting a tech monarchist, openly calling for the president to ignore the Constitution—and, if the judiciary steps in, advising his future running mate to defy the courts, inviting a full-scale constitutional catastrophe. It's a vision of the presidency with no checks or balances, something like Vermeule's unbound executive. Vance explained it this way in a 2024 *Politico* interview:

> The counterargument is, you know, "Aren't you promoting a constitutional crisis?" And my response is no—I'm recognizing a constitutional crisis. If the elected president says, "I get to control the staff of my own government," and the Supreme Court steps in and says, "You're not allowed to do that"—like, that is the constitutional crisis. It's not whatever Trump or whoever else does in response. When the Supreme Court tells the president he can't control the government anymore, we need to be honest about what's actually going on.[12]

The suggestion is made more disturbing by the underlying hints of violence. Vance references the fact that the Supreme Court has no means other than the rule of law to enforce its decisions. By contrast, the president is the commander-in-chief of the military, the overseer of the Department of Justice, and has national guard troops at his ready. If, Vance suggests, the president disagrees with the Supreme Court justices, he should challenge them not on the cogency of their ruling, but on the basis of brute force. Following the blueprint of figures like Yarvin, Project 2025 architects like Roberts, and postliberal Catholics like Vermeule, Vance favors a unified executive branch that has incredible power over the federal government—even if it means the functional collapse of the separation of powers.

"I think the basic idea is that we have to seize the institutions and make them actually work for our people," he said in a 2022 interview.[13]

In ways in line with Yarvin, Vermuele, and others, Vance envisions a chief executive with the power to make sweeping changes to American life through government policy, executive orders, and institutional transformation.

* * *

In 2019, eight years after his first meeting with Thiel, Vance was received into the Catholic Church. He grew up as a kind of nondenominational Protestant, and by the time he entered law school described himself as an angry atheist. However, in Vance's telling, Catholicism began to appeal to him because of its intellectual approach to faith and human life. Soon after he converted, Vance ran for the Senate in Ohio (a campaign to which Thiel donated millions of dollars). In 2021, the newly converted candidate spoke to the Napa Institute, a network of conservative Catholics who are known for defying the Pope, largely opposing the reforms of the Second Vatican Council, and being backed by billionaire donors who are sympathetic to a Christian nationalist vision. "The bishops and laypeople who fill Napa's speaking roster generally do not support Vatican II," writes journalist Mary Jo McConaughey in *Playing God: American Catholic Bishops and the Far Right*. "One of them, Bishop Chaput, put it this way. 'We got friendlier. We opened the doors of the church to the world and they didn't come. But many of us went out.'"[14] According to McConaughey, the Napa Institute and similar organizations linked to it offer Catholics "what amounts to a parallel magisterium teaching and sacramental formation" that is closer to a strict and defensive pre–Vatican II ethos "than it is to the ecumenical, mercy-centered church led by Pope Francis."[15]

In his speech at the Napa Institute, Vance showed how far his politics are from the libertarian economics championed by Reagan and a former generation of conservatives. He griped that "the business community is actively pro-abortion in this country."[16] His solution would be to take active measures against businesses that use their First Amendment rights to express pro-choice positions. "If our answer is to continue to give more power to the business community that's combating our values, what we're doing is sacrificing the life of the unborn and our future on the altar of these companies."[17] Vance, in other words, is more of a Brent Bozell Catholic than a Pope Francis Catholic. He is willing to contour and even limit the free market in order to legislate morality and impose a certain set of values on American citizens.

He is also willing to criticize the Catholic Church directly and publicly disagree with the Pope. In his first interview after becoming vice president, Vance attacked the US Conference of Catholic Bishops on the issue of immigration.

"I think the US Conference of Catholic Bishops has, frankly, not been a good partner in commonsense immigration enforcement that the American people voted for," said the recent convert. "I hope, again, as a devout Catholic, that they'll do better."[18] Vance is so sure of his theological and political convictions that he is willing to question the highest authorities in the Church, and their revenue streams. "I think that the US Conference of Catholic Bishops needs to actually look in the mirror a little bit and recognize that when they receive over $100 million to help resettle illegal immigrants, are they worried about humanitarian concerns? Or are they actually worried about their bottom line?" Vance asked. "We're going to enforce immigration law. We're going to protect the American people."[19]

In 2021 Vance also appeared at a signature meeting for Teneo, an organization started by the tech investor and author Evan Baehr with the help and guidance of Peter Thiel and Missouri Senator Josh Hawley. Baehr, Hawley, and Thiel envision Teneo as a Federalist Society for venture capitalists. Vance is reportedly a current member. The organization was fledgling until Leonard Leo stepped in to raise funds. Leo, who according to 2022 filings has served on the board of the Napa Institute Legal Foundation, is the infamous leader of the actual Federalist Society, who shepherded Trump's three Supreme Court nominees to the bench. Now Teneo is funded by Leo's dark money networks, the Charles Koch Foundation, the DeVos family, and other big donors. The group is Leo's new conduit for imposing his conservative Catholic agenda on American culture and institutions.

In his remarks at the 2021 Teneo gathering, Vance complained that "virtually every major big corporation in this country felt the need to issue a statement in support not of the unborn babies, but in support of people who might want to abort them." Then he said: "If we're unwilling to make companies that are taking the side of the left in the culture wars feel real economic pain, then we're not serious about winning the culture war."[20] Vance's statements at Teneo and the Napa Institute, in addition to his recent comments on the Conference of Bishops, reveal a Catholic convert willing to publicly disagree with the Pope on immigration, who gathers with anti–Vatican II bishops and funders, and who would like to use the power of the government in order to influence morality in the public sphere. There is deep irony here: A convert—drawn to the Church by its hierarchy and intellectual ethos—publicly challenging the leader of the Church to which he devoted himself almost as soon as he is baptized.

Vance's philosophy is not laissez-faire libertarianism; it's common good conservatism cultivated through a postliberal Catholic conception of what "good" means for everyone. His major concern is not overstepping the American traditions of freedom and choice, but the lack of right-wing oligarchs who are willing to use their power and influence to shape the markets and public square: "One of the things that really does worry me is that we have very few oligarchs on our side. And I don't mean just rich people. I mean, people who are smart about deploying their resources in a way that advances the cause. Maybe only Peter Thiel, on our side, I think."[21]

In 2022, Vance, who was a candidate for the Senate at the time, spoke at a conference at Franciscan University with the intellectual luminaries of the postliberal Catholic movement, including Adrian Vermeule and Patrick Deneen. On one panel, theologian Chad Pecknold argued that the way toward civic happiness "is a public orientation to God" through the restoration of Sabbath laws, religious national holidays, and public liturgies.[22] In a later panel, *Newsweek* editor Josh Hammer maintained that the "the only viable force capable of withstanding and turning back the woke onslaught is religion, which in America means Christianity." Hammer believes that using the state as an arbiter of religion and morality will be "both popular and successful."[23]

* * *

During this time period Vance became close to Deneen, who appeared with Vance and Heritage Foundation leader Kevin Roberts in May 2023 to launch Deneen's book, *Regime Change*. This is the event where Deneen called for something more radical than January 6: "I don't want to violently overthrow the government," he said. "I want something far more revolutionary." Vance has signaled his sympathies with Deneen's approach many times—appearing with him publicly and citing his influence. Deneen put out a statement when Vance was announced as Trump's running mate: "JD combines a dedication to domestic productivity, foreign policy realism, and a deep commitment to strengthening American families and the communities that sustain them. He is a man of deep personal faith and integrity, a devoted family man, a generous friend, and a genuine patriot."[24]

One of Roberts's political heroes is Pat Buchanan (also Catholic)—the former aide to presidents Nixon, Ford, and Reagan who ran for president in 1992, 1996, and 2000—who he believes was right to call for a border wall and draconian immigration policies. In his remarks at *The American*

Conservative's annual gala in 2023, Roberts quoted Buchanan extensively.

"There is a religious war going on in this country. It is a cultural war, as critical to the kind of nation we shall be as was the Cold War itself, for this war is for the soul of America," Buchanan said infamously at the 1992 Republican National Convention.[25] Buchanan wrote *A Republic, Not an Empire,* a screed against the United States's international entanglements from World War II to NATO and the Cold War. In it, Buchanan praised Charles Lindbergh for arguing that the country should stay out of World War II.

It's worth noting that when asked about Russia's invasion of Ukraine in 2022, Vance proclaimed, "I don't really care what happens to Ukraine one way or another."[26] This was a stunning turn away from Reagan's vision for American leadership and toward Buchanan's America First isolationism. Vance reiterated this idea in a February 2024 interview with Rod Dreher: "I think that there is a real desire, especially among people who are older than fifty, to dwell in the glory years of American foreign policy. You know, the fall of the Berlin Wall and the 1990s, when America was the true global hegemon. . . . Those days are over," Vance opined.[27]

In ways that Buchanan never developed, Kevin Roberts has a plan for the second American revolution. Project 2025, published by the Heritage Foundation, is a handbook for building the unbound executive through the Trump presidency—and a guide for the founding of a new America. In essence, Project 2025 is a 922-page blueprint for an American regime change by way of a president who is neither checked nor balanced by the other branches of government—what one might see as a practical application of the type of conservatism articulated philosophically by Adrian Vermeule or theologically by Stephen Wolfe.

When Vance was announced as Trump's running mate, Roberts said, "he understands the moment we are in in this country, which is that we have a limited amount of time to implement great policy on behalf of forgotten Americans, someone JD Vance personifies. At Heritage, we could not be happier."[28] The admiration goes both ways. As I examined earlier, Vance wrote the foreword to Roberts's 2024 book, *Dawn's Early Light,* which closes with a violent image of loading guns in order to engage in the fights ahead.

In another era, a conservative viewing government as the answer to human problems would have been unthinkable. But for Vance, the solution to what he sees as the decline of the American dream is *more government* shaping the country actively in service of a higher power.

"When we think about Christian conservatism, we think of sanctity of marriage, sanctity of life," Vance said in an interview for *First Things.* "Of course, these things are important and I certainly believe the Church's teachings on all of these things. And yet, there's an entire Christian moral and economic worldview that is completely cut out of modern American politics, and I think it's important to try to bring that back."[29]

Following Roberts, Deneen, and Vermeule (and unintentionally Rushdoony), Vance sees the government's role not as progress toward a society where humans can exercise their rights freely, but where humans are forced by their government to live in accordance with God's divine order. As the Catholic theologian Massimo Faggioli puts it, "For Vance, Christianity and the church are not the problem but the solution to the ills of the political-religious project called the United States of America."[30]

✦ ✦ ✦

Vance has won the admiration of Christian Reconstructionists by outlining a vision of the United States as "a people" with a specific history, way of life, and religious identity. During the 2024 campaign, Vance consistently articulated the idea that the United States is not an experiment based on lofty ideals—as outlined in the Constitution, expressed in the Declaration of Independence, and discussed at length by the Founders in the Federalist papers and elsewhere—but "a group of people."[31] In his speech at the Republican National Convention in which he accepted the nomination for vice president, Vance mentioned his wife Usha and her family's South Asian heritage, but then quickly pivoted to the fact that you can find five generations of his ancestors in a Kentucky cemetery. "That is the source of America's greatness," Vance said. "That is a homeland, that is our homeland. . . . People will not fight for abstractions but they will fight for their home."[32]

✦ ✦ ✦

In chapter 5, I noted that William Wolfe was one of the fifteen leaders invited to meet and pray with President Trump in March 2025. Wolfe is also one of the editors of the "Statement on Christian Nationalism" published in 2023 by a group of Protestant Christian nationalist leaders. The statement matches Vance's conception of the United States's ethnic foundation:

> WE AFFIRM that a nation is not merely an idea, abstract principle, or ideology but tangibly defined by a particular body of people in a particular place. We affirm that a particular people are necessarily bound together by a shared culture, customs, history, and lineage while sharing common interests, virtues, languages, and worship. We affirm, in regards to "place" that a nation is definitively set by both its borders and times physically defined by God (Acts 17:26).[33]

Vance's view of the United States as a White Christian homeland resonates with Christian Reconstructionists; they also applaud his retrograde views of women's role in society. In the 2024 election, Vance's previous comments about "childless cat ladies" and women over fifty having the "primary function" of caring for their grandchildren made headlines. For the disciple of Doug Wilson, who believes that votes should be cast by household—and that men should lead all households—or Joel Webbon, who believes that women's suffrage should be revoked, these comments were welcome openings to a new structure of American society.

Finally, there are glimmers of ethnonationalism in Vance's understanding of ethnicity and US culture. On January 30, 2025, the vice president started a social media spat with Rory Stewart, a former Conservative member of the British parliament.

Vance tweeted about the principle of "ordo amoris," or order of affections, the theological notion that there should be an order of love that prioritizes Christian affection from family to neighbor to society—and that if all people ordered their loves rightly, they would enjoy freedom. This is a certain reiteration of Aristotle's political philosophy, St. Augustine's political theology, and Calvin's anthropology through a nationalist politics and common good philosophy. In what many interpreted as a response to Vance, Pope Francis soon offered his own interpretation of the concept: "The true ordo amoris that must be promoted is that which we discover by meditating constantly on the parable of the 'good Samaritan' (cf. Lk 10:25–37), that is, by meditating on the love that builds a fraternity open to all, without exception."[34]

But Christian nationalist Protestants praised Vance for his rendering of Christian love as a personal hierarchy. "JD Vance is of course correct about the hierarchy of love," Matt Walsh, the right-wing Christian nationalist blogger and author, wrote soon after Vance's post. "You are called to love your family first. And your nation before the nations of the world."[35] Six months later, Walsh affirmed this position again. Walsh, who boasts four million social media followers, said in November 2025 that if American politicians "could choose between helping ten million foreigners or one million American families, they should choose the American family without hesitation."[36]

Walsh isn't alone in this sentiment. Vance's Catholic conception of the "ordo amoris" is nearly identical to Stephen Wolfe's Protestant ethnonationalist rendering. "A Christian should love his children over other children, his parents over other parents, his kin over other kin, his nation over other nations," Wolfe writes in *The Case for Christian Nationalism*. "The instincts that lead one to these unequal loves are reliable."[37] As I have pointed out, for Wolfe, "the human instinct to socialize and dwell with similar people is universal. Though for many today, especially Westerners, this instinct is understood as evil or pathological."[38] In sum, Vance's formulation of Christian love as a love of one's own before all else corresponds to the ethnonationalist theologies of Rushdoony's Reconstructionist heirs.

* * *

Vance practices his theology of the family, even if it makes for uncomfortable spousal dynamics. On October 29, 2025, Vance spoke at a Turning Point USA (which was founded by Charlie Kirk) event at the University of Mississippi. He was asked a question about his wife's religion. Usha Vance is of South Asian descent and grew up in a Hindu household. She now identifies as an agnostic. Vance outlined how most Sundays Usha comes with him to mass, how they are raising their kids as Christians and sending them to private religious schools, and how he hopes that one day Usha will decide to convert to Catholicism.

"Absolute[ly] amazing for the Vice President to speak about his faith and his family like this in public," William Wolfe posted to X in a seemingly now deleted response to a clip of Vance's remarks. "May God bring Usha to a saving knowledge of Jesus Christ!" Wolfe's comrade in arms Andrew Isker went even further: "Total loyalty to President JD Vance."[39]

These instances reveal how Protestant Reconstructionists recognize Vance as part of their political posse—a patriarchal Christian willing to set the world right by taking away individual freedoms for the "good" of society and the institution of God's—or someone's—kingdom. So far, his Catholicism isn't a problem for them. He is part of their civil kinship, even if he's not part of their church.

> "I feel like I've got a really good sense of senators, and he's by far the smartest and the deepest of any I've ever met."
>
> —TUCKER CARLSON

> "He is absolutely going to be one of the leaders—if not the leader—of our movement."
>
> —KEVIN ROBERTS

> "I'm sure he'll run for the presidency one day."
>
> —STEVE BANNON[40]

While he is too savvy a politician to call for something like a monarchy, integralist government, or a Christian prince, JD Vance is highly aware of the technocrat, Protestant, and Catholic voices clamoring for them. They are his friends and mentors, his sources and influences, and in turn he represents their dream of a radical American future after Donald Trump.

JD Vance has inherited the theology and philosophy of the family that has been the foundation of the Catholic postliberal movement since the 1960s. In his foreword to Kevin Roberts's *Dawn's Early Light,* Vance recalls the "old American Right's" emphasis on family, marriage, and a society based on the virtues therefrom. Vance praises Roberts for recognizing that individual liberty and free enterprise are not the pathways to "recultivating" the garden of the American republic. What is needed is a government willing to prioritize morality and a certain type of family (built in a traditional Catholic image) over personal freedoms. In ways that would please Paul Weyrich, Vance has said that parents should have their vote count for more than Americans without children and that the Democrats are run by "a bunch of childless cat ladies who are miserable at their own lives and the choices that they've made and so they want to make the rest of the country miserable, too."[41] In response, Vance wants to use the power of the state to quell individual liberty in the name of instituting a "Christian view of culture and economics." This is not just a postliberal vision—a model of what comes after liberalism. It is an illiberal vision—a model that negates the promises of liberal democracy in the name of inflicting a communitarian conception of family, sex, and the good life on every American.

Vance's opposition to liberalism goes hand in hand with the postlibertarian turn on the postliberal Right. Vance gives credit to Brent Bozell for "dismantling" the argument that libertarian economics can be the basis for a good society. For Vance, Bozell's key insight is that if the government wants people to behave "well" then it should use "cultural and legal pressures to encourage them to do it." Instead of letting the invisible hand do the work, Vance advocates for the government's closed fist to punch big business in the mouth.

If Vance is cavalier about state intervention in the market, he is too smart a politician to call for the overthrow of US democracy. However, as we examined above, he is willing to encourage the president not to abide by legal rulings of the Supreme Court. Moreover, unlike his predecessor Mike Pence, Vance claims that he would not have certified the election in 2020.[42] These comments are enough for the antidemocratic figures on the postliberal Right to recognize Vance as the elected official willing to take whatever steps necessary to institute the "common good" in American society.

"We are in a late republican period," Vance said to the journalist James Pogue in 2022. By his saying so, Pogue observes, Vance "evoked the common New Right view of America as Rome awaiting its Caesar." Vance continued: "If we're going to push back against it, we're going to have to get pretty wild, and pretty far out there, and go in directions that a lot of conservatives right now are uncomfortable with."[43]

* * *

While Vance speaks carefully about democracy, he is an open advocate of Western supremacy. In the United States, Western supremacists often refer to the country not only as a Christian nation, but also part of a "Western civilization" that stretches back to medieval Christendom and the Greek and Roman empires. They claim that elites have allowed an "invasion" of immigrants to destroy the American "way of life" and that the only way to rescue Western civilization, and the United States, is to purify the country of foreign elements. Vance sometimes uses race to frame the betrayal of "real Americans" by traitorous elites.

> Here's what the elites do. When they say that those people are white privileged, they shut them up. Look, you're unhappy about your job being shipped overseas? You're worried that a lawless southern border is going to cause the same poison that killed your daughter to also affect your grandbaby? Don't you dare complain about that stuff. You are white privileged. You suffer

> from white rage. . . . What they do is use it as a power play so they can get us to shut up. So they can get us to stop complaining about our own country. And they get to run things without any control, without any pushback from the real people.[44]

Vance's claim is that any reference to "White privilege" is an elitist tactic designed to preemptively mitigate "real people" from expressing a desire for a working economy. In sum, elites sell out White Americans, who are the "real people," by telling them that any complaint they have is illegitimate in public discourse.

Vance also sees elites selling out the United States and Western civilization by advocating for rights and representation to immigrants and other historically marginalized groups. In an interview at *First Things,* Vance argues that progressive policies are "a recipe for colonizing your own people." When Democrats are willing to support Ukraine, Vance sees it not as lending aid to a fellow democratic state, fighting off the invasion of an autocratic regime, but "militaristic adventurism overseas," in order to wage "war with your own people at home."[45] When asked about sending aid to an ally, Vance responded: "I will be damned if I am going to prioritize Ukraine's eastern border right now when our own southern border is engulfed by a human tsunami of illegal migrants."[46]

At times, Vance seems like a textbook isolationist with no interest in forging American relationships with historical allies in Europe. However, beneath the surface of his occasional "America First" rhetoric is the belief that Europe "is the cradle of Western civilization." Like his fellow Western supremacists Kevin Roberts, Adrian Vermeule, Alex Karp, and C. Jay Engel,

Vance sees Europe as the source of "the entire idea of Christian civilization that led to the founding of the United States of America."[47] There are unique cultural and religious bonds that in Vance's mind connect the US to Europe. This family resemblance and shared heritage mean Vance has, in his perspective, license to criticize Europe's leaders for allowing widespread immigration. His favorite example is Germany:

> So look, I want Europe to thrive. I want them to be an important ally. Part of that is gonna be Europe respecting its own people, respecting its own sovereignty, and America can't do that job for them. If you have a country like Germany, where you have another few million immigrants come in from countries that are totally culturally incompatible with Germany, then it doesn't matter what I think about Europe, Germany will have killed itself, and I hope they don't do that because I love Germany and I want Germany to thrive.[48]

Naturally, Vance feels the same way about immigrants coming to the US.

During the 2024 campaign, Vance amplified a story about Haitian immigrants eating cats and dogs. Even after it was discredited, he continued peddling it. For Vance, the Haitian immigrants in question are a perfect example of the kinds of "legal" migrants to the United States who are culturally misaligned with the foundations of American society. Even if they have documentation to reside here, he sees them as an "illegal" threat to the good of our society.[49] In a November 2025 interview, Vance claimed that thirty million undocumented immigrants are in the United States—an entirely made-up number—which is the reason for expensive housing prices and a lack of well-paying jobs for Americans. Once again, he blames elites for allowing invaders to ruin the lives of the "real people."

"We cannot rebuild Western civilization. We cannot rebuild the United States of America or Europe by letting millions and millions of unvetted illegal migrants come into our country," Vance says. "It has to stop."[50]

* * *

Seeing Vance as a Western supremacist is a decoder ring for understanding how someone like Yarvin views him as a leader who can, in the words of St. Paul, become all things to all people. Vance can speak the populist language of Appalachia to the masses. When Charlie Kirk was assassinated, it was Vance who stepped in to host Kirk's show, acting as both the vice president and the mouthpiece of a young generation of Christian conservatives. Vance is young enough, and chronically online enough, to speak to Gen Z, but he is also fluent in elite jargon, making him a foil to the Ivy Leaguers and coastal political classes whom he, and many others, sees as selling out the country to foreigners. Moreover, his conception of the United States as an outgrowth of "the cradle of Western civilization" provides a wide angle for nonreligious and heterodox technocrats, as well as America First Reconstructionists and reactionary Catholics, to fit into his vision for the country. He is not simply a Christian nationalist. He is not only an intellectual Catholic. He is not just a good old boy from middle America. He is not just a Peter Thiel Manchurian candidate. Vance sells himself as everything all at once—a Western Christian man of the people who is conversant with, and receptive to, the whole of the postliberal American Right.

In this sense, Vance is not a complement to Trump's MAGA agenda. He is the bridge to something more radical. "Trump will, at most, serve four years in the White House," Vance told Ian Ward in early 2024. "There is a big question about what comes after him."[51] If Vance is the candidate to succeed Trump, he will do so as the figure who convenes the interests of Silicon Valley technocrats, common good Catholics, and all those who are hoping for a second American revolution.

If Trump was crowned the MAGA messiah at the 2024 Republican National Convention, then it seems Vance is the apostle who will bring forth a conservative vision more extreme than even the MAGA Chosen One imagines.

"You know, Jesus played the small rooms until St. Paul came around," Steve Bannon told Ian Ward in 2024, referencing Vance. "It took the zeal of St. Paul to turn Jesus into a headliner."[52]

Catholic integralists see in him a statesman willing to use the government as a weapon to moralize markets and enforce virtue on wayward citizens. Protestant ethnonationalists see a "real American" who understands that the United States is not based on ideas, but on blood, land, and kin. Tech monarchists see an executive willing to defy courts, purge institutions, and treat the state as a corporate entity to be seized and reprogrammed. In this sense, Vance is more dangerous than Trump. In place of the promise to restore American greatness, Vance proposes a civilizational crusade in which faith, ethnicity, and executive power determine who belongs and who does not. He is not simply Trump's heir apparent. He is the blueprint to permanent postliberal rule. This is not a crusade for a Christian nation. It's a march toward something like Western American Christendom. Time will tell whether or not he is *popular* enough to be the *populist* leader for which they long. For now, he's vice president. Someday, he (or someone like him) may be something else altogether.

EPILOGUE

DIGNITY IS WORTH THE MESS: A CALL TO RESIST MONARCHY

> **Many forms of Government have been tried, and will be tried in this world of sin and woe. No one pretends that democracy is perfect or all-wise. Indeed it has been said that democracy is the worst form of Government except for all those other forms that have been tried from time to time.**
>
> —WINSTON CHURCHILL[1]

In the year before the 2024 election, I traveled the country giving lectures and participating in panels on Christian nationalism and the state of American democracy, from Ivy League universities to small civic groups in tiny towns. At each stop I tried to convince my audience that what we were facing was not simply a group of religious Americans who believed they had a right to the head seat at the roundtable of American democracy. Instead, I warned, it's a group who believes they have an inherent superior status to all others around them—and when it's time, they will sacrifice democracy for power. They believe, I said repeatedly, that they have the right to turn over the table and lead by force if they feel it necessary. There were skeptics in every audience. It's one thing to face down the second coming of the Religious Right, but did these people really want an authoritarian government? Would they really tear down the status, wealth, and power of the United States just to win the culture wars? Is a monarch worth it?

"I identify more with Putin's Christian values than Joe Biden's," says Lauren Witzke, the 2020 GOP nominee for the US Senate in Delaware, in a widely shared YouTube interview. "Putin takes care of his people." In another video she asks Putin to invade our territory to liberate the United States from then-President Joe Biden's globalist regime. When I showed these videos to audiences in 2024, they began to see the threat ahead—a Christian movement based not on a return to the 1950s, but on a revolution toward nondemocratic forms of governance. Her comments mirror a video by the media group the Young Turks at an event before the Iowa caucuses in January 2024, in which person after person says on camera that they prefer Donald Trump as a dictator forever than four more years of Joe Biden. "This country needs a dictator," a man in a leather jacket and red MAGA hat says. "I hate to say it."[2]

Why do aspiring leaders like Witzke and men on the street in Iowa think that the United States needs a dictator? What is the appeal of the postliberal story?

There are three aspects of the postliberal worldview that beguile everyday people. First, postliberals offer a cosmic story in which to play a part. They offer a meaningful life by extending an invitation into an epic narrative of the utmost significance. One of the things liberalism and capitalism do poorly is provide an overarching frame to individual and collective life. There is a sense among those seduced by the postliberal Right that modern human existence is nothing more than strip malls, streaming videos, Tinder hookups, and cheap goods from China.

In response, postliberalism promises to do something magical: to return us all to an idyllic time in medieval Christendom, or Calvin's Geneva, or the Massachusetts Bay Colony, when the world was about sacred things—God, family, and parish. A peaceful European village where hearth, home, and church bells are the central objects, not a smartphone screen or a Twitch stream. It's like an offer to live inside Disneyland; to get lost in a world that promises enchantment, clear distinctions between "good" guys and "bad" guys, and a pretty castle from where the noble king and queen look down on their subjects. Postliberalism plays on our escapist impulses by offering a simplified view of the past and an unreachable vision of the future.

I'm not immune to these instincts. The first time I read the word "postliberal" was 2005, during the dark night of the soul that eventually led me out of evangelicalism. By that time, I had been on staff at Rose Drive Friends Church for almost seven years. My life was consumed by ministry. I was a respected part of the community where I grew up. On Sundays, I led prayers in front of two hundred kids in the youth group and two thousand people in the services for the church.

But I wasn't sure I still believed in God. I'd spent two years in seminary reading everything possible about the history of Christianity, the modern United States, and twentieth-century philosophy. Most Thursdays (my pastor's day off) I camped out at a coffee shop with a stack of books, trying to figure out what kind of Christianity I could believe in. The center of evangelicalism didn't hold. I knew that. But what else was there?

On one of those Thursdays I discovered "postliberal theology" in the work of the Yale theologian George Lindbeck.[3] What Lindbeck and other theologians prescribed was a Christianity that absorbed the world through the biblical text. In other words, to pretend we were living in the world centered on Christ and church without concern for persuading others to join us or defending our faith rationally or scientifically. I was initially drawn to Lindbeck's idea: Instead of trying to persuade the world to come to Christ, we could build communities that looked like the ones Christ envisioned. We would forgo democracy and pluralism and the whole messy business of living with neighbors who weren't like us in order to return to the sacredness of a time before. Eventually, the nonbelievers around us would either choose to join our Christ-centered community or need to figure out another place to live.

I soon realized that this was a fantasy. Even when I decamped to Oxford in September 2005 to pursue a master's degree and was surrounded by thousand-year-old libraries, soaring spires, and cobblestone streets, there was no way to pretend that our twenty-first-century world is a homogenous European Christendom with no need to engage the contours of modern life. Ignoring the realities of the global community wasn't going to make them go away. Moreover, I knew the beauty of difference firsthand. My mom is a White woman from the South. My father is a Japanese American from Maui. I grew up toggling between meals of sashimi and grits; kalua pork and homemade biscuits. I knew the wonder and richness of both my parents' cultures, the ways they'd given me a unique identity. There would be no trading that for a pared-down version of myself.

Yet, as much as I hate what this postliberal story does to the "others" who don't fit into the narrative, the appeal makes sense. For a twenty-something young man searching for identity and meaning like me, the postliberal path presented a grand metanarrative in which I would fight the savagery of liberalism in order to help reinstitute the lost world of Christendom as part of a tight-knit community. Democracy and capitalism could be pushed aside in order to expand the sectarian community of the church into the wider world. It would be, as the theologian John Milbank called it, a "radical orthodoxy" based on an imperial faith. My life would be part of a grand epic. It would be meaningful. And at the end of my days I would know clearly if I had been one of the "good" guys.

This is the second aspect of postliberalism that charms everyday people. Postliberal figures, whether theologians, technocrats, or pastors, are willing to offer specific and practical advice for how to live a good life. If the civilizational story that postliberalism invites you into gives you a meaningful role to play, it also provides a sense of how to live the right way. We live in a time of overwhelming uncertainty. Global inequalities. Climate disasters. The onset of AI. Unregulated social media. Our physical and online environments are beset by crisis, misinformation, and rapid change. Liberalism doesn't fill in the content of your life. Liberalism offers human rights and a chance to live without interference from the state or persecution from other citizens. In its most basic form, the deal is that as long as you live in a way that doesn't hurt others, your way of life won't be outlawed or regulated—regardless of what religion you practice or creed you abide by. That worldview is the basis for the separation of church and state, the idea of human rights, and the modern democracies characterized by pluralism and the rule of law.

But it doesn't always offer an ethic. A code. A set of prescriptions for how to live a dutiful life in a world that feels like it changes by the second. Above all else, postliberalism is an offer to return to a time when the state and its leaders told citizens how to live meaningful and virtuous lives. It demands the sacrifice of personal freedom, expression, and for many, identity. But those who take the postliberal bet are willing to forgo those things in order to get a world that makes sense to them—or makes sense of them—in return. When liberals are too afraid to offer visions of the good life, the worst people imaginable for the job step in to tell the masses how to be "real men," "Alpha males," "trad wives," and "biblically feminine." Postliberals are among the many figures on the American Right who offer a robust, if dangerously reductive, understanding of how to be virtuous, dutiful, and righteous.

The final aspect of postliberalism that seduces ordinary citizens into the hands of a dictator is the fact that for many Americans "democracy" has become an empty signifier. The first time I realized this was during a virtual lecture I gave to a group of humanists in the Upper Midwest in spring of 2024. I was caught off guard when a retired humanities professor asked me why defending democracy was so important. Why, in other words, should we go so far to defend democracy, since it is as susceptible to abuse as any other form of government. The questioner made it clear he thought Donald Trump would be destructive if he won another term, but he didn't see the point of basing the opposition around the idea of democracy.

A month or so later, I led a seminar put together by a

number of Asian American churches near my house in the Bay Area. They asked me to speak about the dangers of Christian nationalism to both the Church and to the United States. In my presentation, I made the point that for many Christian nationalists democracy isn't a sacred value—that if they could seize power by other means, they would do so. At the midway point of the seminar, everyone broke into small groups to discuss what they had learned and how it touched their lives and communities. As I paced around the room, I heard a middle-aged Asian American man admit that for him democracy wasn't necessarily a sacred value either. When pushed by the others in his group, he pointed to the lack of government effectiveness, Congress's inaction and unending bureaucratic infighting, and the lack of contact he felt with elected officials.

Soon after, Kamala Harris replaced Joe Biden on the presidential ticket. In the short time her campaign had to form a message ahead of the election, they landed on telling a story of celebrating choice, difference, and freedom in contrast to the myopic vision Trump would impose on the nation. Her rallies became celebrations—full of cheering, chanting, and dancing, manifestations of American diversity and individuality. The message seemed to be that by preserving democracy, we could preserve the liberal order that allows for all of us to live our stories, form our families, and fall in love however we chose. In the face of Trump's threats and the outlines of Project 2025, it was almost—but not quite—the pathway to preventing him from gaining power and changing the fundamental makeup of the United States. When the dust settled after election night, I reflected on the everyday Americans I'd encountered who were not in favor of Trump or his policies, but who nevertheless didn't feel as if liberal democracy was sacred to them.

* * *

Postliberalism is persuasive because it offers meaning at scale: an epic, a war between good and evil, a role to play in history. The liberal response too often sounds like a shrug—*just live your life*—which doesn't feel like enough in a collapsing world. The answer is not to abandon grand narrative, but to provide a better, truer, more humane one.

Mythic purity or medieval reenactment are not going to save us. Instead, we need to renovate the story of democracy in which normal people band together to fight imperial powers and colonizing kingdoms. The history of democracy across the globe is about human beings working in solidarity to topple seemingly insurmountable forces. Democracy holds open a tenuous space where everyone shares power, follows the rule of law, and agrees that everyone is equal under it. The protagonists are not kings and crusaders but ordinary patriots who refuse subservience even when it would be easier to give in. It promises not to restore a lost golden age, but to decide—again and again—that a free society is worth the work.

There's no need to "other" certain religious or ethnic groups in order to tell the story. There are readily available "bad guys" against which we can form a unified, coherent mission to save We the People and build a sustainable future for everyone. The enemies? Billionaires—anyone who hoards enough wealth to wield it as a tool of domination; those who prioritize profit over human life, denying the catastrophic effects of climate change and refusing to build the infrastructure needed to handle floods, fires, and famines; and unregulated forms of AI that threaten the dignity of both humans and the planet.

Where postliberalism offers a Disneyland version of Western civilization, democracy offers something riskier and more adult: a story in which meaning comes not from playing an imposed role, limited by gender, sexuality, ethnicity, and migration status, but from taking responsibility for a shared world none of us can either control or escape. That story is less enchanting—but it is genuine. And it is the only one that doesn't require demonizing minorities or making second-class citizens out of half the population to make sense. But we cannot simply trot out the story of the American Revolutionary War or World War II and think that anyone—especially those folks under forty—is going to believe that democracy simply works for them. We need to reinvigorate the narrative, fill it in with a renewed sense of what we stand for, who we are fighting, and why it matters. That means wading into the waters of what it means to be a "good" person.

Postliberalism offers the illusion of clarity by reducing moral formation to obedience. Democracy insists that goodness is more demanding than that. The response to "liberalism doesn't tell me how to live" is not "let the state decide," but the recognition that democracy depends on moral communities capable of forming people without coercion. We have forgotten how to speak of democracy not as permission to "do you," but as a shared project—one in which freedom is secured together by resisting those who would make us subservient.

When people say democracy isn't sacred, they're often right—*if* democracy means nothing more than billboards and yard signs, gridlock and corruption, out-of-touch elites and expensive consultants. Democracy becomes sacred when it is understood as the fragile structure that reveres truth as the only royalty, sees leaders as removable, and promises to keep violence in check. A dictator resolves conflict by treating citizens as obstacles to overcome. Democracy feels frustrating because it refuses to view anyone as less than equal. Postliberalism thrives when democracy is reduced to slogans, elections, and vibes. When democracy is experienced only as gridlock and bureaucracy, a ruler who promises decisiveness becomes intriguing. The response must be to resignify democracy as a discipline against dehumanization. Democracy matters because it institutionalizes the idea that no one is entitled to rule you by nature, virtue, or divine fiat. The postliberal wager is that submission will make life coherent. The democratic wager is that dignity is worth the mess. Postliberalism succeeds by offering a binary worldview full of morality and meaning at the price of freedom and equality. The democratic response must stop pretending those hungers are illegitimate—and start answering them without nostalgia, misinformation, or manipulation.

We can't turn away from existential questions of meaning and civilizational questions of purpose. We can't make the story smaller. We don't need a thinner story. We need a more powerful one.

ACKNOWLEDGMENTS

Like all of my work, this book is the result of rich conversations with colleagues and friends. I am indebted to Daniel Miller, my *Straight White American Jesus* cohost, who has been discussing religion and politics in America with me for two decades now—and the SWAJ community that nourishes and sustains our work. (There are way too many of you to name!) I am particularly thankful for colleagues whose work and comments provided the spark for the book's core argument: Chelsea Ebin, Sarah Posner, Julie Ingersoll, Phil Williams, Phil Gorski, Laura K. Field, David Congdon, Jerome Copulsky, Andrew Whitehead, Sam Perry, Sarah Stankorb, Matthew D. Taylor, and many others. My team at Axis Mundi Media is nimble, hardworking, and brilliant—thank you Kari Onishi, Scott Okamoto, Andrew Gill, Sam Kang, Leah Payne, Annika Brockschmidt, and Kevin Crowe for making it all happen. To everyone at APARRI, especially Carolyn Chen, Khyati Joshi, Tammy Ho, Jane Iwamura, and Jane Hong—thank you for an academic home I never expected but can't imagine being without.

So much gratitude for my editor, Elisabeth Dyssegaard, and the entire team at St. Martin's for bringing this text to life. And to my agent, Mark Tauber, for seeing the vision for it and taking the ride with me. Most of all, I am grateful to Kendra, Kaia, and Kasia for endless support, belief, and joy. Writing about this stuff is not easy, but you make it worth it.

NOTES

PROLOGUE

1. "'Get the F*** Out of My Country': Republican Senate Candidate Jake Lang's Fiery Dearborn Speech," *APT,* November 20, 2025, https://youtu.be/vd5jM6H1rdM?si=cd1HfvsSY5LeEqE-.
2. Ibid.
3. Robert P. Jones, "White Christian America Ended in the 2010s," NBC News, December 27, 2019, https://www.nbcnews.com/think/opinion/2010s-spelled-end-white-christian-america-ncna1106936.

INTRODUCTION

1. "Dwarkesh Patel: Tech and the American Republic," *Kevin Roberts Show,* October 2, 2024, https://youtu.be/5NZ8LcZdkAw?si=I8eyEztKyalfjUyt.
2. Letter from Thomas Jefferson to George Washington, May 2, 1788, https://founders.archives.gov/documents/Jefferson/01-13-02-0059.
3. Andrew L. Whitehead et al., "Make America Christian Again: Christian Nationalism and Voting for Donald Trump in the 2016 Presidential Election," *Sociology of Religion* 79, no. 2 (Summer 2018): 147–171.
4. Robert P. Jones, "The Divide Over America's Future: 1950 or 2050? Findings from the 2016 American Values Survey," PRRI,

October 25, 2016, https://www.prri.org/research/poll-1950s-2050-divided-nations-direction-post-election/.

5. One of the most important works on this topic is Matthew D. Taylor's *The Violent Take It By Force: The Christian Movement That Is Threatening Our Democracy* (Broadleaf, 2024). Taylor traces the independent charismatic movement called the New Apostolic Reformation, which is related to, but distinct from, mainstream American evangelicalism and thoroughly multi-ethnic in its makeup.
6. David Grann, "The Robespierre of the Right," *New Republic*, October 26, 1997, https://newrepublic.com/article/61338/robespierre-the-right.
7. "Dwarkesh Patel: Tech and the American Republic."
8. L. Brent Bozell Jr., "The Confessional Tribe," *Triumph*, July 1970.
9. Edmund Waldstein, "What Is Integralism Today?," *Church Life Journal*, October 2018.
10. See "Christian Nationalist Pastor Joel Webbon Says America Needs a Dictator," *Right Wing Watch*, May 8, 2024, https://youtu.be/LRL7WxKK-8k?si=69Z0Itfv90w6OF9a.
11. Peter Thiel, "The Education of a Libertarian," *Cato Unbound*, April 13, 2009, https://www.cato-unbound.org/2009/04/13/peter-thiel/education-libertarian/.
12. Julian G. Waller, "Postliberalism and the 2024 Election," George Washington Institute for European, Russian, and Eurasian Studies, June 12, 2025, https://www.illiberalism.org/postliberalism-and-the-2024-election/.
13. Ibid.

1. VIVA CRISTO REY

1. Daniel Kelly, *Living on Fire: The Life of Brent Bozell Jr.* (Intercollegiate Studies Institute, 2014), 23.
2. A. Brad Matthew Schwartz, "The Media Spawned McCarthyism. Now History Is Repeating Itself," *Time*, February 9, 2025, https://time.com/7213586/media-mccarthyism/.
3. Jacob Heilbrunn, *America Last: The Right's Century-Long Romance with Foreign Dictators* (Liveright Books, 2024), 143.
4. Kelly, *Living on Fire*, 66.
5. Ibid., 67.

6. Heilbrunn, *America Last,* 157.
7. L. Brent Bozell Jr., "Freedom or Virtue?" *National Review,* September 11, 1962, https://www.nationalreview.com/2017/01/freedom-virtue-conservatism-goal-society-freedom-or-virtue/.
8. Ibid.
9. Ibid.
10. Patrick Allitt, *Catholic Intellectuals and Conservative Politics in America, 1950–1985* (Cornell University Press, 1993), 144.
11. L. Brent Bozell Jr., "Letter to Yourselves," *Triumph,* March–April 1969.
12. L. Brent Bozell Jr., "Letter to Yourselves Part II: Politics of the Poor," *Triumph,* March–April 1969.
13. L. Brent Bozell Jr., "The Confessional Tribe," *Triumph,* July 1970.
14. Ibid.
15. Ibid.
16. William H. Marshner, "Liberty and Social Order," *Triumph,* May 1973.
17. Ibid.
18. Seth Dowland, "'Family Values' and the Formation of a Christian Right Agenda," *Church History* 78 (September 2009), 607.
19. "A Protestant Affirmation on the Control of Human Reproduction," *Christianity Today,* August 27, 1968, https://www.christianitytoday.com/1968/11/protestant-affirmation-on-control-of-human-reproduction/.
20. "Southern Baptists Approve Abortion In Certain Cases," *The New York Times,* June 3, 1971, https://www.nytimes.com/1971/06/03/archives/southern-baptists-approve-abortion-in-certain-cases.html.
21. David Roach, "How Southern Baptists Became Pro-Life," *Baptist Press,* January 16, 2015, https://www.baptistpress.com/resource-library/news/how-southern-baptists-became-pro-life/.
22. Dowland, "Family Values," 607.
23. Chelsea Ebin, *The Radical Mind: The Origins of the Right-Wing Catholic and Protestant Coalition Building* (University Press of Kansas, 2024), 146.
24. Sophie Bjork-James, *The Divine Institution: White Evangelicalism's Politics of the Family* (Rutgers University Press, 2021).
25. Ebin, *Radical Mind,* 152.

26. Dowland, "Family Values," 606.
27. Ebin, *Radical Mind,* 152.
28. Paul Weyrich, "Comments," in *No Longer Exiles: The Religious New Right in American Politics,* ed. Michael Cromartie (Ethics and Public Policy Center, 1993), 53.
29. Ibid., 53–54.
30. William S. Lind and William H. Marshner, *Cultural Conservatism: Toward a New National Agenda* (Free Congress Research and Education Foundation, 1987), 1.
31. Ibid., 35.
32. Ibid., 145–146.
33. Paul Weyrich, "Letter to Conservatives," 1999, https://nationalcenter.org/ncppr/1999/02/16/letter-to-conservatives-by-paul-m-weyrich/.
34. L. Brent Bozell Jr., "The Death of the Constitution," *Triumph,* February 1968.
35. Eric Heubeck, *Integration of Theory and Practice: A Program for the New Traditionalist Movement* (Free Congress Foundation, 2001), https://web.archive.org/web/20010713152425/http://www.freecongress.org/centers/conservatism/traditionalist.htm#1.
36. Heubeck, *Integration of Theory and Practice.*
37. Ebin, *Radical Mind,* 151.
38. Ibid.
39. Anne Nelson, *Shadow Network: Media, Money, and the Secret Hub of the Radical Right* (Bloomsbury, 2019), 97.
40. Bradley Onishi, *Preparing for War: The Extremist History of White Christian Nationalism—And What Comes Next* (Broadleaf Books, 2023), 125.

2. KING JESUS

1. Samuel Perry, "What Is CREC?," *The Conversation,* June 20, 2025. https://theconversation.com/what-is-crec-the-christian-nationalist-group-has-a-vision-for-america-and-defense-secretary-pete-hegseths-support-258273.
2. Ian Ward, "Doug Wilson Has Spent Decades Pushing for a Christian Theocracy. In Trump's DC, the New Right Is Listening," *Politico Magazine,* May 23, 2025, https://www.politico.com/news/magazine/2025/05/23/doug-wilson-new-right-pastor-hegseth-trump-officials-00355376.

3. Julie J. Ingersoll, *Building God's Kingdom: Inside the World of Christian Reconstructionism* (Oxford University Press, 2015), 1.
4. Molly Worthen, "The Chalcedon Problem: Rousas John Rushdoony and the Origins of Christian Reconstructionism," *Church History* 77, no. 2 (June 2008).
5. Rousas John Rushdoony, *This Independent Republic: Studies in the Nature and Meaning of American History* (Chalcedon Press, 1964), 184.
6. Rousas John Rushdoony, *The Institutes of Biblical Law*, vol. 1 (Chalcedon Books, 1973), 16.
7. Ibid., 16.
8. Ibid., 31.
9. Ibid., 275.
10. Michael J. McVicar, *Christian Reconstruction: RJ Rushdoony and the Making of American Religious Conservatism* (University of North Carolina Press, 2015), 120.
11. Rushdoony, *This Independent Republic*, 184.
12. McVicar, *Christian Reconstruction*, 42.
13. Rousas John Rushdoony, *The Institutes of Biblical Law*, vol. 3 (Chalcedon Books, 1999), 121.
14. Ibid., 121.
15. Rushdoony, *Institutes*, vol. 1, 238.
16. Rushdoony, *Institutes*, vol. 3, 290.
17. Rushdoony, *This Independent Republic*, 11.
18. Rushdoony, *Institutes*, vol. 1, 238.
19. Ibid., 56.
20. Ibid., 12.
21. Ibid., 134.
22. Worthen, "Chalcedon."
23. Rushdoony, *This Independent Republic*, 31.
24. Ibid., 109.
25. Hal Lindsey, *The Road to Holocaust* (Bantam Books, 1989).
26. Rodney Clapp, "Democracy as Heresy," *Christianity Today* 31, no. 3 (February 1987).
27. Worthen, "Chalcedon."
28. Crawford Gribben, *Survival and Resistance in Evangelical America: Christian Reconstruction in the Pacific Northwest* (Oxford University Press, 2021), 49.
29. Ibid., 49.

30. Ibid., 139.
31. Chris Hume, "Poison Pills, Theonomy, and Doug Wilson," *Future of Christendom,* https://futureofchristendom.org/poison-pills-theonomy-and-doug-wilson/, accessed August 2025.
32. Doug Wilson, *Mere Christendom: The Case for Bringing Christianity Back Into Modern Culture* (Canon Press, 2023), 78.
33. Ibid., 75.
34. Ibid., 78.
35. Ibid., 112–113.
36. Ibid., 195.
37. Tia Levings, "Doug Wilson Plays Humble and Reasonable for the CNN Cameras," Substack, August 8, 2025, https://tialevings.substack.com/p/doug-wilson-plays-humble-and-reasonable.
38. Doug Wilson, *Federal Husband: Covenant Headship and the Christian Man* (Canon Press, 1999), 81.
39. Ibid., 80.
40. Doug Wilson, "Recovering the Masculine Mind," *Blog and Mablog,* June 19, 2024, https://www.youtube.com/watch?v=7a11j3rctcI.
41. Doug Wilson, *Reforming Marriage* (Canon Press, 2099), 50.
42. Sarah Stankorb, "Inside the Church That Preaches 'Wives Need to Be Led with a Firm Hand,'" *Vice,* September 2021, https://www.vice.com/en/article/inside-the-church-that-preaches-wives-need-to-be-led-with-a-firm-hand/.
43. Ibid.
44. Franziska Wild, "'Christ or Chaos': A Conservative Church with Political Ties Comes to Washington," *Washingtonian,* July 16, 2025, https://www.washingtonian.com/2025/07/16/christ-or-chaos-a-conservative-church-with-political-ties-comes-to-washington/.
45. Doug Wilson, "A Mission to Babylon," *Blog and Mablog,* May 12, 2025, https://dougwils.com/books-and-culture/s7-engaging-the-culture/a-mission-to-babylon.html.
46. Peter Bell, *Sons of Patriarchy,* podcast, season 1, episode 1, October 28, 2024, https://podcasts.apple.com/us/podcast/the-war-on-the-evangellyfish/id1772141068?i=1000674622288.
47. CNN, "The Christian Nationalist Pastor with Ties to Defense Secretary Pete Hegseth," August 8, 2025, https://www.cnn.com/2025/08/08/politics/video/christian-nationalist-doug-wilson-pam-brown-digvid.

3. PETER THIEL'S TECHNO-MONARCHISM

1. George Packer, "No Death, No Taxes," *The New Yorker*, November 20, 2011.
2. Ross Douthat, "Peter Thiel and the Antichrist," *The New York Times*, June 26, 2025, https://www.nytimes.com/2025/06/26/opinion/peter-thiel-antichrist-ross-douthat.html.
3. Steven Hubbard, "ICE to Use ImmigrationOS by Palantir, a New AI System, to Track Immigrants' Movements," American Immigration Council, August 21, 2025, https://www.americanimmigrationcouncil.org/blog/ice-immigrationos-palantir-ai-track-immigrants/.
4. See the *Conversations with Tyler* podcast, episode 210, "Peter Thiel and Political Theology," https://conversationswithtyler.com/episodes/peter-thiel-political-theology/.
5. Alex Picquard, "Peter Thiel, the Libertarian Billionaire Waging War on Government," *Le Monde*, July 22, 2025, https://www.lemonde.fr/en/summer-reads/article/2025/07/22/peter-thiel-the-libertarian-billionaire-waging-war-on-government_6743617_183.html.
6. Max Chafkin, *The Contrarian: Peter Thiel and Silicon Valley's Pursuit of Power* (Penguin Press 2021).
7. Emma Goldberg, "Seeking God, or Peter Thiel, in Silicon Valley," *The New York Times*, February 11, 2025, https://www.nytimes.com/2025/02/11/business/silicon-valley-christianity.html.
8. Rod Dreher, "Stranger to Himself on a Train," *Rod Dreher's Diary*, February 12, 2025, https://roddreher.substack.com/p/stranger-to-himself-on-a-train?open=false#%C2%A7peter-thiel-and-silicon-valley-christianity.
9. See "Remarks by Commencement Speaker Peter Thiel," *Hamilton College*, May 22, 2016, https://youtu.be/id4ywg5oemc?si=QT161uNymx4rFC14.
10. Ibid. Italics mine.
11. Even in this case, Thiel didn't totally play by the rules. He paid for the symposium at Stanford that ultimately led to the publication of *Politics and Apocalypse*. Laura Bullard summarizes in an investigative piece on Thiel and Girard for *Wired*: "In the summer of 2004, Thiel and his old mentor Hamerton-Kelly organized a weeklong Girardian seminar at Stanford and invited Girard and Palaver to take part. The gathering was a small, closed symposium with only

eight participants and served as Thiel's self-orchestrated debut as a Girardian intellectual. Newly wealthy after having sold PayPal in a deal valued at $1.5 billion, he footed the bill for the week and also helped underwrite the publication of a book that would collect all the papers presented at the seminar." https://www.wired.com/story/the-real-stakes-real-story-peter-thiels-antichrist-obsession/ https://www.jstor.org/stable/10.14321/j.ctt7zt6qq

12. Paul Leslie, "From Philosophy to Power: The Misuse of René Girard by Peter Thiel, JD Vance and the American Right," *Salgamundi* 226–227 (Spring–Summer 2025), https://salmagundi.skidmore.edu/articles/1176-from-philosophy-to-power.
13. Peter Thiel, "The Straussian Moment," in *Politics and Apocalypse*, ed. Robert Hamerton-Kelly (Michigan State University Press, 2007), 189–218.
14. Ibid.
15. See Gil Duran, "Silicon Valley Holy War," *The Nerd Reich*, September 10, 2025. https://www.thenerdreich.com/silicon-valley-holy-war/.
16. Thiel, "Straussian Moment." Italics mine.
17. Max Chafkin, *The Contrarian: Peter Thiel and Silicon Valley's Pursuit of Power* (Penguin Press 2021), 20.
18. Ibid., 20.
19. Ibid., 10.
20. See Tyler Cowen, "Peter Thiel on Political Theology," *Conversations with Tyler*, podcast, April 17, 2024, https://conversationswithtyler.com/episodes/peter-thiel-political-theology/.
21. Thiel, "Straussian Moment."
22. Quentin Hardy, "René Girard, French Theorist of the Social Sciences, Dies at 91," *The New York Times*, November 10, 2015, https://www.nytimes.com/2015/11/11/arts/international/rene-girard-french-theorist-of-the-social-sciences-dies-at-91.html?_r=0.
23. Thiel, "Straussian Moment."
24. Ibid.
25. Peter Thiel, "Founder as Victim, Founder as God," class lecture at Stanford University, 2012. See Blake Masters, "CS183: Startup - Peter Thiel Class Notes," Tumblr, June 6, 2012, https://blakemasters.tumblr.com/post/24578683805/peter-thiels-cs183-startup-class-18-notes.

26. Ibid.
27. Douthat, "Peter Thiel and the Antichrist."
28. Ibid.
29. Packer, "No Death, No Taxes."
30. Thiel, "Founder as Victim."
31. Ibid.
32. Ibid.
33. Hoover Institution, "Make Ticker Tape Parades Great Again: A Conversation with Peter Thiel," December 17, 2021, https://www.hoover.org/research/make-ticker-tape-parades-great-again-conversation-peter-thiel-0.
34. Thiel, "Founder as Victim."
35. Douthat, "Peter Thiel and the Antichrist."
36. See Nick Bostrom, "The Vulnerable World Hypothesis," in *Global Policy* 10, no. 4 (2019): 455–476. See also "Peter Thiel on 'Anti-Anti-Anti-Anti Classical Liberalism,'" *Oxford Union*, January 27, 2023, https://youtu.be/fQ4rc7npiXQ?si=uuzYS1EOZ0SMwTol.
37. "Peter Thiel on 'Anti-Anti-Anti-Anti Classical Liberalism.'"
38. Ibid.
39. Cowen, "Peter Thiel on Political Theology."
40. Peter Thiel, "A Time for Truth and Reconciliation," *Financial Times*, January 10, 2025, https://www.ft.com/content/a46cb128-1f74-4621-ab0b-242a76583105.
41. See Blake Masters, "CS183: Startup."
42. Peter Thiel, "The Education of a Libertarian," *Cato Unbound*, April 13, 2009, https: //www.cato-unbound.org/2009/04/13/peter-thiel/education-libertarian/.
43. Ibid.
44. Ibid.
45. Ibid.
46. Packer, "No Death, No Taxes."

4. A POSTLIBERAL CATHOLIC KINGDOM

1. "Regime Change and the Future of Liberalism," Intercollegiate Studies Institute, https://www.youtube.com/watch?v=2ZbsiKEhy-8.
2. "Heritage Foundation President Celebrates Supreme Court Immunity Decision: "We Are in the Process of the Second American Revolution," *Media Matters*, July 2, 2024, https://www.mediamatters

.org/project-2025/heritage-foundation-president-celebrates-supreme-court-immunity-decision-we-are.

3. "J. D. Vance—JML #070," *Jack Murphy Live*, September 21, 2021, https://www.youtube.com/watch?v=PMq1ZEcyztY&t=1s.
4. "Regime Change and the Future of Liberalism."
5. Chelsea Ebin, *The Radical Mind: The Origins of the Right-Wing Catholic and Protestant Coalition Building* (University Press of Kansas, 2024), 168.
6. Damon Linker, "The Post-Liberal Catholics Find Their Man," *The Atlantic*, August 8, 2024, https://www.theatlantic.com/ideas/archive/2024/08/J.D.-vance-post-liberal-catholics-thiel/679388/.
7. Kevin Gallagher, "The Eclipse of Catholic Fusionism," *American Affairs*, August 20, 2018, https://americanaffairsjournal.org/2018/08/the-eclipse-of-catholic-fusionism/.
8. Patrick Deneen, *Why Liberalism Failed* (Yale University Press, 2019), 47.
9. Sohrab Ahmari, "Against David French–ism," *First Things*, May 29, 2019, https://firstthings.com/against-david-french-ism/.
10. Vermeule, "Liberalism's Good and Faithful Servants." Deneen, *Why Liberalism Failed*, 38.
11. Ibid., 40.
12. Laura K. Field, "Revisiting Why Liberalism Failed Part 2: Distorted Methods, Disorienting History—Deneen on the Past, Present, and Future," Niskanen Center, December 21, 2020, https://www.niskanencenter.org/revisiting-why-liberalism-failed-distorted-methods-disorienting-history-deneen-on-the-past-present-and-future/.
13. Ahmari, "Against David French–ism."
14. Deneen, *Why Liberalism Failed*, xiii–xiv.
15. Ibid., 10.
16. Adrian Vermeule, "A Christian Strategy," *First Things*, November 1, 2017, https://firstthings.com/a-christian-strategy/.
17. Ibid.
18. Ahmari, "Against David French–ism."
19. Matthew J. Peterson, "America Needs a New Re-Founding," *The American Conservative*, July 25, 2020, https://www.theamericanconservative.com/america-needs-a-re-founding/.
20. Vermeule, "Liberalism's Good and Faithful Servants."

21. Ibid.
22. Deneen, *Why Liberalism Failed*, 4.
23. Adrian Vermeule, *Common Good Constitutionalism* (Polity Press, 2022), p. 37. Though all the current conservative justices on the Supreme Court identify as originalists, rather than common good constitutionalists, in *Trump v. United States*, all six of them voted to grant presidents immunity from prosecution: "A former president is entitled to absolute immunity from criminal prosecution for actions within his 'conclusive and preclusive constitutional authority.'" Five of the six conservative justices are Catholic; Neil Gorsuch, who was born and raised Catholic, now identifies as Episcopalian.
24. Kyrion Huigens, "Theistic Illiberal Constitutionalism: A Review of Adrian Vermeul's *Common Good Constitutionalism*," *University of Louisville Law Review* 63, no. 1 (fall 2024), 3.
25. Adrian Vermeule, "What Common Good?," *American Prospect*, April 7, 2022.
26. Vermeule, *Common Good Constitutionalism*, 48.
27. Adrian Vermeule, "Beyond Originalism," *The Atlantic*, March 31, 2020.
28. Ibid.
29. Vermeule, *Common Good Constitutionalism*, 37.
30. Vermeule, "Beyond Originalism."
31. Ian Ward, "Critics Call It Theocratic and Authoritarian. Young Conservatives Call It an Exciting New Legal Theory," *Politico*, December 9, 2022, https://www.politico.com/news/magazine/2022/12/09/revolutionary-conservative-legal-philosophy-courts-00069201.
32. Vermeule, *Common Good Constitutionalism*, 157.
33. David Dyzenhaus, "The Snake Charmers," *Verfassung Blog*, March 7, 2022, https://verfassungsblog.de/os5-snake-charmers/.
34. Ibid.
35. Molly Ball, "The Fall of the Heritage Foundation and the Death of Republican Ideas," *The Atlantic*, September 25, 2013, https://www.theatlantic.com/politics/archive/2013/09/the-fall-of-the-heritage-foundation-and-the-death-of-republican-ideas/279955/.
36. Andrew Blasko, "Reagan and Heritage: A Unique Partnership," Heritage Foundation, June 7, 2004, https://www.heritage.org/conservatism/commentary/reagan-and-heritage-unique-partnership.

37. Kevin Roberts, foreword to *Project 2025: Mandate for Leadership* (Heritage Foundation, 2024), 3.
38. Liset Cruz et al., "37 Ways Project 2025 Has Shown Up in Trump's Executive Orders," *Politico*, February 5, 2025, https://www.politico.com/interactives/2025/trump-executive-orders-project-2025/.
39. Kevin Roberts, *Dawn's Early Light: Taking Back Washington to Save America* (Broadside Books, 2024), 3.
40. Ibid., 4.
41. Ibid., 17.
42. Ibid., 17–18.
43. Ibid., 18, 131.
44. Kevin Roberts, "The Future of Conservatism: Community, the Common Good, and State Power," *Public Discourse*, May 19, 2022, https://www.thepublicdiscourse.com/2022/05/82357/.
45. Ibid.
46. Kevin Roberts, foreword to *Project 2025*, 13. Italics mine.
47. Roberts, *Dawn's Early Light*, 19.
48. JD Vance, foreword to Roberts, *Dawn's Early Light*, xi.

5. THEOCRATIC CAESARISM

1. Samantha Rutt, "Trump's Prayer Army: Spiritual Leaders Who Are Guiding the President Through His 2nd Term," *Daily Mail*, March 22, 2025, https://www.dailymail.co.uk/news/article-14519421/trump-prayer-army-faith-leaders-advising-president.html.
2. James Silberman (@JSilbermanFTS), "Very happy to announce that this is now official! We'll call this Project 2035.," X, November 6, 2024, https://x.com/JSilbermanFTS/status/1854330969475735985.
3. James Silberman and Dusty Deevers, *The Statement on Christian Nationalism and the Gospel*. https://www.statementonchristiannationalism.com/.
4. Ibid.
5. Ibid.
6. Phil Williams, "Aiming to 'Radicalize Main Street,' Christian Nationalists Set Sights on Tiny Jackson County, Tennessee," *News Channel* 5, November 18, 2024, https://www.newschannel5.com/news/newschannel-5-investigates/confronting-hate/aiming

-to-radicalize-main-street-christian-nationalists-set-sights-on-tiny-jackson-county-tennessee.

7. Kiera Butler, "Christian 'TheoBros' Are Building a Tech Utopia in Appalachia," *Mother Jones*, April 8, 2025.
8. Doug Wilson, "Isker, Dreher, and Me," *Blog and Mablog*, September 11, 2023, https://dougwils.com/books-and-culture/books/isker-review.html.
9. Jack Jenkins, "The Second Coming of Doug Wilson," *Church Leaders*, June 3, 2024, https://churchleaders.com/news/486644-the-second-coming-of-doug-wilson-rns.html/2.
10. Andrew Isker, *The Boniface Option* (self-published, 2023), 104.
11. Ibid., 19. Italics are mine.
12. Ibid., 81–82.
13. Ibid., 16.
14. Ibid., 130.
15. Ibid., 9.
16. Ibid., 130.
17. Ibid., 24.
18. Ibid., 133.
19. Ibid., 133.
20. Ibid., 100.
21. Ibid., 101.
22. Once again, Carl Schmitt appears as a favorite among postliberal thinkers. The reader will recall that Schmitt is an important influence on Adrian Vermeule, the Catholic integralist Harvard law professor profiled in chapter 4 and Peter Thiel, the tech investor from chapter 3.
23. C. Jay Engel, "Carl Schmitt and the Political," *American Reformer*, June 15, 2024.
24. C. Jay Engel, "Why I'm Not a Libertarian," *Contra Mordor*, February 26, 2024, https://writing.cjayengel.com/p/why-im-not-a-libertarian.
25. C. Jay Engel (@contramordor), "When I say Heritage American, this is what I mean: those who are ethno-culturally tied to the ethos and spirit of the United States prior to its definitional transformation . . . ," X, May 26, 2024, https://x.com/contramordor/status/1794811572684263627.
26. Phil Williams, "Men Behind Tennessee's Christian Nationalist

Settlement: 'This Country Belongs to Jesus,' Not the Jews," *News Channel* 5, April 14, 2025, https://www.newschannel5.com/news/newschannel-5-investigates/confronting-hate/men-behind-tennessees-christian-nationalist-settlement-this-country-belongs-to-jesus-not-the-jews.

27. C. Jay Engel (@contramordor), "The Jews as a collective have largely operated at odds with the Old American way of life, rooted as it is in European Christendom," X, November 9, 2024, https://x.com/contramordor/status/1855242893817983217.
28. C. Jay Engel (@contramordor), X, November 9, 2024, https://x.com/contramordor/status/1855245894989336828.
29. C. Jay Engel, "Revolution from the Middle," *American Reformer*, May 7, 2024, https://americanreformer.org/2024/05/revolution-from-the-middle/.
30. Dave Forsythe, "A Pastoral Response to Wolfe's Christian Nationalism," Ezra Institute, July 15, 2025, https://www.ezrainstitute.com/a-pastoral-response-to-wolfes-christian-nationalism/.
31. Stephen Wolfe, *The Case for Christian Nationalism* (Canon Press, 2022), 159.
32. Wolfe, *Case for Christian Nationalism*, 22.
33. In what he describes as a work of political theory, Wolfe spends very little time reflecting on the development of modern nation-states and what we mean today when we use the word "nation." There's scant discussion of the concept of a nation-state beyond the idea of a group of people who occupy a place for generations and develop a particular way of doing life. In other words, the path from Adam and Eve to the contemporary nation-state isn't mediated by Rousseau, Hobbes, or any reckoning with the long lineage of political theory that has contributed to the cultivation of the nation-state as we've come to understand it; there's no substantive discussion of the differences among communities, cities, people groups, nations, states, and countries. Instead, he uses the term "nation" synonymously with the term "ethnicity": "I use the terms ethnicity and nation almost synonymously," Wolfe writes. "Ethnicity, as something experienced, is familiarity with others based in common language, manners, customs, stories, taboos, rituals, calendars, social expectations, duties, loves, and religion." See Wolfe, *Case for Christian Nationalism*, 135–136.
34. Wolfe, *Case for Christian Nationalism*, 22.

35. Ibid., 23.
36. Ibid., 74.
37. Ibid., 101.
38. Ibid., 142.
39. Wolfe deleted the tweets in which he offered this view. See Samuel Sey, "Why Some Evangelicals Are Embracing Racism," *Christian Post,* August 28, 2023, https://www.christianpost.com/voices/why-some-evangelicals-are-embracing-racism.html.
40. Stephen Wolfe, "The Possibility of Christian Peoples," *American Reformer,* March 16, 2023, https://americanreformer.org/2023/03/the-possibility-of-christian-peoples/.
41. Stephen Wolfe, "Why Multiculturalist Pluralism Fails and What to Build Instead," *New Christendom Press,* July 1, 2024, https://www.youtube.com/watch?v=i1ruwS_D1-I.
42. See "Christian Nationalism: Faith or Agenda? | Michael Bird vs. Stephen Wolfe, Hosted by Billy Hallowell," *Unbelievable?,* March 22, 2024, https://youtu.be/zieWeTqe2qc?si=DgsyUz98oq-MBZR9.
43. See Right Wing Watch (@RightRingWatch), "Joel Webbon explaining what 'true revival' in America would look like . . . ," X, July 23, 2024, https://x.com/RightWingWatch/status/1815767515579974061?s=20.
44. See "Owen Strachan, Immigration, and the Great Commission" *Right Response Ministries,* July 10, 2024, https://www.youtube.com/watch?v=rCF9flZR7dk.
45. Ibid.
46. "Contra Mundum Election Night Livestream," *Contra Mundum* podcast, November 5, 2024, https://www.youtube.com/watch?v=0j5_i1hqJRQ.
47. "Christian Nationalist Pastor Joel Webbon Says America Needs a Dictator," *Right Wing Watch,* May 8, 2024, https://www.youtube.com/watch?v=LRL7WxKK-8k.
48. C. Jay Engel (@contramordor), "The use of Protestant Franco—or Appalachian Pinochet—shall be to crush the Administrative State . . . ," X, October 6, 2023, https://x.com/contramordor/status/1710392424311451782.
49. Wolfe, *Case for Christian Nationalism,* 278.
50. Ibid., 280.

51. Ibid., 286.
52. Ibid., 287.
53. Ibid., 286.
54. Ibid., 287.
55. Ibid., 291.
56. Kelly J. Baker, "The Artifacts of White Supremacy," *Religion and Culture Forum*, June 14, 2017, https://voices.uchicago.edu/religionculture/2017/06/14/813/.

6. TECHNO-FEUDALISM

1. John Carey, *A Little History of Poetry* (Yale University Press, 2020). https://yalebooks.yale.edu/2020/04/30/the-epic-of-gilgamesh/.
2. Samantha Subin, "Palantir's Stock Is up 1,700% Since Its NYSE Debut Five Years Ago. Here's How It Got There," *CNBC*, September 30, 2025.
3. Barton Gellman, "Peter Thiel Is Taking a Break from Democracy," *The Atlantic*, November 9, 2023.
4. Gideon Lewis-Kraus, "The Palantir Guide to Saving America's Soul," *The New Yorker*, February 19, 2025.
5. Andy Greenberg, "How a 'Deviant' Philosopher Built Palantir, A CIA-Funded Data-Mining Juggernaut," *Forbes*, August 14, 2013.
6. Kari Paul, "Tech Workers Protest Data Mining Firm Palantir for Role in Immigrant Arrests," *The Guardian*, May 13, 2019.
7. Sam Biddle and Ryan Devereaux, "Peter Thiel's Palantir Was Used to Bust Relatives of Migrant Children, New Documents Show," *Intercept*, May 2, 2019.
8. Spencer Woodman, "Palantir Provides the Engine for Donald Trump's Deportation Machine," *Intercept*, March 2, 2017.
9. Sheera Frenkel and Aaron Krolik, "Trump Taps Palantir to Compile Data on Americans," *The New York Times*, May 30, 2025.
10. Peter Thiel, "The Straussian Moment," in *Politics and Apocalypse*, ed. Robert Hamerton-Kelly (Michigan State University Press, 2007).
11. Ibid.
12. Noel Castree, "Tech Giant Palantir Helps the US Government Monitor Its Citizens. Its CEO Wants Silicon Valley to Find Its Moral Compass" *Conversation*, July 28, 2025.

13. Maureen Dowd, "Alex Karp Has Money and Power. So What Does He Want?," *The New York Times*, August 17, 2025.
14. Alexander C. Karp and Nicholas W. Zamiska, *The Technological Republic: Hard Power, Soft Belief, and the Future of the West* (Crown Currency, 2025) 17.
15. Ibid., 15.
16. Ibid., 15.
17. Ibid., 33.
18. Ibid., 232.
19. Steven Levy, "Alex Karp Goes to War," *Wired*, November 10, 2025.
20. Karp and Zamiska, *Technological Republic*, 233.
21. Jack McCordick, "Alex Karp's War for the West," *New Republic*, February 28, 2025.
22. Karp and Zamiska, *Technological Republic*, 248.
23. Ibid., 249.
24. Ibid., 248–249.
25. "Alex Karp: Why the Woke Left Lost," *Ronald Reagan Presidential Foundation and Institute*, December 7, 2024, https://www.youtube.com/watch?v=Q07voo-CFYc.
26. McCordick, "Alex Karp's War for the West."
27. "Palantir Technologies: Q3 2024 Earnings Webcast, YouTube, November 4, 2024, https://www.youtube.com/watch?v=StuGNHgrDn8.
28. William D. Hartung, "At This Point, Silicon Valley Militarists Aren't Just Greedy—They're Bloodthirsty," *Nation*, March 21, 2025.
29. Elon Musk (@elonmusk), "Western Civilization is doomed, unless the core weakness of suicidal empathy is recognized and actions are taken . . . ," X, November 5, 2025, https://x.com/elonmusk/status/1986103240187064654?s=20.
30. Elon Musk (@elonmusk), "The doom of Western Civilization must be averted!," X, December 11, 2025, https://x.com/elonmusk/status/1999018146322166248?s=20.
31. Thiel, "Straussian Moment."
32. James Dale Davidson and William Rees-Mogg, *The Sovereign Individual: Mastering the Transition to the Information Age* (Touchstone, 1997), 14.
33. Ibid., 15.

34. Ibid., 19.
35. Ibid., 20.
36. See Gil Duran, "The Sovereign Individual: Radical Bible of Tech's 'Cognitive Elite,'" *Nerd Reich*, February 25, 2025.
37. Peter Thiel, "Preface," in James Dale Davidson and William Rees-Mogg, *The Sovereign Individual: Mastering the Transition to the Information Age* (1997; Touchstone, 2020), 9.
38. See Duran, "Sovereign Individual."
39. Ibid.
40. Mencius Moldbug, "A Formalist Manifesto," *Unqualified Reservations*, April 24, 2007.
41. Ibid.
42. Ava Kofman, "Curtis Yarvin's Plot Against America," *The New Yorker*, June 2, 2025.
43. Moldbug, "Formalist Manifesto."
44. Ibid.
45. Ibid.
46. Ibid.
47. Ibid.
48. Mencius Moldbug, "Patchwork: A Political System for the 21st Century: Chapter 1," *Unqualified Reservations*, November 13, 2008.
49. Ibid.
50. Lomez, "The Dissident Interviews: Curtis Yarvin on Libertarianism, the Cathedral, Poetry and More," *IM—1776*, https://im1776.com/2021/09/03/curtis-yarvin-interview/.
51. Kofman, "Yarvin's Plot Against America."
52. Mencius Moldbug, "Patchwork: A Political System for the 21st Century Chapter 3: What We Have and What's So Bad About It," *Unqualified Reservations*, November 27, 2008.
53. Ian Ward, "Curtis Yarvin's Ideas Were Fringe. Now They're Coursing Through Trump's Washington," *Politico*, January 30, 2025.
54. Ed Simon, "What We Must Understand About the Dark Enlightenment Movement," *Time*, March 24, 2025.
55. Peter Jamison and Elizabeth Dwoskin, "Curtis Yarvin Helped Inspire DOGE. Now He Scorns It," *The Washington Post*, May 8, 2025.
56. Curtis Yarvin, "A Conversation About Monarchy," *Gray Mirror*, March 12, 2024.
57. Ibid.

58. Doina Chiacu, "Trump: If It Saves the Country, It's Not Illegal," *Reuters*, February 16, 2025.
59. Presidential Executive Order, "Ensuring Accountability for All Agencies," February 18, 2025, https://www.whitehouse.gov/presidential-actions/2025/02/ensuring-accountability-for-all-agencies/.
60. Yarvin, "Conversation About Monarchy."
61. Jacob Knutson, "What Is Unitary Executive Theory? How Is Trump Using It to Push His Agenda?" *Democracy Docket*, February 20, 2025.
62. Yarvin, "Conversation About Monarchy."
63. George Chidi, "US Immigration Enforcement Using Military Hardware and Tactics on Civilians," *The Guardian*, October 10, 2025.
64. Melissa Sanchez et al., "'I Lost Everything': Venezuelans Were Rounded Up in a Dramatic Midnight Raid but Never Charged With a Crime," *Pro Publica*, November 13, 2025.
65. Ibid.

7. THE THREADS OF THE POSTLIBERAL ALLIANCE

1. Julian Waller, "On the Postliberal Turn: One Implication of the Vance Nomination," *Political Orders*, July 19, 2024, https://politicalorders.substack.com/p/on-the-postliberal-turn.
2. R. R. Reno, *Return of the Strong Gods: Nationalism, Populism, and the Future of the West* (Regnery, 2021), xxi.
3. L. Brent Bozell Jr., "Freedom or Virtue?" *National Review*, September 11, 1962.
4. JD Vance, "End the Globalization Gravy Train," *American Mind*, April 21, 2020.
5. Peter Thiel, "The Education of a Libertarian," *Cato Unbound*, April 13, 2009, https: //www.cato-unbound.org/2009/04/13/peter-thiel/education-libertarian/.
6. C. Jay Engel, "Why I'm Not a Libertarian," at *Contra Mordor*, February 26, 2024, https://writing.cjayengel.com/p/why-im-not-a-libertarian.
7. AF Post (@AFpost), "Pastor Joel Webbon said that Christian nationalists should be allowed to impose their values on others . . . ," X, November 14, 2025, https://x.com/AFpost/status/1989455341948371059?s=20.
8. "Against the Dead Consensus," *First Things*, March 21, 2019.
9. Thiel, "Education of a Libertarian."

10. Mencius Moldbug, "A Formalist Manifesto," *Unqualified Reservations*, April 24, 2007.
11. Ava Kofman, "Curtis Yarvin's Plot Against America," *The New Yorker*, June 2, 2025.
12. Curtis Yarvin, "The Historical Guilt of the Old Regime," *Gray Mirror* (blog), January 26, 2023; David Marchese, "Curtis Yarvin Says Democracy Is Done," *The New York Times*, January 18, 2025.
13. C. Jay Engel, "To Celebrate Our Western Patrimony," *Contra Mordor*, February 9, 2024. https://writing.cjayengel.com/p/to-celebrate-our-western-patrimony.
14. Maureen Dowd, "Alex Karp Has Money and Power. So What Does He Want?," *The New York Times*, August 17, 2025.
15. Ihsan Yilmaz and Nicholas Morieson, "Civilizational Populism: Definition, Literature, Theory, and Practice," *Religions* 13, no. 11 (2022).
16. Ihsan Yilmaz and Nicholas Morieson, "Civilizational Populism Around the World," *Populism & Politics: European Center for Populism Studies*, July 31, 2022, 6.
17. "Christian Nationalism: Faith or Agenda? | Michael Bird vs. Stephen Wolfe, Hosted by Billy Hallowell," *Unbelievable?*, March 22, 2024, https://youtu.be/zieWeTqe2qc?si=DgsyUz98oq-MBZR9.
18. Mencius Moldbug, "An Open Letter to Open-Minded Progressives: Chapter XIV: Rules for Reactionaries," *Unqualified Reservations*, July 17, 2008.
19. Moldbug, "Open Letter: Chapter XIV."
20. R. J. Rushdoony, *God's Plan for Victory: The Meaning of Postmillennialism* (Chalcedon Press, 1977), 28.
21. Émile P. Torres, "The Acronym Behind Our Wildest AI Dreams and Nightmares," *Truthdig*, June 15, 2023.
22. Associated Press, "How Silicon Valley Is Using Religious Language to Talk About AI," *NBC News*, August 29, 2025.
23. Nick Bilton, "Artificial Intelligence May Be Humanity's Most Ingenious Invention—And Its Last," *Vanity Fair*, September 13, 2023.
24. lukeprog, "So You Want to Save the World," *Less Wrong*, December 31, 2011. https://www.lesswrong.com/posts/5BJvusxdwNXYQ4L9L/so-you-want-to-save-the-world.
25. Torres, "The Acronym Behind Our Wildest AI Dreams and Nightmares."

26. Kevin Roberts, *Dawn's Early Light* (Broadside Books, 2024), xii.
27. Kevin Roberts, foreword to *Project 2025*, 13. Italics mine.
28. Adrian Vermeule, "Beyond Originalism," *The Atlantic*, March 31, 2020.
29. Joakim Scheffer, "JD Vance Could Lead the Post-Liberal Elite—An Interview with Patrick Deneen," *Hungarian Conservative*, April 8, 2025.
30. Ian Ward, "Doug Wilson Has Spent Decades Pushing for a Christian Theocracy. In Trump's DC, the New Right Is Listening," *Politico*, May 23, 2025.
31. Barton Gellman, "Peter Thiel is Taking a Break From Democracy," *The Atlantic*, November 9, 2023.
32. Boris Muñoz, "Curtis Yarvin's Brave New World: 'We Need a Corporate Dictatorship to Replace a Dying Democracy,'" *El País*, August 19, 2025.
33. Curtis Yarvin, "You Can't Handle the Truth," *Gray Mirror*, October 5, 2025.
34. Greg Sargent, "Trump's Shocking Brawl with Laura Ingraham on Fox Exposes His Weakness," *New Republic*, November 12, 2025.
35. Joel Webbon (@JoelWebbon), "It is long past time to admit that Donald Trump is NOT our guy . . . ," X, November 12, 2025, https://x.com/rightresponsem/status/1988605999733977237?s=20.
36. C. Jay Engel (@contramordor), "This is always what he was. Some of us have been saying this since the beginning . . . , X, November 12, 2025, https://x.com/contramordor/status/1988645122586669372?s=20.
37. C. Jay Engel (@contramordor), "The Trump people don't realize that we are not interested in compromises or halfway deals with corporations . . . ," X, November 12, 2025, https://x.com/contramordor/status/1988697398357418159?s=20.
38. T. S. Flanders, "The Danger of Trump to Postliberal Catholicism," *OnePeterFive*, May 6, 2024.

8. JD VANCE: CROWN PRINCE OF POSTLIBERAL AMERICA

1. David Marchese, "Curtis Yarvin Says Democracy Is Done," *The New York Times*, January 18, 2025.
2. Ibid.

3. McKay Coppins, "God's Plan for Mike Pence," *The Atlantic*, January/February Issue, 2018.
4. See Nick Evans, "Vance Wondered Whether Trump Was 'America's Hitler,' Says Former Roommate Sharing Screenshot," *Ohio Capital Journal*, April 19, 2022.
5. JD Vance, "How I Joined the Resistance," *Lamp*, April 1, 2020.
6. Ibid.
7. Ibid.
8. Ibid.
9. See https://x.com/JDVance/status/1887958058342502623?s=20, accessed February 2026.
10. See "VP Vance Responds to 'Young Republicans' Leaked Messages," *Charlie Kirk*, October 15, 2025, https://www.youtube.com/watch?v=h_9FposK2p4.
11. See "J. D. Vance—JML #070," Jack Murphy Live, September 21, 2021, https: //www.youtube.com/watch?v=PMq1ZEcyztY&t=1s.
12. Ankush Khardori, "JD Vance's 'Constitutional Crisis' in the Making," *Politico*, August 12, 2024.
13. James Pogue, "Inside the New Right, Where Peter Thiel Is Placing His Biggest Bets," *Vanity Fair*, May 2022.
14. Mary Jo McConaughey, *Playing God: American Catholic Bishops and the Far Right* (Melville House, 2023), 61.
15. Ibid.
16. See "A Conversation with JD Vance at the Napa Institute 2021 Summer Conference," Napa Institute, February 6, 2023, https://youtu.be/Mhgz-03M-7w?si=tyeJ6OgB3nb0XKj9.
17. Ibid.
18. See Maria Wiering, "JD Vance Suggests U.S. Bishops Only Care for Immigrants to Protect 'Their Bottom Line," *America Magazine*, January 26, 2025.
19. Ibid.
20. Andy Kroll, "Transcript of JD Vance Teneo Network 2021 Speech," DocumentCloud, July 16, 2024, https://www.documentcloud.org/documents/24815790-J.D.-vance-teneo-network-2021-speech/.
21. Ibid.
22. "The Perfect Society: Church, State, and the Common Good," *Franciscan University of Steubenville*, November 9, 2022, https://www.youtube.com/watch?v=uXrBbap0YFI.

23. See Brian Fraga, "'New Right' Academics Argue for Biblical Lawmaking at Steubenville Conference," *New Catholic Register*, October 17, 2022.
24. Anastasia Kaliabakos and Bradley Devlin, "The Right Reacts to 'Vice President J. D. Vance,'" *American Conservative*, July 15, 2024.
25. Patrick J. Buchanan, *A Republic, Not an Empire: Reclaiming America's Destiny* (Regnery, 2002).
26. Kelsey Vlamis, "GOP Senate Candidate JD Vance Said He Doesn't 'Really Care What Happens to Ukraine,'" *Business Insider*, February 2, 2022, https://www.businessinsider.com/gop-candidate-J.D.-vance-i-dont-care-what-happens-ukraine-2022–2.
27. Rod Dreher, "'I Would Like to See European Elites Actually Listen to Their People for a Change': An Interview with J. D. Vance," *European Conservative*, February 22, 2024.
28. See Kamala HQ (@KamalaHQ), "Trump's Project 2025 leader: 'We have confirmed news that Senator JD Vance is the Vice Presidential running mate. You will see a broad smile on my face . . . ,'" X, July 15, 2024, https://x.com/KamalaHQ/status/1812955816372367465?s=20.
29. Matthew Schmitz, "JD Vance, Religious Populist," *First Things*, May 1, 2024.
30. Massimo Faggioli, "JD Vance's Catholicism: Theological Profile of Trump's Heir Apparent," *Catholic Outlook*, July 24, 2024.
31. See Jamelle Bouie, "JD Vance Claims One of Our Worst Traditions as His Own," *The New York Times*, July 23, 2025.
32. Schmitz, "JD Vance, Religious Populist."
33. James Silberman and Dusty Deevers, *The Statement on Christian Nationalism and the Gospel*, https://www.statementonchristiannationalism.com/.
34. Pope Francis, "Letter of the Holy Father Francis to the Bishops of the United States of America," February 10, 2025, https://www.vatican.va/content/francesco/en/letters/2025/documents/20250210-lettera-vescovi-usa.html.
35. Matt Walsh, "JD Vance is of course correct about the hierarchy of love . . . ," Facebook, February 2, 2025, https://www.facebook.com/MattWalshBlog/posts/J.D.-vance-is-of-course-correct-about-the-hierarchy-of-love-you-are-called-to-love/1215761006572945/.

36. RedWave Press (@RedWavePress), "The Daily Wire's Matt Walsh: 'I'm America only in the same sort of sense that I'm my family only . . . ,'" X, November 17, 2025, https://x.com/RedWave_Press/status/1990547641285972223?s=20.
37. Stephen Wolfe, *The Case for Christian Nationalism* (Canon Press, 2022), 101.
38. Ibid., 142.
39. Andrew Isker (@BonifaceOption), "Total loyalty to President JD Vance," October 29, 2025. https://x.com/BonifaceOption/status/1983715409023939034?s=20.
40. Ian Ward, "Is There Something More Radical than MAGA? J. D. Vance Is Dreaming It," *Politico*, March 15, 2025.
41. See "Senator JD Vance 'Childless Cat Lady' Comments Cause Stir," *WWLTV*, July 26, 2024, https://youtu.be/XiuQ4nOyqZk?si=7XW00woFNvrqLXdX.
42. Tal Axelrod, "J. D. Vance Says He Wouldn't Have Certified 2020 Race Until States Submitted Pro-Trump Electors," *ABC News*, February 4, 2024.
43. James Pogue, "Inside the New Right, Where Peter Thiel Is Placing His Biggest Bets," *Vanity Fair*, May 2022.
44. See David Corn, "JD Vance's Racist Populism," *Mother Jones*, July 3, 2024.
45. Schmitz, "JD Vance, Religious Populist."
46. JD Vance, "'I Will Be Damned' if Ukraine Prioritized over 'Tsunami of Illegal Migrants,'" *Columbus Dispatch*, March 31, 2022.
47. "Europe Is 'at Risk' of 'Engaging in Civilizational Suicide,' JD Vance Says," *Fox News*, March 14, 2025, https://www.foxnews.com/video/6370057044112.
48. Ibid.
49. See Stephen Fowler, "Vance Says Haitian Migrants with Protected Status Are 'Illegal Aliens' to Be Deported," *NPR*, September 18, 2024.
50. "'We Cannot Rebuild Western Civilization . . .' JD Vance's 'No-Nonsense' Take on Illegal Migrants," *ANI News*, February 20, 2025, https://youtu.be/WHEt0mdNG4M?si=5GPj-grlBp-S4RJo.
51. Ward, "Is There Something More Radical Than MAGA?"
52. Ibid.

EPILOGUE

1. UK Parliament Hansard, Commons, vol. 444, Orders of the Day, Parliament Bill, Speaker Winston Churchill, November 11, 1947, https://hansard.parliament.uk/commons/1947-11-11/debates/110a3531-22eb-4dff-9ff3-041c29e16967/OrdersOfTheDay.
2 Reich Wing Watch, "Nothing But Praise for Putin," https://www.youtube.com/watch?v=Lau_V2_Wl80; Rob Port, "This Country Needs a Dictator," Inforum, January 15, 2024, https://www.inforum.com/opinion/columns/port-this-country-needs-a-dictator.
3. George Lindbeck, *The Nature of Doctrine: Religion and Theology in a Postliberal Age* (Westminster John Knox Press, 1984).

INDEX